Polish Traditions with American Additions

Polish Traditions
with American Additions

©2015 Jean Marie Miscisin

All Rights Reserved

ISBN: 13: 978 – 1514258712

ISBN: 10: 1514258714

CONTENTS	Page
DEDICATION and INTRODUCTION	6
January Kindness	13
Fruit of the Holy Spirit = Kindness	14
Liturgical Calendar = Holy Name of Jesus	15
Devotions and Celebrations = Polish Little Christmas	19
Polish–American Recipe = Golabki: Cabbage Rolls	22
Polish–American Activity = Busia Aprons	24
People of Polish Heritage = My Great-Grandmothers and	26
My Grandmothers	26
February Love	29
Fruit of the Holy Spirit = Love	30
Liturgical Calendar = Holy Family	31
Devotions and Celebrations = God is Love	33
Polish–American Recipe = *Zupa = Kury z Jarzynami*:	35
Chicken Soup	35
First Day - Braised Chicken Thighs	35
Second Day - Soup from Braised Chicken Thighs	36
Polish–American Activity = Wycinanki - Valentines	37
People of Polish Heritage = Dzia Dzia Walenty, Busia Helen, & Uncles	38
March Self-Control	39
Fruit of the Holy Spirit = Self-Control	40
Liturgical Calendar = Saint Joseph	41
Devotions and Celebrations = Lent	49
Polish–American Recipe = *Paczki:* Fried Doughnuts	50
Polish–American Activity = Palm Weaving	52
People of Polish Heritage = Uncle Steve and Aunt Irene	56
April Faithfulness	57
Fruit of the Holy Spirit = Faithfulness	58
Liturgical Calendar = The Holy Spirit	59
Devotions and Celebrations = Divine Mercy	66
Easter and Basket for Easter Breakfast	69
Polish–American Recipe = *Zupa z Sliwek*: Prune Soup	70
Polish–American Activity = Wycinanki – Kwiat - Flower	72
People of Polish Heritage = My Mother's side of My Family	73

May Modesty	75
Fruit of the Holy Spirit = Modesty	76
Liturgical Calendar = The Blessed Virgin Mary	77
Devotions and Celebrations = First Communions	81
Wianek – Children of Mary	82
Young Ladies Sodality	83
Polish–American Recipe = *Ciasto Szybki*: Quick Cake	85
Coffee Cake Variations = Pineapple Upside Down Cake	85
Coffee Cake Variations = Huckleberry Muffins	87
Polish–American Activity = Garden Flowers on the Table	88
People of Polish Heritage = My Mother	90
June Purity	93
Fruit of the Holy Spirit = Purity	94
Liturgical Calendar = The Sacred Heart of Jesus	95
Devotions and Celebrations = Corpus Christi Procession	98
Polish–American Recipe = *Kapusta*: Cabbage Side Dish	100
Polish–American Activity = Wycinanki – Wstazka = Ribbon Style	102
People of Polish Heritage = Sisters of Saint Joseph	103
July Joy	107
Fruit of the Holy Spirit = Joy	108
Liturgical Calendar = The Precious Blood of Jesus	109
Devotions and Celebrations = Independence Day / God and Country	111
Polish–American Recipe = *Wieprzowa Przyjecie*: Pork Barbeque	113
Melt in Your Mouth Ribs & My Special BAR-B-Q Sauce	114
Polish–American Activity = Patriotic – American Flags	115
People of Polish Heritage = My Daddy's side of My Family	116
August Goodness	119
Fruit of the Holy Spirit = Goodness	120
Liturgical Calendar = The Immaculate Heart of Mary	121
Devotions and Celebrations = Sacrament of Matrimony	123
Mary – Queen of Heaven and Earth	123
Polish–American Recipe = *Ciastka z Owsiane*: Oatmeal Cookies	125
Polish–American Activity = Companion Gardening	128
People of Polish Heritage = My Polish Wedding Reception	129
September Gentleness	132
Fruit of the Holy Spirit = Gentleness	133
Liturgical Calendar = Our Lady of Sorrows	134
Devotions and Celebrations = Immaculate Conception	136
Polish–American Recipe = *Zupa = Krupnik*: Barley Soup	137
First Day - Braised Beef Short Ribs	137
Second Day – Krupnik = Barley Soup from Braised Beef Short Ribs	138
Polish–American Activity = Stage Dramatic Productions	139
People of Polish Heritage = All Saints Parish	140

October Patience	143
Fruit of the Holy Spirit = Patience	144
Liturgical Calendar = Holy Rosary	145
Devotions and Celebrations = Rosary a Photo Album of the Life of Jesus	146 146
Polish–American Recipe = *Jablko Kruchy*: Apple Crisp	157
Apple Crisp with American Additions by Jean Marie Miscisin	158
Polish–American Activity = Wycinanki – Sceneria = Scenery with Leaves	160 160
People of Polish Heritage = Grandparents and the Rosary	161
November Generosity	162
Fruit of the Holy Spirit = Generosity	163
Liturgical Calendar = Souls in Purgatory	164
Devotions and Celebrations = All Saints Day	166
Polish–American Recipe = *Pasztecik*: Pasty and Pasty Roll	169
Turnover Pasties - Modified from Busia Pearl's Recipe	169
Pasty Vege – Roll	171
Pasty Dough	172
Polish–American Activity = House Plants Care with Prayer	173
People of Polish Heritage = Uncles, Aunts & Cousins	174
December Peace	178
Fruit of the Holy Spirit = Peace	179
Liturgical Calendar = Immaculate Conception of Mary	180
Devotions and Celebrations = Advent and Christmas Traditions	184
Polish–American Recipe = *Chrust – Faworki*: Favors	186
Polish–American Recipe = Kolacky = Thumbprint Cookies	188
Polish–American Activity = Wycinanki – Sniegu-platek = Snowflake	190 190
People of Polish Heritage = My Daddy	192

DEDICATION and INTRODUCTION

The Lord takes delight in His people.
Let the faithful exalt in glory; let them sing for joy upon their couches;
Let the high praises of God be in their throats.
This is the glory of all the faithful.
(Excerpts from PSALM 149)

My book is dedicated to every living person. Each one of you is an unrepeatable gift to the world created out of God's love; to know, love and serve God in this world and to go back to be with God for all eternity.

Every beat of our hearts and every breath that we take is a gift of love from God.

Growing up in a large extended Polish Catholic Community, I learned that the people who lived and loved each other from first through fifth generations delighted in their God. They lived in an awareness of God's love and the shortness of earthly life. At the end of every party and visit to friends' homes they sang the lyrics of, "How Swiftly the Moments Pass Waltz."
The chorus refrain words are = "In a year, in a day, in a moment, together we will not be."

Everybody knew that all people are sinners in need of God's love and mercy.
They also knew that God was always ready to enter the hearts of the people who opened the doors to their own hearts even just a little. As you read through my book you will notice that I chose only examples of the virtues that I believe will lead toward becoming a more loving and obedient child of God.

The Holy Spirit who lives in you is strong, loving, and wise. (2 Timothy 2: 7)
Take as your norm the sound words that you heard from me, in the Faith and Love that are in Christ Jesus. Guard this rich trust with the help of the Holy Spirit who dwells within us.
(2 Timothy 2: 13-14)

Come Holy Spirit! Come live in me. Come with your Gifts and Heavenly Aid.
Come fill my heart which you have made.

This is my version of a prayer that was taught to me by the Sisters of Saint Joseph, a Polish Order of Nuns, who were serving at All Saints Catholic School from 1941 to 1954, when I was in their loving care.. I owe a debt of gratitude to the Sisters of Saint Joseph, who served by cooking, cleaning, and other necessary tasks in their convent and All Saints Catholic Church; also Sister Mary Avila who was organist after my grandfather died, in addition to All the Classroom Teachers in grades Kindergarten through Twelfth Grade. All of these Sisters lavished their unconditional love on ME, a small child of God. By their expressions of love they were living examples of the Fruits of the Holy Spirit. Faith without works is dead. (James 2: 14-16)

What are the Gifts of the Holy Spirit?

Faith, Hope, Love, Knowledge, Understanding, Wisdom, Counsel, Fortitude, Piety, and Filial Fear of the Lord are the Gifts of the Holy Spirit.

"By their fruits you will know them." The Twelve Fruits of the Holy Spirit are basically character traits of a good person. In the Children of Mary Organization at All Saints Catholic School, I learned to call these Twelve Fruits of the Holy Spirit = "Virtues" of a Child of Mary.

What are the Fruits of the Holy Spirit?

For each Month of Our Calendar Year,
I chose one of the Twelve Fruits of the Holy Spirit

January = Kindness	February = Love	March = Self-Control
April = Faithfulness	May = Modesty	June = Purity
July = Joy	August = Goodness	September = Gentleness
October = Patience	November = Generosity	December = Peace

The organization of my book is inspired by Biblical Verses. Although I am notating the Book, Chapter and Verses where specific wording of the Biblical Verses can be found in most translations of the Holy Bible, the wording may be different. Within my book there are references to verses in both the Old Testament and the New Testament of the Holy Bible. Please read all of these verses in your Holy Bible, so that you may understand the context of each verse. To my knowledge, there are no direct quotations; instead I present my synthesis, interpretation, and application of the Biblical references to the Fruits of the Holy Spirit.

Peace I leave with you; my peace I give to you. Not as the world gives do I give it to you. Do not let your hearts be troubled or afraid. (John 14: 27)

I am the vine and my Father is the grower. He takes away every branch in me that does not bear fruit, and every one that does bear fruit he prunes so that it bears more fruit.

You are already pruned because of the word I spoke to you. Remain in me, as I remain in you. Just as a branch cannot bear fruit on its own unless it remains on the vine, so neither can you unless you remain in me. I am the vine you are the branches. Whoever remains in me and I in him will bear much fruit, because without me you can do nothing that is good. If you remain in me and my words remain in you, ask for whatever you want and it will be done for you.

By this is my Father glorified, that you bear much fruit and become my disciples. As the Father Loves me, so I also Love you. Remain in my Love. If you keep my commandments, you will remain in my Love, just as I have kept my Father's commandments and remain in his Love. (John 15: 1 – 10)

I have told you this so that my Joy might be in you and your Joy might be complete. This is my commandment: Love one another as I Love you. No one has greater Love than this to lay down one's life for one's friends. You are my friends if you do what I command you. This I command you Love one another. (John 15: 11 – 14, 17)

Jesus said: It was not you who chose me, but I who chose you and appointed you to go and bear fruit that will remain, so that whatever you ask in my name he may give you. (John 15: 16)

My Questions: What is meant by Fruit?   What should I ask for in the name of Jesus?

A tree is known by its Fruit. A good tree does not bear rotten fruit, nor does a rotten tree bear good fruit. For every tree is known by its own fruit. For people do not pick figs from thornbushes, nor do they gather grapes from brambles. A good person out of the store of goodness in his heart produces good, but an evil person out of a store of evil produces evil; for from the fullness of the heart the mouth speaks. (Luke 6: 43 – 45)

And I tell you, ask and you will receive; seek and you will find; knock and the door will be opened to you. For everyone who asks, receives; and the one who seeks, finds; and to the one who knocks, the door will be opened.

What father among you would hand his son a snake when he asks for a fish? Or hand him a scorpion when he asks for an egg? If you then, who are wicked, know how to give good Gifts to your children, how much more will the Father in heaven give the Holy Spirit to those who ask him? (Luke 11: 9 – 13)

MY REASONING:

We are to obey the commandments to Love God and Love One Another.
We are to ask for the Holy Spirit to come Live in Our Hearts.
When the Holy Spirit is Living in Our Hearts, the Holy Spirit will bring HIS Gifts, bestow blessings on our lives, and we will bear Fruit abundantly.

How will we know that the Holy Spirit is dwelling in a person?
The Fruits of Holy Spirit will be evident in their lives.

What are the Fruits of Holy Spirit?

Jesus mentions three of the Fruits of Holy Spirit in the verses presented above.
Joy, Peace, and Love are three of the Twelve Fruits of Holy Spirit. The other nine are Kindness, Self-Control, Faithfulness, Modesty, Purity, Goodness, Gentleness, Patience, and Generosity. When we demonstrate these virtues by our lives other people can know by our "Good Fruit" that we are following the teachings of Jesus.

So, the conclusions I can draw are: When we pray we are to ask the Holy Spirit to come into our lives and we will receive the Gifts of the Holy Spirit.

When we diligently seek the Truth we will find that Jesus is the Way, the Truth, and the Life.

When we open our hearts to Love God and Love One Another we are knocking on the door to the Kingdom of God and the door will be opened.

How did I decide the Contents of this book?
Again I turned to the Holy Bible for inspiration:
Whatever is true, whatever is honorable, whatever is just, whatever is pure, whatever is lovely, whatever is gracious, if there is any excellence and if there is anything worthy of praise, think about these things. (Philippians 4: 8)

My Polish version of these Bible verses in Ecclesiastes 3: 1-8
:
For everything there is a season, and a time for every matter under heaven:
A time to be born and a time to die; both Baptisms and Funerals were times for Family gatherings.

A time to plant, and a time to pluck up what is planted; every family I knew had a home garden or a farm.

A time to break down the outhouse, and a time to build an in-door bathroom was common.

It was time to weep at accidents and deaths; and a time to laugh every day.

It was time to mourn at "wakes," and a time to dance at weddings.

It was always time to embrace other people, even when we didn't feel like doing it.

A time to keep or recycle, and the time to throw away was only unusable garbage.

It was time to tear worn out cloths into rags for cleaning, and a time to sew curtains and broomstick skirts out of "Flour Sacks."

It was time to keep silence in Church, and a time to speak only with permission.

It was time to love even our enemies, and a time to hate the devil and evil deeds.

It was time for World War II and time to pray for Peace on earth. It was time for peace except for the "Cold War" with the Soviet Republic.

To be Polish meant to be Catholic so I looked back on the beautiful cycle of Polish Celebrations that were found in All Saints Catholic Church, a Juridical Polish National Parish, a Catholic Parish founded by a Bishop from Poland in 1910. All Saints Catholic Church is in full communion with the Pope and the Catholic Church in Rome, and not completely under the jurisdiction of the Diocesan Bishop.

There I found the Liturgical Calendar =

January = Holy Name of Jesus
March = Saint Joseph
May = The Blessed Virgin Mary
July = The Precious Blood of Jesus
September = Our Lady of Sorrows
November = Souls in Purgatory

February = Holy Family
April = The Holy Spirit
June = The Sacred Heart of Jesus
August = The Immaculate Heart of Mary
October = Holy Rosary
December = Immaculate Conception of Mary

It would take volumes of books to describe every Liturgical Devotion and Celebration in the Catholic Church. Three Liturgical Year Calendars provide lists of the Biblical Proclamations for the Sundays and Feast Days of the Universal Catholic Church, providing world wide unity on those days. The year 2014 was designated as Liturgical Year Calendar A, 2015 as Liturgical Year Calendar B, and 2016 will use Liturgical Year Calendar C. There are various choices for the week day Masses.

At least One Litany or One Novena is included in each month with a brief description of some Scriptural Readings designated for each month. This book is not intended to provide instruction in the theological Mysteries of the Catholic Faith, such as the Incarnation and Resurrection of our Savior Jesus Christ, and the Sacred Mysteries of the Holy Sacrifice of the Mass and the Sacraments. These Mysteries are unfathomed by any intellect, human or angelic, and require the grace of Faith. If these Mysteries could be completely understood, then they would no longer be mysteries which require Faith.

A Litany is a traditional list of short prayers. There are two basic forms; the first litanies of adoration and petition are addressed to God in the Mystery of the Trinity, God the Father, God the Son our Savior, and the Holy Spirit the Paraclete. The second form consists of Prayers of Intercession where we ask the Saints to Pray for and with us.

Novenas are Prayers that are recited once each day for Nine (9) Days. Other Novenas are said: once each hour on one day, or once each week for nine weeks, or once each month nine months. Frequently the same set of prayers is said each time. On the other hand, a different prayer is frequently said on each day of a Novena.

Novenas originated with Jesus when He ordered the apostles not to leave Jerusalem, but to wait there for the promise of the Father. "This," Jesus said, "is what you have heard from me; for John baptized with water, but you will be baptized with the Holy Spirit not many days from now." (Acts 1: 4-5) These instructions were given before Jesus Ascended back into Heaven. Between the Ascension of Jesus and the Feast of Pentecost are Nine Days of Prayer.

Jesus said, "It is not for you to know the times or periods that the Father has set by his own authority. But you will receive power when the Holy Spirit has come upon you; and you will be my witnesses in Jerusalem, in all Judea and Samaria, and to the ends of the earth." When he had said this, as they were watching, he was lifted up, and a cloud took him out of their sight. While he was going and they were gazing up toward heaven, suddenly two men in white robes stood by them. They said, "Men of Galilee, why do you stand looking up toward heaven? This Jesus, who has been taken up from you into heaven, will come in the same way as you saw him go into heaven."
(Acts 1: 7-11)

Then they returned to Jerusalem from the mount called Olivet, which is near Jerusalem. When they had entered the city, they went to the room upstairs where they were staying, Peter, and John, James, Andrew, Philip, Thomas, Matthew, Bartholomew, and others. All these were constantly devoting themselves to prayer, together with certain women, including Mary the mother of Jesus. (Acts 1: 1-4)

Between the Ascension and the day of Pentecost they had spent nine (9) days in prayer. We spend nine days in prayer before many feasts in the Polish Catholic Traditions. This practice is not a requirement of the Universal Catholic Church. It is a beautiful pious practice that helps present truths about our faith.

The apostles and the others were all together in one place. Suddenly from heaven there came a sound like the rush of a violent wind, and it filled the entire house where they were sitting. Divided tongues, as of fire, appeared among them, and a tongue rested on each of them. All of them were filled with the Holy Spirit and began to speak in other languages, as the Spirit gave them ability. (Acts 2: 12-14)

Each country may celebrate the Memorial Feast Day of different Saints who have been canonized in the Catholic Church. There are four required steps for a person to be declared a Canonized Saint and it is frequently a lengthy process taking many years; the steps are Servant of God, Venerable, Blessed, and Canonization. All Baptized Christians are called to accept the love, mercy, and grace from God to follow Jesus Christ. The Saints are people who have demonstrated heroic virtue at least the last ten years of their lives or have been martyred for their beliefs in the teachings of Jesus Christ. As Catholics we are encouraged to imitate their virtues while they were living on earth.

The Bible Readings for that day could be chosen because the particular Saint had taught, lived, or clarified the message from a particular passage or verse. I am including at least one Feast Day Celebration for each month that had special Polish cultural facets.

Devotions and Celebrations =
January = Three Kings -The Epiphany
February = God's Love
March = Lent
April = Easter
May = May Procession
June = Corpus Christi Procession
July = God and Country
August = Mary – Queen of Heaven and Earth
September = Immaculate Conception
October = Holy Rosary – Photo Album of the Life of Jesus
November = Thanksgiving for God's Blessings
December = Advent and Christmas Traditions

The endearing term for grandmother is Busia (boo-sha) and for grandfather is Dzia Dzia (jaj-jah as in "jar" without the "r").

Polish–American Recipes = Please refer to the CONTENTS pages.

Jesus stresses the need for inner purity of heart, not ritual purity of the body. He called the people to him and said to them, "Hear and understand: not what goes into the mouth defiles a man, but what comes out of the mouth, this defiles a man." (Matthew 15:10-11)

There are many Polish Cookbooks available from the various regions of Poland. When the three super powers, Russia, Prussia, and Austria, divided Poland, the Polish people modified some of their traditional recipes. I only included the Polish recipes that were prepared by my two Busias and to my knowledge they were not found in a cook book. I learned the methods for preparing the recipes by watching or helping my Mother and Grandmothers in their kitchens. To my knowledge the recipes were not written down until I asked my Mother and Grandmothers to tell me the ingredients. When it came to proportions, that information was variable from "about ..." to "a pinch of ..." or "a dash of something". Some times they said, "... when and if available" because both grandmothers had their own fruit and vegetable gardens. They both lived in Flint, Michigan when I was growing up, where the one growing season were short; many had "Hot Houses" similar to today's Greenhouses, and smaller. To me they had plenty of food. I was very small for my age so both Busias were always trying to "fatten me up".

Polish–American Activity = Please refer to the CONTENTS pages.

The hands-on activity that I chose for each Month, I originally learned from one or both of my Busias. Over the years I modified the process as I learned more about each activity.

People of Polish Heritage =

Every person who lives is an unrepeatable gift to the world created out of God's Love to Know, Love and Serve God in This World and to go back to be with God . Every beat of our hearts and every breath that we take is a Gift of Love from God.

For just as the body is one and has many members, and all the members of the body, though many, are one body, so it is with Christ. For in the one Spirit we were all baptized into one body with Jesus as our Head and we were all made to drink of one Spirit. Indeed, the body does not consist of one member but of many. If the foot would say, "Because I am not a hand, I do not belong to the body," that would not make it any less a part of the body. If the ear would say, "Because I am not an eye, I do not belong to the body," that would not make it any less a part of the body. If the whole body were an eye, where would the hearing be? If the whole body were hearing, where would the sense of smell be? God arranged the members in the body, each one of them, as he chose. There are many members, yet one body in Jesus Christ.
(1 Corinthians 12: 12-20)

If one part suffers, all the parts suffer with it; if one part is honored all the parts share its joy.
(1 Corinthians 12: 26)

You are the light of the world. No one after lighting a lamp puts it under the bushel basket, but on the lampstand, and it gives light to all in the house. In the same way, let your light shine before others, so that they may see your good works and give glory to your Father in heaven. (Matthew 5: 13-16)

Each Month ends with a trip down memory lane with dozens of People of Polish Heritage who had a positive influence on my character and my World View. My book, Polish Traditions with American Additions, is only possible because I have loving memories of the many People of Polish Ancestry their friends, and neighbors, mostly immigrants from many other countries.

It would take volumes to introduce the readers of my books to the hundreds of people of Polish Ancestry who had a positive influence on my life. In this book I provide only a brief glimpse into the lives of some of the people of Polish Ancestry from whom I learned to live with an awareness of God's presence, God's love, God's mercy, and God's promises.

January   Kindness

Day Lilies in My Backyard

Fruit of the Holy Spirit = Kindness

Liturgical Calendar = Holy Name of Jesus

Devotions and Celebrations = Polish Little Christmas

Polish–American Recipe = Gola̱mpki – Cabbage Rolls

Polish–American Activity = Busia Aprons

People of Polish Heritage = My Great-Grandmothers and My Grandmothers

January   Kindness

Fruit of the Holy Spirit = Kindness

Prayer:

    Holy Spirit, eternal Love of the Father and the Son, kindly bestow on us the fruit of kindness, that we may willingly help our neighbor.

Kindness = goodness in words and actions.

Kindness = to live the virtue of kindness by treating others as we want to be treated.

Kindness = doing something good and not expecting anything in return.

Kindness = helping others without waiting for someone to help back.

Kindness = also shown in polite speech, respectful conduct, and forgiveness for injuries sustained.

Do not let kindness and truth leave you. (Proverbs 3:3-4)

He who pursues justice and kindness will find life and honor. (Proverbs 21:20-22)

But the fruit of the Spirit is love, joy, peace, patience, kindness, goodness, faithfulness. (Galatians 5:21-23)

Put on then, as God's chosen ones, holy and beloved, compassion, kindness, lowliness, meekness, and patience. (Colossians 3:11-13)

January   Kindness

Liturgical Calendar = Holy Name of Jesus

"... God greatly exalted him and bestowed on him the name that is above every name, that at the name of Jesus every knee shall bend, of those in heaven and on earth and under the earth, and every tongue confess that Jesus Christ is Lord, to the glory of God the Father." (Philippians 2: 9 – 11)

Litany of the Most Holy Name of Jesus

This is an old and popular form of prayer in honor of the Name of Jesus.
The author is not known.

LEADER PRAYS.	FAITHFUL RESPOND.
Lord, have mercy on us.	*Lord, have mercy on us.*
Christ, have mercy on us.	*Christ, have mercy on us.*
Lord, have mercy on us.	*Lord, have mercy on us.*
Christ, hear us.	*Christ, graciously hear us.*
God the Father of Heaven,	*Have mercy on us.*
God the Son, Redeemer of the world,	*Have mercy on us.*
God the Holy Spirit,	*Have mercy on us.*
Holy Trinity, One God,	*Have mercy on us.*
Jesus, Son of the living God,	*Have mercy on us.*
Jesus, Splendor of the Father,	*Have mercy on us.*
Jesus, Brightness of eternal Light,	*Have mercy on us.*
Jesus, King of Glory,	*Have mercy on us.*
Jesus, Sun of Justice,	*Have mercy on us.*
Jesus, Son of the Virgin Mary,	*Have mercy on us.*
Jesus, most amiable,	*Have mercy on us.*
Jesus, most admirable,	*Have mercy on us.*
Jesus, the mighty God,	*Have mercy on us.*
Jesus, Father of the world to come,	*Have mercy on us.*
Jesus, angel of great counsel,	*Have mercy on us.*
Jesus, most powerful,	*Have mercy on us.*
Jesus, most patient,	*Have mercy on us.*
Jesus, most obedient,	*Have mercy on us.*
Jesus, meek and humble of heart,	*Have mercy on us.*
Jesus, Lover of Chastity,	*Have mercy on us.*
Jesus, our Lover,	*Have mercy on us.*
Jesus, God of Peace,	*Have mercy on us.*
Jesus, Author of Life,	*Have mercy on us.*
Jesus, Model of Virtues,	*Have mercy on us.*
Jesus, zealous for souls,	*Have mercy on us.*
Jesus, our God,	*Have mercy on us.*
Jesus, our Refuge,	*Have mercy on us.*
Jesus, Father of the Poor,	*Have mercy on us.*
Jesus, Treasure of the Faithful,	*Have mercy on us.*
Jesus, good Shepherd,	*Have mercy on us.*
Jesus, true Light,	*Have mercy on us.*

Jesus, eternal Wisdom,	*Have mercy on us.*
Jesus, infinite Goodness,	*Have mercy on us.*
Jesus, our Way and our Life.	*Have mercy on us.*
Jesus, joy of the Angels,	*Have mercy on us.*
Jesus, King of the Patriarchs,	*Have mercy on us.*
Jesus, Master of the Apostles,	*Have mercy on us.*
Jesus, Teacher of the Evangelists,	*Have mercy on us.*
Jesus, Strength of Martyrs,	*Have mercy on us.*
Jesus, Light of Confessors,	*Have mercy on us.*
Jesus, Purity of Virgins,	*Have mercy on us.*
Jesus, Crown of all Saints,	*Have mercy on us.*
Be merciful,	*Spare us, O Jesus.*
Be merciful,	*Graciously spare us, O Jesus.*
From all evil,	*Deliver us, O Jesus.*
From Your wrath,	*Deliver us, O Jesus*
From all sin,	*Deliver us, O Jesus.*
From the snares of the devil,	*Deliver us, O Jesus*
From the spirit of fornication,	*Deliver us, O Jesus*
From everlasting death,	*Deliver us, O Jesus*
From the neglect of Your inspirations,	*Deliver us, O Jesus*
Through the mystery of Your Holy Incarnation,	*Deliver us, O Jesus*
Through Your Nativity,	*Deliver us, O Jesus*
Through Your Infancy,	*Deliver us, O Jesus*
Through Your most divine Life,	*Deliver us, O Jesus*
Through Your Labors,	*Deliver us, O Jesus*
Through Your Agony and Passion,	*Deliver us, O Jesus*
Through Your cross and Dereliction,	*Deliver us, O Jesus*
Through your Sufferings,	*Deliver us, O Jesus*
Through Your Death and Burial,	*Deliver us, O Jesus*
Through Your Resurrection,	*Deliver us, O Jesus*
Through Your Ascension,	*Deliver us, O Jesus*
Through Your Institution of the Most Holy Eucharist,	*Deliver us, O Jesus*
Through Your Joys,	*Deliver us, O Jesus*
Through Your Glory,	*Deliver us, O Jesus*
Lamb of God, Who takes away the sins of the world,	*Spare us, O Jesus!*
Lamb of God, Who takes away the sins of the world,	*Graciously hear us, O Jesus!*
Lamb of God, Who takes away the sins of the world,	*Have mercy on us, O Jesus!*
Jesus, hear us.	*Jesus, graciously hear us.*

Let us pray.

    Lord Jesus Christ, You have said, "Ask and you shall receive; seek and you shall find; knock and it shall be opened to you"; mercifully attend to our supplications, and grant us the grace of Your most divine love, that we may love You with all our hearts, and in all our words and actions, and always praise You. Make us, O Lord, to have a perpetual fear and love of Your holy name, for You never fail to govern those whom You establish in Your love. You, Who live and reign forever and ever. Amen.

    Fear in this prayer was explained as: being afraid of separating ourselves from the Love of God by deliberately disobeying one or more of the Ten Commandments.

Novena of Confidence to the Sacred Heart

O Lord Jesus Christ, to your most Sacred Heart, I confide this/these intentions.
(*mention your intention/s*)

Only look upon me, and then do what your Sacred Heart inspires.

Let your Sacred Heart decide; I count on it, I trust in it.

I throw myself on Your mercy, Lord Jesus! You will not fail me.

Sacred Heart of Jesus, I trust in You.
Sacred Heart of Jesus, I believe in Your love for me.
Sacred Heart of Jesus, Your Kingdom come.

O Sacred Heart of Jesus, I have asked you for many favors, and I earnestly implore this one.

Take it, place it in Your open, broken Heart, and, when the Eternal Father looks upon It, covered with Your Precious Blood, He will not refuse it.

It will be no longer my prayer, but Yours, O Jesus.
O Sacred Heart of Jesus, I place all my trust in You.
Let me not be disappointed. Amen.

     Growing up with Polish Traditions within the Roman Catholic Church; the Liturgical Year, the Vestment Colors, and the Monthly Special Holy Days were and are the same all over the world. The events in the Life of Jesus that are celebrated can vary only in the "external" facets; for example processions can be very elaborate or not even occur.

     In ethnic cultures around the world there are special Devotions, Litanies, Novenas, Hymns, and Celebrations to commemorate the events in the life of Jesus designated for each month of the Calendar Year. In addition, on Feast Days of Saints canonized by the Catholic Church, and Angels; special prayers either in public or private are recited, but not required.

     In Michigan, January was usually very cold with blustery winds and snow. Our Catholic Churches and our homes still continued to glow with the warmth, peace, and joy of Christmas.

WE ONLY ADORE GOD.

     The New Year is dedicated to Mary on January 1 - When we celebrated the wonderful feast of Mary, Mother of God, where we honor Mary's highest title. The whole month of January is dedicated to the Holy Name of Jesus, which is celebrated on January 3.

     The first eleven days of January fall during the liturgical season known as Christmas which is represented by the liturgical color white. In the first part of January we continue to rejoice and celebrate Christ's coming to Bethlehem and into our hearts. My memories of childhood church processions in the Polish Traditions are still remembered with mostly "Black and white snapshots" while the vivid, beautiful colors linger in my heart.

January 6, the Solemnity of Epiphany, we rejoice with Mary as her Son is adored by the three Wise Men. We follow the Magi to the crib as they bring their gifts of gold, frankincense, and myrrh. In the next section of this book, Devotions and Celebrations = Three Kings Feast of the Epiphany, I will describe the Polish traditions for "Little Christmas" and the American Additions and changes, that were made by my American family of Polish ancestry.

Finally we reach the culmination of this season with the Baptism of Our Lord by St. John the Baptist. He points to Jesus, the Lamb of God who unites time and eternity in the Eucharistic Sacrifice and even January's diminishing darkness seems to echo St. John's prayer:

"Jesus must increase and I must decrease."

In this liturgical season the Church eagerly follows Our Lord as he gathers his apostles and announces his mission. At Cana's wedding feast Jesus performs his first public miracle at the request of his Mother, and his disciples saw his glory and believed in him. We, his present-day disciples, pray for faith as we contemplate the eternal wedding feast and the unique role of the Blessed Mother in the plan of salvation. May we wholeheartedly obey her words of counsel: "Do whatever he tells you."

The remaining days of January are the beginning of Ordinary Time. With a touch of sadness we take down our decorations and enter into the liturgical period known as Ordinary Time where we will devote ourselves to the mystery of Christ in its entirety. The liturgical color changes to green — a symbol of the hope of eternal rest in heaven, especially the hope of a glorious resurrection.

January   Kindness

Devotions and Celebrations =

Polish - Little Christmas

1. Polish - Little Christmas

2. Ornaments that hung on Our Christmas Tree

    In the first picture from left to right, Raymond Anthony age 3. Christian Valentine age 5, Jean Marie age 15, and Barbara Joan age 17 in our living room on Little Christmas. How do I know? Look at the drooping branches on our Balsam Spruce Christmas Tree. It has been up since the first Sunday in Advent until January 6, the day that we celebrated the visit to the Holy Family by the three Kings, Kasper, Melchior, and Balthazar. The controversy about the time of their visit didn't bother us. We were sure that Saint Joseph was a great Foster-Father for Jesus or he would not have been chosen to protect Jesus from King Herod. We were also sure that Saint Joseph found a nice place for them to live in Bethlehem, even though he might not have known that the three Kings were traveling a long way to find Jesus. We knew that Our Manger Scene was just there to help us remember the events more easily.

    Three years before my Mother died she gave one fourth of her ornaments to each of her children. Some Christmas seasons I hung them on a large tree. Two of my retirement years they were hung on a table top tree, and one year displayed in a basket.

    Before my sister Barbara started school, we only opened All Christmas Presents on January 6. When my sister was in First Grade, she went back to school after Christmas Vacation before January 6. Even though All Saints School was taught by Polish Nuns, many of the students were not Polish. Most of the children came from first or second generation immigrant families with different traditions. While we received instruction in the Polish Language those students were given extra instruction in reading English.

When it came to SHOW and TELL the other students brought in some of their Christmas Presents. The Polish children shared their Christmas Caroling at the International Institute, visits to family members and friends, and the twelve kinds of food on the table on Christmas Day to remember the first twelve years in the life of Jesus.

The next year we opened all except one gift on either Christmas Day or on the day we received it, and before my sister went back to school so she could choose to talk about a gift. I don't remember what I shared in Kindergarten.

Shirley Temple Dolls – PUZZLES

When I was in First Grade, I shared the gift of Shirley Temple Dolls – Puzzles which I received from Santa Claus. That was the first Christmas that I knew that Santa didn't live at the North Pole. He was my best friend's Uncle Frank. I didn't tell anyone about the secret, because I liked "playing make believe" with the other children. Madeline and I were playing in the basement of her home, where her Uncle Frank had an apartment. We were curious and found a big cabinet that divided off the apartment from the children's play room. One day in early December that year we found the door to the cabinet unlocked. Inside was a Santa Claus suit, placed across some boxes and shiny black boots on the floor. We quickly closed the door and promised to keep Sana's identity a secret. When my children were young I taught them that everybody could BE Santa Claus if they had love in their hearts and the spirit of giving.

One Polish Tradition that is still carried on in our homes is the use of "Blest Chalk" to place these markings on the inside frame of all exterior doors = 20 – K – M – B – 14. This indicates the year and a message to the THREE KINGS that they can find the HOLY FAMILY, Jesus, Mary, and Joseph living with us in our home life.

Sacraments

Sacraments are visible signs of invisible realities of the Catholic Faith. Please refer to the Catechism of the Catholic Church for more information or the director of RCIA = Rite of Christian Initiation for Adults. When searching the Internet it is best to go to CatholicsComeHome.org. This book is simply my sharing of the Polish Traditions that are directly connected to my Catholic Faith and are not intended to be considered a theological treatise.

Polish - American Baptisms

The Baptismal Rite for an infant is the same in all Catholic Churches throughout the world. A white garment is placed on the baby a symbol of cleansing the soul of all stain of sin. The candle held by an adult symbolizes Jesus Light of the World.

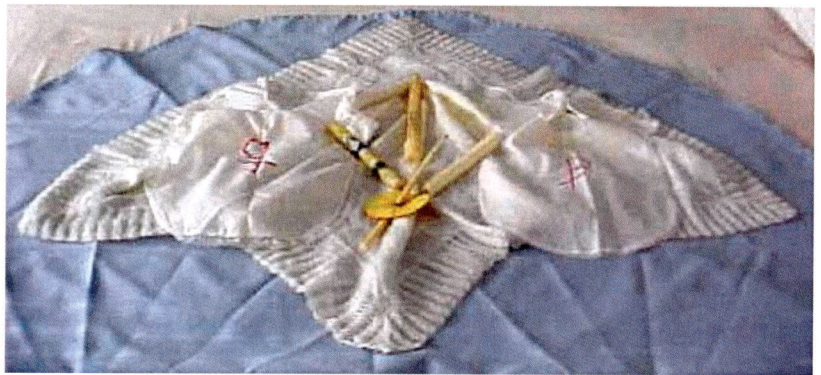

The celebrations after the Baptismal Rite in Church can be different. American families might not even have a celebration. Some families of Polish descent might have the "party" in the Church Hall/Family Center, in a home or even at a restaurant.

Baptismal Clothing

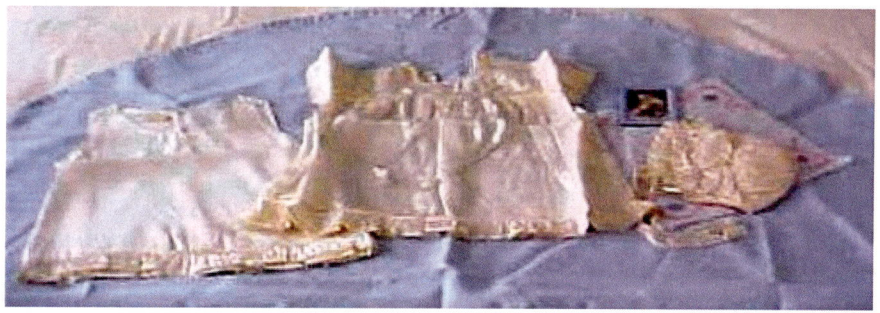

Jean Marie 1936

Jean Marie's Daughters - All Five

Jean Marie's Sons - All Five

January Kindness

Polish–American Recipe = *Golabki*: Cabbage Rolls

The ingredients are the same as those used by both of my grandmothers.
One sunny day, My Mother was preparing Golabki using a pressure cooker. My Daddy said, "It's a beautiful day. Let's go on a picnic." So My Mother packed up the pressure cooker and all the side dishes. My Daddy made a special set of coals in the park Grill. Then he lit them so they would be hot on one half of the grill and lower the heat on the other side, because the pressure in the cooker needed to be heated to raise the pressure and then lowered for about twenty minutes. In a regular oven Golabki need to be baked for at least one hour.

While my sister and I played, My Daddy helped My Mother set out the other side dishes. People would stop and stare at us and all of us would just laugh and start singing Polish songs like we couldn't speak English.

FILLING:
4 pounds ground beef (Angus Beef 20% fat preferred)
2 pounds ground pork
1 pound bacon
2 cups of each before stir-frying = celery, onions, green bell peppers
3 cups cooked rice (cooked very well done so it sticks together)

SEASONINGS = 1 teaspoon of **Mixed Blend of Seasonings** for General cooking (Alphabetical Order: Basil, Bay Leaves, Carrots, Cayenne Pepper, Celery Seed, Citric Acid, Coriander, Cumin, Garlic, Lemon Juice Powder, Lemon Oil, Marjoram, Mustard, Onion, Orange Peel, Oregano, Rosemary, Savory Thyme, and Tomato) into the ground beef before dividing in half.
Plus = ½ teaspoon of **Poultry Seasoning Mix** (Proportioned most to least: Thyme, Sage, Marjoram, Rosemary, Black Pepper, and Nutmeg), into the ground pork before dividing in half.

1 pound Bacon (Original, Thin Sliced, and Smoked) cut into tiny pieces and fry to a crisp and drain. Salt each of the vegetables lightly to bring out the "Caramel Sweetness" Stir-Fry in one tablespoon bacon grease for each vegetable.
Divide the meat in half place into two big bowls.
Cool everything in the refrigerator then place half of each of the ingredients into each bowl of beef/pork mixture. Blend the mixture with the vegetables and seasonings by using your fingers or two big spoons.

WRAPPING:

One head of Cabbage take off the top two outer layers of Cabbage leaves. Pick up the head and "slam" the core on a hard flat surface. This will separate the core from most of the other leaves. Carefully cut away the pieces of core.

Place the whole head of cabbage in a steamer, core side down, until outer leaves are soft and easy to peel off without falling apart. The leaves will have to be peeled off two or three layers at a time. Allow cooling time between peeling off the leaves. If the leaf is difficult to roll, trim off some of the thick rib of the leaf.

A temporary steamer can be made by placing four forks poked into the bottom of the head of cabbage and placing the cabbage head in a large kettle with purified water. The leaves will have to be peeled off two or three layers at a time. Allow cooling time between peeling off the leaves. If the leaf is difficult to roll trim off some of the thick rib of the leaf.

I made Golabki at least seven times before I was married, and the first time I made them as a newly wed, I cut my thumb and needed fourteen stitches.

Butter the bottom and sides of a casserole dish that has a cover. Take each leaf and fill just enough to overlap the cabbage leaf. Place the leaf rib side down, place the meat mixture in the "bowl-part of the leaf" and roll up only once over the meat. Take each side of the leaf and overlap on top. Place the Golabek in the dish with the lapping facing up. Top with tomato and vegetables mixture.

TOPPING:

Use one (1) tablespoon or more of canned Petite Diced Tomatoes, with celery, onions, & green bell peppers to top each Golabek depending on the size of the cabbage leaf.

Before I found this canned product, I would make my own topping using two cups fresh diced tomatoes, and one cup of each of the following celery, onions and green bell peppers stir-frying them separately before mixing them together. I prepared the topping the day before I actually made the Golabki and let the mixture cool overnight.

Preheat oven to 350º before rolling the Golabki.

Fill the casserole dish as evenly as possible.
If more than one layer, place one layer vertical and the second layer horizontal.
Bake covered for one hour and then shut off oven, place cover ajar and let stand for at least ten minutes in the oven before serving. Use a large "strainer" spoon to scoop out each Golabek.

The stuffing inside the cabbage leaves tastes "GREAT" and frequently crumbles apart; but we have to cut them apart anyway to eat them.

As far as I know, only my Mother made Golabki in a pressure cooker.

January   Kindness

Polish–American Activity = Busia Aprons

Viewer's Left to Right =
My Great-Grandmother Josephine
My Grandmother Pearl

Viewer's Left to Right =
Me, Jean Marie
My second daughter, Mary

Yellow Flowered Apron was the second apron that I had made upon my retirement from classroom teaching. The Blue Apron, I had worn out before I decided to write this book.

Yes, I laid the aprons on my bed to take the following pictures.

Yellow Flowered Apron

Front View

Back view showing the overlap of the two sides

Plaid Busia Apron

Front View

Back view showing the overlap of the two sides

Newspaper Pattern

Since I made a newspaper pattern from memory, I improved the "fit" with each pattern that I made. I saved the pattern for the Plaid Busia Apron because it fits my body best.

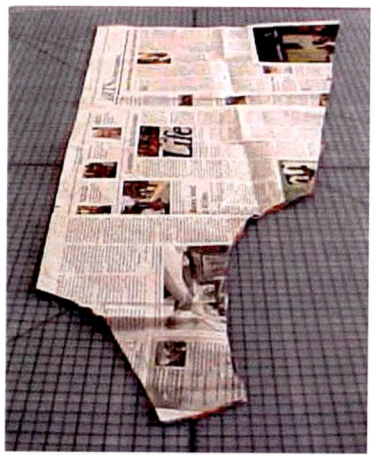

Front Panel = Straight edge is placed on the fold edge of the fabric and is one/third of the apron.

Side/Back Panels = Straight edge is placed on the open edge of the fabric to make the two sides. Each side is one/third of the apron.

    The Straight edge of each Side/Back Panel is sewn to the slant sides of the Front Panel.

To measure a person for a custom made Busia Apron measure around the largest part of the person's body; that most likely be the stomach or the hips. Divide that number by two and the result of the calculation is the width of the Front Panel and each Side/Back Panel at the widest point.

A Busia Apron usually covers the person down to the knees or lower. If the apron is too long it will get in the way when bending to reach low cupboards and when using the oven putting in and taking out pots and pans.

Busia Apron for a Small Child

January   Kindness

People of Polish Heritage = My Great-Grandmothers and My Grandmothers

1. Left to right = My Daddy's Grandmother with My Daddy's Mother = Busia Pearl

2. Left to right = My Mother's Grandmother with My Mother's Mother = Busia Helen

    All of my Grandmothers lived the example of Kindness. Yes, I know they had faults, but my purpose is to present the character traits and virtues that I recognized and wish to emulate not merely imitate. From my two Grandmothers, I learned much about being a woman, and now realize it was a special blessing, for I also learned how to grow old "peacefully" even when my body isn't cooperating.

My Daddy's Mother, Busia Pearl lived to the age of one-hundred-two (102) in her own home.
My Mother's Mother, Busia Helen lived to the age of ninety-eight (98) in her own home.
From my two Busias I received unconditional love and observed many acts of kindness.

1. The picture of my Busia Pearl with her Mother, my Great-grandmother, are wearing aprons made in the pattern of the aprons that both of my Busias made for me. I learned the basics of sewing by watching my two Grandmothers sew and mend clothing for their large families and grandchildren.
1. For Christmas presents, when my three eldest daughters were very young, I sewed matching aprons for each of them and my sister's three daughters. Yes, we made the patterns from newspaper back then too. By the time our last two daughters were born I was sewing Halloween Costumes instead of aprons.
1. I didn't learn to walk until I was almost two years old, and I didn't talk much, so my Daddy said, "Once I learned to talk and walk they couldn't get me to shut up or sit down." I was a very lively child, and frequently got on my Mother's nerves so my Daddy would take me for walks to his Mother's house while my Mother was preparing dinner. My Daddy would talk to me about all the things that we saw along the route, which was a little shorter than one mile. I share more memories about my Daddy in my other book, "God Carries Me Like My Daddy."   Once we got to Busia Pearl's house, if it was raining we would go inside the back door which opened into a "Pullman Kitchen," long and narrow, along the outside wall was a long window with glass shelves that held many pots of plants. Some were filled with herbs others held flowers, and vines including a "sweet potato vine."
1. Busia Pearl had a wooden step stool high enough to reach the counter, so a person could sit on it and work on the counter. The steps were used by Busia to reach the high shelves in the kitchen. When I came over, Busia was usually also preparing dinner, but she would pop an apron (Just my size) over my head and set me up on the stool. Depending on what she was preparing she would tell me the steps for each ingredient. In this book, I give the complete recipe for "Pasties" that I learned from Busia Pearl. The first steps are to prepare the vegetables. While Busia peeled

potatoes she would give me the carrots to brush off the roots in a bowl of cool water. While Busia chopped the carrots and potatoes, she would give the celery to me and taught me to carefully peel each stalk away from the center, then break each stalk in half to take off the "strings" and set the halves in the bowl of water, when I got older she would add another chore, such as cutting the different vegetables in "bite size pieces." The strings and peelings went into a large bowl and were taken out and placed in the compost bin behind the back porch.

1. The walks with my Daddy took place from the time I was three until I reached ten years old. My brother Chris was born in May after I had turned ten. After my brother was born, my Mother realized that I could be "helpful" both in the kitchen and by entertaining my little brother, while she prepared dinner. I remember those days fondly. The walks with my Daddy were fewer but we still found time to talk with each other.

2. During the day when my Daddy was at work, My Mother would call someone on the telephone and say, "I will be right over as soon as I dump Jean Marie off at Busia's house." I was elated and literally danced around singing, "I'm going to play with Busia today." When I got to Busia Helen's house, it was full of activity. Starting at the age of three years old when I was dumped off at Busia's house, she too would pop-on my special apron. I am including a short story based on these visits.

Only Busia Bakes Bread

My Mother, my sister, and I would bake Christmas cookies together by the time I was three years old. On other occasions we would bake Chocolate Chips cookies. One day when we were baking Chocolate Chip Cookies, I asked my Mother why she didn't bake bread she responded with, "Only Busia bakes bread." I accepted the answer and promised myself that I would find out "Why only 'Mine Busia' bakes bread." It must have been quite a while before Busia baked bread. One rainy day, when "I was dumped off at Busia Helen's house," she asked me, "What do you want to do today?" Of course, I responded with, "Let's bake bread." We went into the kitchen. She got out my apron and popped it over my head, set me on a metal step stool, all painted white, and got out the ingredients. She told me the name of each ingredient and measurement as she did each step, and I watched her. Finally, she had the dough all mixed in a big bowl and she went into the dining room, and cleared off the beautiful lace tablecloth and put what looked like a white sheet for a bed on the big wooden, dining room table. I learned later that it was called a "pedestal table" because it had one big fat leg right smack dab in the middle of the table top with claws sticking out in four directions for balance.

Busia Helen brought the metal stool with her on the next trip into the kitchen. She went back and brought two big flat boards that were wrapped in white towels and placed the biggest board at one end of the table and the smaller of the two on one side. Busia set me on the metal stool with the smaller cutting board in front of me.

Busia Helen took a big round ball of dough out of her bowl and set it on her board with the towel. I noticed she had sprinkled the towel with a handful of flour. She patted the dough down then rolled up one end of the dough and pushed the dough with the "heels" of both hands and the table made a loud squeak, and when she lifted her hands to turn the dough the table made two smaller squeaks. She continued "kneading" the dough this way for a short while.

She smiled at me and took a smaller ball of dough out of the big dough in which she had mixed the ingredients for bread. She had set aside the first ball of dough and took another big ball of dough. She smiled and nodded to me so I knew that she wanted me to copy her movements. She prepared six big loaves of bread and I prepared three small loaves of bread. She covered the loaves with warm wet towels and set them back on the kitchen table.

Busia then took me into the living room where we prayed the Rosary together. Praying made me drowsy so Busia took me into her bedroom and tossed me on her "Down Bed" with a "Down Comforter" on top. I felt like I had been tossed on a cloud and soon fell asleep. I woke up later to the wonderful aroma of fresh baked bread. Busia smiled when I peeked into the kitchen and patted the stool and she set me by the kitchen table. She cut off both ends of one of the loaves of bread and slathered on home-made butter and gave one slice to me and sat down and told jokes as we enjoyed the "Best part of the Bread."

It seemed like just a short time and my Mother came in the front door of Busia's house. I ran up to my Mother and said, "I know why only Busia bakes bread!" My Mother smiled and asked, "You do?" Nodding vigorously I said, "You don't have a squeaky table." Actually, I remembered most of these events and my Daddy and Mother loved repeating this story to their friends. It was a long time before I understood why their friends laughed every time they heard this story.

2. On some sunny days when I was six years young, see picture in May Chapter, Busia Helen would take off my light blue dress, white shoes, and white socks. She would take out my hair ribbon and tie my hair back in a pony tail with a "strip of cloth". She would then dress me in Uncle Danny's out grown shirt, blue jeans, socks and tennis shoes send me outside to play baseball with Uncle Danny and his friends. For more details refer to April Chapter.

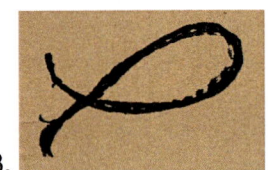

1. & 2.   3.   4.

1. Top Picture = Front of my Mother's Parents' Home on Industrial Avenue in Flint, Michigan.
2. Bottom Picture = Back of my Mother's Parents' Home with the big back porch screened and storm windows for winter.
3. Busia Helen had a large back porch. On the porch corner post facing the side street was this Fish Symbol which was used by early Christians who knew that most of the first Apostles chosen by Jesus were fishermen. It was used by my Busias to signal the Hoboes who had hopped off the freight trains that they could get food at that home. My Busia felt safe because she had her Guardian Angel and a Big Dog. Her first dog was Cubby a Siberian Husky that looked like a little bear cub when he was a puppy. The second dog was Ziggy who was a purebred Collie. When a Hobo knocked on the porch door, Busia would tell him to wait until she was back in her house before coming into the porch and she made sure that he saw her dog. Both dogs were trained to growl at strangers. Busia would go into the house lock the door, warm up a big bowl of soup, unlock the door with her dog close by her, place the soup on a cabinet close to the door, tell the Hobo to leave the bowl there, and finally say, "Go with God and pray for me." Busia never had any trouble when she was home, and she was sure that the one time that her home was robbed when she wasn't at home that it was a "stranger" who didn't recognize the Fish Symbol.
4. My sister Barbara and I are bundled up for winter, Polish style.

There are more Busia stories interspersed throughout this book. Both of my Busias were kind to others and generous with their time and food to help family, friends, neighbors, and even strangers.

Jesus said, "What you did to others you did it to ME."

Living the virtue of Kindness means doing something good and not expecting anything in return.

February   Love

Columbine in Neighbor's Yard

Fruit of the Holy Spirit = Love

Liturgical Calendar = Holy Family

Devotions and Celebrations = God is Love

Polish–American Recipe = Chicken Soup

Polish–American Activity = Wycinanki - Valentines

People of Polish Heritage = Dzia Dzia Walenty, Busia Helen, and Uncles

February Love

Fruit of the Holy Spirit = Love

Prayer:

     Holy Spirit, eternal Love of the Father and the Son, kindly bestow on us the fruit of charity, that we may be united to You by divine Love.

Love = to perform ALL our actions out of love for God.

Love = to exhibit the virtue of charity, or love, by our unselfish devotion and care for our neighbor.

A new commandment I give to you, that you love one another; even as I have loved you, that you also love one another. By this all men will know that you are my disciples, if you have love for one another." (John 13: 33-36)

"Teacher, which commandment in the law is the greatest?" Jesus said to him, "You shall love the Lord your God with all your heart, and with all your soul, and with all your mind.' This is the greatest and first commandment. The second is: 'You shall love your neighbor as yourself.' (Matthew 22: 36 – 40)

Little children, let us not love in word or speech but in deed and in truth. (1 John 3: 17-19)

Beloved, let us love one another; for love is of God, and he who loves is born of God and knows God. (1 John 4: 6-8)

So we know and believe the love God has for us. God is Love, and they who abide in love abide in God, and God abides in them. (1 John 4:15 – 17)

St. Paul told us: "Faith, hope, love abide, these three; but the greatest of these is love." (1 Corinthians 13: 13)

Charity is our love for God above all things for His own sake, and our neighbor as ourselves for the love of God. Jesus told His apostles. (John 13: 34)

St. Paul told us. "Love one another; even as I have loved you, that you also love one another. By this all men will know that you are My disciples, if you have love for one another." (1 Corinthians 13: 13)

"Faith, hope, love abide, these three, but the greatest of these is love." Charity is a gift to us from God wrapped in Sanctifying Grace. Charity like hope resides in the will. (John 15: 9 – 17)

February Love

Liturgical Calendar = Holy Family

Holy Family Litany

LEADER PRAYS.	FAITHFUL RESPOND.
Lord, have mercy on us.	Christ, have mercy on us.
Lord, have mercy on us. Jesus, hear us.	Jesus, graciously hear us.
God the Father of Heaven,	have mercy on us.
God the Son, Redeemer of the world,	have mercy on us.
God the Holy Spirit,	have mercy on us.
Holy Trinity, One God,	have mercy on us.
Infant, Jesus Christ,	have mercy on us.
Infant, true God,	have mercy on us.
Infant, Son of the living God,	have mercy on us.
Infant, Son of the Virgin Mary,	have mercy on us.
Infant, strong in weakness,	have mercy on us.
Infant, powerful in tenderness,	have mercy on us.
Infant, Treasure of grace,	have mercy on us.
Infant, Fountain of love,	have mercy on us.
Infant, Renewer of the heavens,	have mercy on us.
Infant, Repairer of the evils of the earth,	have mercy on us.
Infant, Head of the angels,	have mercy on us.
Infant, Root of the patriarchs,	have mercy on us.
Infant, Speech of the prophets,	have mercy on us.
Infant, Desire of the Gentiles,	have mercy on us.
Infant, Joy of shepherds,	have mercy on us.
Infant, Light of the Magi,	have mercy on us.
Infant, Salvation of infants,	have mercy on us.
Infant, Expectation of the just,	have mercy on us.
Infant, Instructor of the wise,	have mercy on us.
Infant, First-fruit of all saints,	have mercy on us.
Be merciful,	spare us, O Infant Jesus.
Be merciful,	graciously hear us, O Infant Jesus.
From the slavery of the children of Adam,	Infant Jesus, deliver us.
From the slavery of the devil,	Infant Jesus, deliver us.
From the evil desires of the flesh,	Infant Jesus, deliver us.
From the malice of the world,	Infant Jesus, deliver us.
From the pride of life,	Infant Jesus, deliver us.
From the inordinate desire of knowing,	Infant Jesus, deliver us.
From blindness of spirit,	Infant Jesus, deliver us.
From an evil will,	Infant Jesus, deliver us.
From our sins,	Infant Jesus, deliver us.
Through Thy most pure Conception,	Infant Jesus, deliver us.
Through Thy most humble Nativity,	Infant Jesus, deliver us.
Through Thy tears,	Infant Jesus, deliver us.
Through Thy most painful Circumcision,	Infant Jesus, deliver us.

Through Thy most glorious Epiphany,	Infant Jesus, deliver us.
Through Thy most pious Presentation,	Infant Jesus, deliver us.
Through Thy most divine life,	Infant Jesus, deliver us.
Through Thy poverty,	Infant Jesus, deliver us.
Through Thy many sufferings,	Infant Jesus, deliver us.
Through Thy labors and travels,	Infant Jesus, deliver us.
Lamb of God, Who takes away the sins of the world,	have mercy on us, O Infant Jesus.
Lamb of God, Who takes away the sins of the world,	graciously hear us, O Infant Jesus.
Lamb of God, Who takes away the sins of the world,	have mercy on us.
Jesus, Infant, hear us.	Jesus, Infant, graciously hear us.

Let Us Pray

O Lord Christ, Thou were pleased so to humble Thyself in Thine incarnate divinity and most sacred humanity as to be born in time and become a little child. Grant that we may acknowledge infinite wisdom in the silence of a child, power in weakness, and majesty in humiliation. Adoring Thy humiliations on earth, may we contemplate Thy glories in Heaven, Who with the Father and the Holy Spirit, lives and reigns forever. Amen.

Holy Family Novena

Jesus, Mary, and Joseph, bless me and grant me the grace of loving Holy Church as I should, above every earthly thing, and of ever showing my love by deeds.

Jesus, Mary, and Joseph, bless me and grant me the grace of openly professing as I should, with courage and without human respect, the faith that I received as your gift in holy Baptism.

Jesus, Mary, and Joseph, bless me and grant me the grace of sharing as I should in the defense and propagation of the Faith when duty calls, whether by word or by the sacrifice of my possessions and my life.

Jesus, Mary, and Joseph, bless me and grant me the grace of loving my family and others in mutual charity as I should, and establish us in perfect harmony of thought, will, and action, under the rule and guidance of the shepherds of the Church.

Jesus, Mary, and Joseph, bless me and grant me the grace of conforming my life fully as I should to the commandments of God's law and those of His Holy Church, so as to live always in that charity which they set forth.

Jesus, Mary, and Joseph, I ask in particular this special favor: *(Mention your favor).*

The month of February is traditionally dedicated to the Holy Family. Between the events which marked Christmas and the beginning of Christ's public life, the Catholic Church turns our attention toward the Holy Family to inspire the Christian family to strive to live unconditional love for All Human Beings from conception to natural death.

February usually begins in one Liturgical Season - Ordinary Time and ends in another, Lent. In February the feast, Presentation of our Lord is celebrated between two other seasons, Christmas and Easter. The Presentation of our Lord includes the prophecy of Simeon when the small Christ Child is being offered to God His Father.

The prophecy of Simeon: "And Simeon blessed them, and said to Mary his mother: Behold this child is set for the fall and for the resurrection of many in Israel, and for a sign which shall be contradicted; And thy own soul a sword shall pierce." (Luke II: 34-35).

The Solemnity of the **Presentation of the Lord** on February 2nd refers back to the Christmas mystery of Light except that now, Christ, the helpless babe, is "the Light of Revelation to the Gentiles who will save his people from their sins." Candles, symbolizing Christ our Light, will be carried in procession on this day. The Paschal candle that was lit during the Easter Vigil Liturgy the Saturday before Easter is included.

"The Light of Revelation" shines more brightly with each successive Sunday of Ordinary Time, until its magnificence – exposing our sinfulness and need for conversion – propels us into the penitential Season of Lent. We prepare to accept the cross of blest ashes on Ash Wednesday and plunge ourselves into the major exercises of Lent – fasting, prayer, almsgiving – laying our thoughts and prayers on the heart of our Mother Mary. She, who offered her Son in the temple and on the Cross, will teach us how to deny ourselves, take up our cross daily, and follow after her Son.

February Love

Devotions and Celebrations = God is Love

The month of February is traditionally dedicated to the Holy Family. Between the events which marked Christmas and the beginning of Christ's public life, the Catholic Church turns our attention toward the Holy Family to inspire the Christian family to strive to live unconditional love for All Human Beings from conception to natural death.

Dedication of One's Family

Most loving Jesus, by Your sublime and beautiful virtues of humility, obedience, poverty, modesty, charity, patience, and gentleness, You blessed with peace and happiness the family which You chose on earth. In Your mercy look upon my family. We belong to You, for we have received Your many blessings over many years and we entrust ourselves to Your loving care. Look upon my family in Your loving kindness, preserve us from danger, give us help in time of need, and grant us the grace to persevere to the end in imitation of Your holy Family, so that having revered You and loved You faithfully on earth, we may praise You eternally in heaven. Mary, dearest Mother, to your intercession we have recourse, knowing that your Divine Son will hear your prayers. Glorious patriarch, Saint Joseph, help us by your powerful prayers and offer our prayers to Jesus through Mary's hands. Amen.

Prayer

Lord Jesus Christ, being subject to Mary and Joseph, You sanctified family life by Your beautiful virtues. Grant that we, with the help of Mary and Joseph, may be taught by the example of Your holy Family, and may after death enjoy its everlasting companionship.
Lord Jesus, help us ever to follow the example of Your holy Family, that in the hour of our death Your glorious Virgin Mother together with Saint Joseph may come to meet us, and we may be worthy to be received by You into the everlasting joys of heaven. You live and reign forever. Amen.

Holy Reminders and Sacramentals

1. Medals   2. Scapulars   3. Rosaries & Chaplet Beads

4. Pictures – Statues – Palms – Candles – Holy Water

Sacramentals are not required by the Catholic Church. Sacramentals are called Holy Reminders, and considered similar to pictures of family members and famous people.

1. **Medals** = Medals have images on both sides: Jesus on one side and his Mother on the other are most common. Some have an image of a Canonized Saint and a short prayer on the reverse side.
2. **Scapulars** = Scapulars for the Lay People are miniature, over the shoulder representations of the long garments worn by men and women who have consecrated their lives in service to God and the Catholic Church.
3. **Rosaries** = Rosary beads have been used to pray the Psalms in the Old Testament of the Holy Bible. See the October Chapter for a more detailed description of the Mysteries of the Rosary and the Scriptural verses that are meditated on during these prayers.
3. **Chaplet Beads** = See the April Chapter in this book for a description of the Divine Mercy Chaplet. The Chaplet Beads of Saint Michael the Archangel surround the regular Rosary Beads in the illustration above. The Lord's Prayer is said on each large bead and three Hail Mary's are said on the small beads. Short prayers asking the different Choirs of Angels to protect us from the snares of the evil ones are said before each large bead.
4. **Pictures** = Pictures of the Holy Family. Jesus, Mary, and Joseph, and others Saints and Angels can be compared to having pictures of Family members, living or dead, hanging or otherwise on display.
4. **Statues** = Just as we have statues of famous people of their heroic deeds, we have statues to remind us of Holy people and Heavenly Beings.
4. **Palms** = Palms are used to remind us of the triumphant entry of Jesus into Jerusalem. The previous years palms are burned and the ashes are used on Ash Wednesday at the beginning of Lent. Please refer to the March chapter for more information.
4. **Candles** = Candles symbolize Jesus the Light of the world. Jesus came into the world to bring to light the Love of God.
4. **Holy Water** = We keep Holy Water in our Churches and in our homes to remind us of our Baptism when we are dedicated to God and marked with an invisible sign as a child of God.

February Love

Polish–American Recipe = *Zupa = Kury z Jarzynami*: Chicken Soup

First Day - Braised Chicken Thighs

Step 7. Tea Ball contents

Step 13. Chicken falls off bone.

Preheat Oven to 275º degrees.
1. Place two tablespoons butter in a medium frying pan. Simmer two (2) cups celery and two (2) cups onions separately; lightly salt and sprinkle with Poultry seasoning while frying.
2. Line the bottom of an oven-proof, square casserole dish with half of the onions and celery. The dimensions of my dish are four (4) inches deep and ten (10) inches square. Save the rest of the onions and celery in a bowl to use for topping.
3. In the same pan without washing it, place four Tablespoons butter. Take ten thawed chicken thighs and cut off the Elimination Tail. Some people suck on them to gross-out others.
4. Take off any pin-feathers with a small bladed knife. Rinse each thigh in purified water and set on a plate to drain. .Sprinkle each thigh with salt and Poultry Seasoning. The commercial brand that I use has the following ingredients = Poultry Seasoning Mix Proportioned most to least: Thyme, Sage, Marjoram, Rosemary, Black Pepper, and Nutmeg.
5. On a medium high heat, brown three or four thighs at a time for five (5) minutes on the skin side down and seven (7) minutes on the bone side down. Turn down the heat if the spices are getting dark brown and sticking.
6. Place one thigh in each of the four corners and one in the middle a little off center, SKIN SIDE DOWN.
7. In a Tea Ball place six (6) or seven (7) Whole Allspice, and the equivalent of two, large, dehydrated, Bay Leaves about three (3) inches long each.
8. Place the filled Tea Ball next to the thigh in the middle of the dish.
9. Brown the rest of the chicken thighs and place them in the dish SKIN SIDE UP between the first batch.
10. Pour one half cup of purified water into the frying pan to dissolve the spices and pour over the filled Tea Ball.
11. Carefully place some onions and celery that were set aside, on top of each thigh.
12. Place casserole dish in the center of the preheated oven, cover and bake for two (2) hours.
13. After two hours, test if done by using tongs to pickup each thigh bone and shake gently. If the meat falls off the bone it is done. If the meat does not fall off continue baking and check a different thigh at half hour intervals. Some thighs took over three hours, but it is worth it.
14. Using a dish and two kettles separate the meat into the dish.

15. Place all of the onions, celery, and all the juices in a small kettle; add one cup cool purified water, pat down the onions and celery below the water level., cover, and set aside to cool before placing the kettle in the refrigerator.
16. In the morning the fat can be lifted off easily with a fork, and discarded.
17. Place skin, bones, cartilage, and solid fat particles into a four quart kettle or slow cooker. Add four cups purified water to the cooker and the Tea Ball.
18. Cook the bones, etc. on low for three more hours. After the three hours strain the clear broth into a large kettle that can be refrigerated and add the Tea Ball. You won't know if it was long enough until the next day. The broth should be semi-solid like Gelatine.
19. Lift off the layers of fat from both kettles and discard the fat.

Second Day - Soup from Braised Chicken Thighs

1. Place two cups Baby Carrots in a steamer or kettle for twenty minutes.
2. When done drain water into the kettle that has the strained chicken broth.
3. Use a fork and small sharp knife to cut the Baby Carrots into bite sized pieces.
4. With the stove element set on Low, heat up the kettle that has the strained chicken broth to simmer.
5. Add the onions, celery, and cut carrots; simmer for twenty minutes and the Chicken Soup is done.
6. At this stage, the Chicken Soup will freeze well.
7. To serve, prepare Kluski, egg noodles, rice or small pasta following the directions on the package. Heat the Chicken Soup from one container.

1. Dry, store purchased Kluski.

2. Kluski boiled and added to bowl of soup.

3. Soup with garden fresh herbs.

4. Steamed rice added to broth with commercial blend of spices.

February Love

Polish–American Activity = Wycinanki - Valentines

Saint Valentines Day February 14, we made Wycinanki cards for special people.

Completed Valentine sample.

Start with a full size square sheet of paper. Colored paper & paper with designs can also be used.

FOLDING INSTRUCTIONS

1. Fold in half.

2. Fold in quarters.

3. Fold diagonally, draw or cut.

Draw or cut the paper when folded in eighths and then refold to add more designs. Personalize each Valentine with other Wycinanki patterns, little flowers, symbols of the person's favorite sport, or little greeting "Talk Bubbles" similar to those in comic books.

February Love

People of Polish Heritage = People Who Lived Unconditional Love
The Unconditional Love from My Mother's Parents & Brothers Sustained Me through the Tumultuous Times of World War II.
My Mother's Parents & Brothers Lived & Loved in This Home That Dzia Dzia Built.

1. Dzia Dzia was my Mother's Tata/Daddy, My grandfather. Dzia Dzia Urbanik helped build their family home and was one of the builders of All Saints Catholic Church where Dzia Dzia Urbanik was organist. When I was only three years old he would set me on the organ bench beside him even during Mass. During the Gospel readings we would turn away from the huge pipe organ and face the altar. One Sunday when we turned I slipped off the bench onto the foot peddles and it blasted out a loud booming sound. Dzia Dzia tenderly picked up me, set me back next to him and hugged me close until it was time to turn back toward the keys. He made sure I was securely situated on the organ bench before playing the next Hymn.

1. When I was seven years young, he died Good Friday morning before I had made my First Holy Communion. Two lessons that he taught me have guided my life. He truly Loved his neighbors. We lived in the integrated part of Flint, Michigan and Dzia Dzia was sitting in his rocker on the front porch and I was sitting on one of the "stoops" when a Policeman was walking the beat. The Policeman had very dark black skin color. My Dzia Dzia with a heavy Polish accent said, "Good morning - good neighbor." I asked, "What's his name?" My Dzia Dzia said, "I don't know." Then I asked, "Where does he live? How do you know he is good?" Dzia Dzia chortled, "There is no such thing as a stranger – we are all God's children." On another occasion Dzia Dzia stated, "Janina you keep busy looking for the good in people and you won't have time to see the bad." Years later, I realized the wisdom in this statement. At first glance it says – the person will have so many Good Qualities you won't notice the Bad. On the other hand the person could have so many Bad habits that it will take along time to find the Good ones.

2. This picture was taken on my twin uncles Eighth Grade Graduation. Back row left to right are Dzia Dzia and Uncle Johnny, Standing are Uncle Benny, Busia Helen, and Uncle Bernard. Holding Cubby is my Uncle Danny. I remember many holidays filled with music. My Uncles didn't "Baby sit" me they called it "Visiting me." Uncle Danny let me play baseball with him and his friends. Read The January Chapter for Busia Helen's and April Chapter for more Uncles' memories.

God is Love and they who live in Love live in God and God lives in them.

March   Self-Control

Marigolds in Neighbor's Yard

Fruit of the Holy Spirit = Self-Control

Liturgical Calendar = Saint Joseph

Devotions and Celebrations = Lent

Polish–American Recipe = *Paczki:* Fried Doughnuts

Polish–American Activity = Palm Weaving

People of Polish Heritage = Uncle Steve and Aunt Irene

March   Self-Control

Fruit of the Holy Spirit = Self-Control

Prayer:

    Holy Spirit, eternal Love of the Father and the Son, kindly bestow on us the the fruits of self-control and chastity, that we may keep our bodies in such holiness as befits your temple, so that having by your assistance preserved our hearts pure on earth, we may merit in Jesus Christ, according to the words of the Gospel, to see God eternally in the glory of his kingdom.

Self-control = to exercise self-control by working to overcome the temptations we face and by trying always to do God's will.

Self-Control = to restrain our negative emotions such as anger.

And if any one loves righteousness, her labors are virtues; for she teaches self-control and prudence, justice and courage; nothing in life is more profitable for men than these. (Wisdom 8:6-8)

But the fruit of the Holy Spirit is love, joy, peace, patience, kindness, goodness, faithfulness, gentleness, self-control, against such there is no law. (Galatians 5: 21-24)

For God did not give us a spirit of timidity but a spirit of power and love and self-control. (Timothy 1:6-8)

For this reason, make every effort to supplement your faith with virtue, virtue with knowledge, knowledge with self-control, self-control with endurance, endurance with devotion, devotion with mutual affection, and mutual affection with love. (2 Peter 1: 5-7)

March Self-Control

Liturgical Calendar = Saint Joseph

We know Joseph was a man of faith, obedient to whatever God asked of him without knowing the outcome. When the angel came to Joseph in a dream and told him the truth about the child Mary was carrying, Joseph immediately and without question or concern for gossip, took Mary as his wife. When the angel came again to tell him that his family was in danger, he immediately left everything he owned, all his family and friends, and fled to a strange country with his young wife and the baby. He waited in Egypt without question until the angel told him it was safe to go back.

The month of March is dedicated to Saint Joseph. The Solemnity of Saint Joseph, March 19, is a special day this month in which we celebrate the great honor bestowed upon the foster father of Jesus. Also on the Solemnity of the Annunciation, March 25, we ponder Our Lady's fiat.

Litany of Saint Joseph

LEADER PRAYS.	**FAITHFUL RESPOND.**
Lord, have mercy.	Lord, have mercy.
Christ, have mercy.	Christ, have mercy.
Lord, have mercy.	Lord, have mercy.
Jesus, hear us. Jesus,	graciously hear us.
God, the Father of Heaven,	Have mercy on us.
God, the Son, Redeemer of the world,	Have mercy on us.
God, the Holy Spirit,	Have mercy on us.
Holy Trinity, One God,	Have mercy on us.
Holy Mary,	pray for us.
St. Joseph,	pray for us.
Renowned offspring of David,	pray for us.
Light of Patriarchs,	pray for us.
Spouse of the Mother of God,	pray for us.
Chaste guardian of the Virgin,	pray for us.
Foster father of the Son of God,	pray for us.
Diligent protector of Christ,	pray for us.

Head of the Holy Family,	pray for us.
Joseph most just,	pray for us.
Joseph most chaste,	pray for us.
Joseph most prudent,	pray for us.
Joseph most strong,	pray for us.
Joseph most obedient,	pray for us.
Joseph most faithful,	pray for us.
Mirror of patience,	pray for us.
Lover of poverty,	pray for us.
Model of artisans,	pray for us.
Glory of home life,	pray for us.
Guardian of virgins,	pray for us.
Pillar of families,	pray for us.
Solace of the wretched,	pray for us.
Hope of the sick,	pray for us.
Patron of the dying,	pray for us.
Terror of demons,	pray for us.
Protector of Holy Church,	pray for us.
Lamb of God, who take away the sins of the world,	spare us, O Lord.
Lamb of God, who take away the sins of the world,	spare us, O Lord.
Lamb of God, who take away the sins of the world.	graciously hear us, O Lord.

He made him the lord of his household, and prince over all his possessions.

Saint Joseph - Novena Prayer

This prayer is said at the end of each day's devotion.

Saint Joseph, I, your child, greet you. You are the faithful protector and intercessor of all who love and venerate you. You know that I have special confidence in you and that, after Jesus and Mary, I place my hope of salvation in you, for you are especially powerful with God and will never abandon your faithful children. Therefore I humbly invoke you and commend myself, with all who are dear to me and all that belong to me, to your intercession. I beg of you, by your love for Jesus and Mary, not to abandon me during life and to assist me at the hour of my death.

Glorious Saint Joseph, spouse of the Immaculate Virgin, intercede for me a pure, humble, charitable mind, and resignation to the divine Will of God. Be my guide, my father, and my model through life that I may merit to die as you did in the arms of Jesus and Mary.

Loving Saint Joseph, faithful follower of Jesus Christ, I raise my heart to you to implore your powerful intercession in obtaining from the Divine Heart of Jesus all the graces necessary for my spiritual and temporal welfare, particularly the grace of a happy death, and the special grace I now implore: (Mention your request).

Guardian of the Word Incarnate, I feel confident that your prayers on my behalf will be graciously heard before the throne of God. Amen.

MEMORARE

Remember, most pure spouse of Mary, ever Virgin, my loving protector, Saint Joseph to whom no one ever had recourse to your protection or asked for your aid without obtaining relief. Confiding, therefore, in your goodness, I come before you and humbly implore you. Despise not my petitions, foster-father of the Redeemer, but graciously receive them. Amen.

First Day = Foster-Father of Jesus

Saint Joseph, you were privileged to share in the mystery of the Incarnation as the foster-father of Jesus. Mary alone was directly connected with the fulfilment of the mystery, in that she gave her consent to Christ's conception and allowed the Holy Spirit to form the sacred humanity of Jesus from her blood. You had a part in this mystery in an indirect manner, by fulfilling the condition necessary for the Incarnation -- the protection of Mary's virginity before and during your married life with her. You made the virginal marriage possible, and this was a part of God's plan, foreseen, willed, and decreed from all eternity.

In a more direct manner you shared in the support, upbringing, and protection of the Divine Child as His earthly foster-father. For this purpose the Heavenly Father gave you a genuine heart of a father -- a heart full of love and self-sacrifice. With the toil of your hands you were obliged to offer protection to the Divine Child, to procure for Him food, clothing, and a home. You were truly the saint of the holy childhood of Jesus -- the living created providence who watched over the Christ-Child.

When Herod sought the Child to put Him to death, the Heavenly Father sent an angel but only as a messenger, giving orders for the flight; the rest He left entirely in your hands. It was that fatherly love which was the only refuge that received and protected the Divine Child. Your fatherly love carried Him through the desert into Egypt until all enemies were removed. Then on your arms the Child returned to Nazareth to be nourished and provided for during many years by the labor of your hands. Whatever a human son owes to a human father for all the benefits of his up-bringing and support, Jesus owed to you, because you were to Him His earthly, foster-father, teacher, and protector.

You served the Divine Child with a singular love. God gave you a heart filled with heavenly, supernatural love -- a love far deeper and more powerful than any biological father's love could be.

You served the Divine Child with great unselfishness, without any regard to self-interest, but not without sacrifices. You did not toil for yourself, but you seemed to be an instrument intended for the benefit of others, to be put aside as soon as it had done its work, for you disappeared from the scene once the childhood of Jesus had passed.

You were the shadow of the Heavenly Father not only as the earthly representative of the authority of the Father, but also by means of your fatherhood -- which only appeared to be natural -- you were to hide for a while the divinity of Jesus. What a wonderfully sublime and divine vocation was yours -- the loving Child who you carried in your arms, and loved and served so faithfully, had God in Heaven as Father and was Himself God!

Yours is a very special rank among the saints of the Kingdom of God, because you were so much a part of the very life of the Word of God made Man. In your house at Nazareth and under your care the redemption of mankind was prepared. What you accomplished, you did for us. You are not only a powerful and great saint in the Kingdom of God, but a benefactor of the whole of Christendom and mankind. Your rank in the Kingdom of God, surpassing far in dignity and honor of all the angels, deserves our very special veneration, love, and gratitude.

Saint Joseph, I thank God for your privilege of having been chosen by God to be the earthly, foster-father of His Divine Son. As a token of your own gratitude to God for this your greatest privilege, obtain for me the grace of a very devoted love for Jesus Christ, my God and my Savior. Help me to serve Him with some of the self-sacrificing love and devotion which you had while on this earth with Him. Grant that through your intercession with Jesus, your foster-Son, I may reach the degree of holiness God has destined for me, and save my soul.

Second Day = Virginal Husband of Mary

Saint Joseph, I honor you as the true husband of Mary. Scripture says: "Jacob begot Joseph, the husband of Mary, and of her was born Jesus who is called Christ" (Matt. 1:16). Your marriage to Mary was a sacred contract by which you and Mary gave yourselves to each other. Mary really belonged to you with all she was and had. You had a right to her love and obedience; and no other person so won her esteem, obedience, and love.

You were also the protector and witness of Mary's virginity. By your marriage you gave to each other your virginity, and also the mutual right over it -- a right to safeguard the other's virtue. This mutual virginity also belonged to the divine plan of the Incarnation, for God sent His angel to assure you that motherhood and virginity in Mary could be united.

This union of marriage not only brought you into daily familiar association with Mary, the loveliest of God's creatures, but also enabled you to share with her a mutual exchange of spiritual goods.

Mary found her edification in your calm, humble, and deep virtue, purity, and sanctity. What a great honor comes to you from this close union with her whom the Son of God calls Mother and whom He declared the Queen of heaven and earth! Whatever Mary had belonged by right to you also, and this included her Son, even though He had been given to her by God in a wonderful way. Jesus belonged to you as His legal, earthly, father. Your marriage was the way which God chose to have Jesus introduced into the world, a great divine mystery from which all benefits have come to us.

God the Son confided the guardianship and the support of His Immaculate Mother to your care. Mary's life was that of the Mother of the Savior, who did not come upon earth to enjoy honors and pleasures, but to redeem the world by hard work, suffering, and the cross. You were the faithful companion, support, and comforter of the Mother of Sorrows. How loyal you were to her in poverty, journeying, work, and pain. Your love for Mary was based upon your esteem for her as Mother of God. After God and the Divine Child, you loved no one as much as her. Mary responded to this love. She submitted to your guidance with naturalness and easy grace and childlike confidence. The Holy Spirit Himself was the bond of the great love which united your hearts. Saint Joseph, I thank God for your privilege of being the virginal husband of Mary. As a token of your own gratitude to God, obtain for me the grace to love Jesus with all my heart, as you did, and love Mary with some of the tenderness and loyalty with which you loved her.

Third Day = Man Chosen by the Blessed Trinity

Saint Joseph, you were the man chosen by God the Father. He selected you to be His representative on earth, hence He granted you all the graces and blessings you needed to be His worthy representative. You were the man chosen by God the Son. Desirous of a worthy, earthly, foster-father, He added His own riches and gifts, and above all, His love. The true measure of your sanctity is to be judged by your imitation of Jesus. You were entirely consecrated to Jesus, working always near Him, offering Him your virtues, your work, your sufferings, your very life. Jesus lived in you perfectly so that you were transformed into Him. In this resides your special glory, and the keynote of your sanctity. Hence, after Mary, you are the holiest of the saints.

You were chosen by the Holy Spirit. He is the mutual Love of the Father and the Son -- the heart of the Holy Trinity. In His wisdom He draws forth all creatures from nothing, guides them to their end in showing them their destiny and giving them the means to reach it. Every vocation and every fulfilment of a vocation proceeds from the Holy Spirit. As a foster-father of Jesus and head of the Holy Family, you had an exalted and most responsible vocation -- to open the way for the redemption of the world and to prepare for it by the education and guidance of the youth of the God-Man. In this work you cooperated as the instrument of the Holy Spirit. The Holy Spirit was the guide; you obeyed and carried out the works. How perfectly you obeyed the guidance of the God of Love.

The words of the Old Testament which Pharaoh spoke concerning Joseph of Egypt can well be applied to you: "Can we find such another man, that is full of the spirit of God, or a wise man like to him?" (Gen. 41:38). No less is your share in the divine work of God than was that of Egypt. You now reign with your foster-Son and see reflected in the mirror of God's Wisdom the Divine Will and what is of benefit to our souls.

Saint Joseph, I thank God for having made you the man specially chosen by Him. As a token of your own gratitude to God, obtain for me the grace to emulate your virtues so that I too may be pleasing to the Heart of God. Help me to give myself entirely to His service and to the accomplishment of His Holy Will, that one day I may reach heaven and be eternally united to God as you are.

Fourth Day = Faithful Servant

Saint Joseph, you lived for one purpose -- to be the personal servant of Jesus Christ, the Word made flesh. Your noble birth and ancestry, the graces and gifts, so generously poured out on you by God -- all this was yours to serve our Lord better. Every thought, word, and action of yours was an homage to the love and glory of the Incarnate Word. You fulfilled most faithfully the role of a good and faithful servant who cared for the House of God.

How perfect was your obedience! Your position in the Holy Family obliged you to command, but besides being the foster-father of Jesus, you were also His disciple. For almost thirty years, you watched the God-Man display a simple and prompt obedience, and you grew to love and practice it yourself. Without exception you submitted to God, to the civil rulers, and to the voice of your conscience.

When God sent an angel to tell you to care for Mary you obeyed in spite of the mystery which surrounded her motherhood. When you were told to flee into Egypt under painful conditions, you obeyed without the slightest word of complaint. When God advised you in a dream to return to Nazareth, you obeyed. In every situation your obedience was as simple as your faith, as humble as your heart, as prompt as your love. It neglected nothing; it took in every command.

You had the virtue of loving devotedness, which marks a good servant. Every moment of your life was consecrated to the service of our Lord: sleep, rest, work, pain. Faithful to your duties, you sacrificed everything unselfishly, even cheerfully. You would have sacrificed even the happiness of being with Mary. The rest and quiet of Nazareth was sacrificed at the call of duty. Your entire life was one generous giving, even to the point of being ready to die in proof of your love for Jesus and Mary. With true unselfish devotedness you worked without praise or reward.

But God wanted you in a certain sense to cooperate in the Redemption of the world. He confided to you the care of nourishing and defending the Divine Child. He wanted you to be poor and to suffer because He destined you to be the earthly, foster-father of His Son, who came into the world to save men by His sufferings and death, and you were to share in His suffering. In all of these important tasks, the Heavenly Father found you a faithful servant!

Saint Joseph, I thank God for your privilege of being God's faithful servant. As a token of your own gratitude to God, obtain for me the grace to be a faithful servant of God as you were. Help me to share, as you did, the obedience of Jesus, who came not to do His Will, but the Will of His Father; to trust in the Providence of God, knowing that if I do His Will, He will provide for all my needs of soul and body; to be calm in my trials and to leave it to our Lord to free me from them when it pleases Him to do so. And help me to imitate your generosity, for there can be no greater reward here on earth than the joy and honor of being a faithful child of God.

Fifth Day = Patron of the Church

Saint Joseph, God has appointed you patron of the Catholic Church because you were the head of the Holy Family, the starting-point of the Church. You were the father, protector, guide and support of the Holy Family. For that reason you belong in a particular way to the Church, which was the purpose of the Holy Family's existence.

I believe that the Church is the family of God on earth. Its government is represented in priestly authority which consists above all in its power over the true Body of Christ, really present in the Blessed Sacrament of the Altar, thus continuing Christ's life in the Church. From this power, too, comes authority over the Mystical Body of Christ, the members of the Church -- the power to teach and govern souls, to reconcile them with God, to bless them, and to pray for them.

You have a special relationship to the priesthood because you possessed a wonderful power from our Savior Himself. Your life and office were of a priestly function and are especially connected with the Blessed Sacrament. To some extent you were the means of bringing the Redeemer to us -- as it is the priest's function to bring Jesus to us in the Mass -- for you reared Jesus, supported, nourished, protected and sheltered Him. You were prefigured by the patriarch Joseph, who kept supplies of wheat for his people. But how much greater than he were you! Joseph of old gave the Egyptians mere bread for their bodies. You nourished, and with the most tender care, preserved for the Church Jesus who is the Bread of Heaven and who gives eternal life in Holy Communion.

God has appointed you patron of the Church because the glorious title of patriarch also falls by special right to you. The patriarchs were the heads of families of the Chosen People, and theirs was the honor to prepare for the Savior's incarnation. You belonged to this line of patriarchs, for you were one of the last descendants of the family of David and one of the nearest forebears of Christ according to the flesh. As husband of Mary, the Mother of God, and as the earthly, foster-father of the Savior, you were directly connected with Christ. Your vocation was especially concerned with the Person of Jesus; your entire life centered around Him. You are, therefore, the closing of the Old Testament and the beginning of the New, which took its rise with the Holy Family of Nazareth. Because the New Testament surpasses the Old in every respect, you are the patriarch of patriarchs, the most venerable, exalted, and amiable of all the patriarchs.

Through Mary, the Church received Christ, and therefore the Church is indebted to her. But the Church owes her debt of gratitude and veneration to you also, for you were the chosen one who enabled Christ to enter into the world according to the laws of order and fitness. It was by you that the patriarchs and the prophets and the faithful reaped the fruit of God's promise. Alone among them all, you saw with your own eyes and possessed the Redeemer promised to the rest of men.

Saint Joseph, I thank God for your privilege of being the Patron of the Church. As a token of your own gratitude to God, obtain for me the grace to live as a worthy member of this Church, so that through it I may save my soul. Bless the priests, the religious, and the laity of the Catholic Church that they may ever grow in God's love and faithfulness in His service. Protect the Church from the evils of our day and from the persecution of her enemies. Through your powerful intercession may the church successfully accomplish its mission in this world -- the glory of God and the salvation of souls.

Sixth Day = Patron of Families

Saint Joseph, I venerate you as the gentle head of the Holy Family. The Holy Family was the scene of your life's work in its origin, in its guidance, in its protection, in your labor for Jesus and Mary, and even in your death in their arms. You lived, moved, and acted in the loving company of Jesus and Mary. The inspired writer describes your life at Nazareth in only a few words: "And Jesus went down with them and came to Nazareth, and was subject to them." (Luke, 2:51) Yet these words tell of your high vocation here on earth, and the abundance of graces which filled your soul during those years spent in Nazareth.

Your family life at Nazareth was radiant with the light of divine charity. There was an intimate union of heart and mind among the members of your Holy Family. There could not have been a closer bond than that uniting you to Jesus, your foster-Son and to Mary, your most loving wife. Jesus chose to fulfill toward you, His foster-father, all the duties of a faithful son, showing you every mark of honor and affection due to a parent. Mary showed you all the signs of respect and love of a devoted wife. You responded to this love and veneration from Jesus and Mary with feelings of deepest love and respect. You had for Jesus a true fatherly love, enkindled and kept aglow in your heart by the Holy Spirit. And you admired the workings of grace in Mary's soul, and this admiration caused the holy love which you had consecrated to her on the day of your wedding grow stronger every day.

God has made you a heavenly patron of family life because you sanctified yourself as head of the Holy Family and thus by your beautiful example sanctified family life. How peacefully and happily the Holy Family rested under the care of your fatherly rule, even in the midst of trials. You were the protector, counselor, and consolation of the Holy Family in every need. Just as you were the model of piety, so you gave us by your zeal, your earnestness and devout trust in God's providence, and especially by your love, the example of labor according to the Will of God. You cherished all the experiences common to family life and the sacred memories of the life, sufferings, and joys in the company of Jesus and Mary. Therefore the family is dear to you as the work of God, and it is of the highest importance in your eyes to promote the honor of God and the well-being of man. In your loving fatherliness and intercession you are the patron and intercessor of families, and you deserve a place in every home.

Saint Joseph, I thank God for your privilege of living in the Holy Family and being its head. As a token of your own gratitude to God, obtain God's blessing upon my own family. Make our home the kingdom of Jesus and Mary -- a kingdom of peace, of joy, and love.

I also pray for all families. Your help is needed in our day when God's enemy has directed his attack against the family in order to desecrate and destroy it. In the face of these evils, as patron of families, be pleased to help; and as of old, you arose to save the Child and His Mother, so today arise to protect the sanctity of the home. Make our homes sanctuaries of prayer, of love, of patient sacrifice, and of work. May they be modeled after your own at Nazareth. Remain with us with Jesus and Mary, so that by your help we may obey the commandments of God and of the Church; receive the holy sacraments of God and of the Church; live a life of prayer; and foster religious instruction in our homes. Grant that we may be reunited in God's Kingdom and eternally live in the company of the Holy Family in heaven.

Seventh Day = Patron of Workers

Saint Joseph, you devoted your time at Nazareth to the work of a carpenter. It was the Will of God that you and your foster-Son should spend your days together in manual labor. What a beautiful example you set for the working classes.

It was especially for the poor, who compose the greater part of mankind, that Jesus came upon earth, for in the synagogue of Nazareth, He read the words of Isaiah and referred them to Himself: "The Spirit of the Lord is upon me, because He has anointed Me to bring good news to the poor..." (Luke 4:18). It was God's Will that you should be occupied with work common to poor people, that in this way Jesus Himself might ennoble it by inheriting it from you, His foster-father, and by freely embracing it. Thus our Lord teaches us that for the humbler class of workmen, He has in store His richest graces, provided they live content in the place God's Providence has assigned them, and remain poor in spirit for He said, "Blessed are the poor in spirit, for theirs is the kingdom of heaven" (Matt. 5:3).

The kind of work to which you devoted your time in the workshop of Nazareth offered you many occasions of practicing humility. You were privileged to see each day the example of humility which Jesus practiced -- a virtue most pleasing to Him. He chose for His earthly surroundings not the courts of princes nor the halls of the learned, but a little workshop of Nazareth. Here you shared for many years the humble and hidden toiling of the God-Man. What a touching example for the worker of today.

While your hands were occupied with manual work, your mind was turned to God in prayer. From the Divine Master, who worked along with you, you learned to work in the presence of God in the spirit of prayer, for as He worked He adored His Father and recommended the welfare of the world to Him, Jesus also instructed you in the wonderful truths of grace and virtue, for you were in close contact with Him who said of Himself, "I am the Way and the Truth and the Life."

As you were working at your trade, you were reminded of the greatness and majesty of God, who, as a most wise Architect, formed this vast universe with wonderful skill and limitless power.

The light of divine faith that filled your mind, did not grow dim when you saw Jesus working as a carpenter. You firmly believed that the saintly Youth working beside you was truly God's own Son.

Saint Joseph, I thank God for your privilege of being able to work side by side with Jesus in the carpenter shop of Nazareth. As a token of your own gratitude to God, obtain for me the grace to respect the dignity of labor and ever to be content with the position in life, however lowly, in which it may please Divine Providence to place me. Teach me to work for God and with God in the spirit of humility and prayer, as you did, so that I may offer my toil in union with the sacrifice of Jesus in the Mass as a reparation for my sins, and gain rich merit for heaven.

Eighth Day = Friend in Suffering

Saint Joseph, your share of suffering was very great because of your close union with the Divine Savior. All the mysteries of His life were more or less mysteries of suffering. Poverty pressed upon you, and the cross of labor followed you everywhere. Nor were you spared domestic crosses, owing to misunderstandings in regard to the holiest and most cherished of all beings, Jesus and Mary, who were all to you. Keen must have been the suffering caused by the uncertainty regarding Mary's virginity; by the bestowal of the name of Jesus, which pointed to future misfortune. Deeply painful must have been the prophecy of Simeon, the flight into Egypt, the disappearance of Jesus at the Paschal feast. To these sufferings were surely added interior sorrows at the sight of the sins of your own people.

You bore all this suffering in a truly Christ-like manner, and in this you are our example. No sound of complaint or impatience escaped you -- you were, indeed, the silent saint! You submitted to all in the spirit of faith, humility, confidence, and love. You cheerfully bore all in union with and for the Savior and His Mother, knowing well that true love is a crucified love. But God never forsook you in your trials. The trials, too, disappeared and were changed at last into consolation and joy.

It seems that God had purposely intended your life to be filled with suffering as well as consolation to keep before my eyes the truth that my life on earth is but a succession of joys and sorrows, and that I must gratefully accept whatever God sends me, and during the time of consolation prepare for suffering. Teach me to bear my cross in the spirit of faith, of confidence, and of gratitude toward God. In a happy eternity, I shall thank God fervently for the sufferings which He deigned to send me during my pilgrimage on earth, and which after your example I endured with patience and heartfelt love for Jesus and Mary.

You were truly the martyr of the hidden life. This was God's Will, for the holier a person is, the more he is tried for the love and glory of God. If suffering is the flowering of God's grace in a soul and the triumph of the soul's love for God, being the greatest of saints after Mary, you suffered more than any of the martyrs.

Because you have experienced the sufferings of this valley of tears, you are most kind and sympathetic toward those in need. Down through the ages souls have turned to you in distress and have always found you a faithful friend in suffering. You have graciously heard their prayers in their needs even though it demanded a miracle. Having been so intimately united with Jesus and Mary in life, your intercession with Them is most powerful.

Saint Joseph, I thank God for your privilege of being able to suffer for Jesus and Mary. As a token of your own gratitude to God, obtain for me the grace to bear my suffering patiently for love of Jesus and Mary. Grant that I may unite the sufferings, works and disappointments of life with the sacrifice of Jesus in the Mass, and share like you in Mary's spirit of sacrifice.

Ninth Day = Patron of a Happy Death

Saint Joseph, how fitting it was that at the hour of your death Jesus should stand at your bedside with Mary, the sweetness and hope of all mankind. You gave your entire life to the service of Jesus and Mary; at death you enjoyed the consolation of dying in Their loving arms. You accepted death in the spirit of loving submission to the Will of God, and this acceptance crowned your hidden life of virtue. Yours was a merciful judgment, for your foster-Son, for whom you had cared so lovingly, was your Judge, and Mary was your advocate. The verdict of the Judge was a word of encouragement to wait for His coming to Limbo, where He would shower you with the choicest fruits of the Redemption, and an embrace of grateful affection before you breathed forth your soul into eternity.

You looked into eternity and to your everlasting reward with confidence. If our Savior blessed the shepherds, the Magi, Simeon, John the Baptist, and others, because they greeted His presence with devoted hearts for a brief passing hour, how much more did He bless you who have sanctified yourself for so many years in His company and that of His Mother? If Jesus regards every corporal and spiritual work of mercy, performed in behalf of our fellow men out of love for Him, as done to Himself, and promises heaven as a reward, what must have been the extent of His gratitude to you who in the truest sense of the word have received Him, given Him shelter, clothed, nourished, and consoled Him at the sacrifice of your strength and rest, and even your life, with a love which surpassed the love of all fathers.

God really and personally made Himself your debtor. Our Divine Savior paid that debt of gratitude by granting you many graces in your lifetime, especially the grace of growing in love, which is the best and most perfect of all gifts. Thus at the end of your life your heart became filled with love, the fervor and longing of which your frail body could not resist. Your soul followed the triumphant impulse of your love and winged its flight from earth to bear the prophets and patriarchs in Limbo the glad tidings of the advent of the Redeemer.

Saint Joseph, I thank God for your privilege of being able to die in the arms of Jesus and Mary. As a token of your own gratitude to God, obtain for me the grace of a happy death. Help me to spend each day in preparation for death. May I, too, accept death in the spirit of resignation to God's Holy Will, and die, as you did, in the arms of Jesus, strengthened by Holy Viaticum, and in the arms of Mary, with her rosary in my hand and her name on my lips!

March   Self-Control

Devotions and Celebrations = Lent

Here and there in the stark March landscape of Michigan, a few plants and trees are beginning to give evidence of the new life that winter's frost and chill had concealed from our eyes. The Church's vibrant new life has been obscured, too, by the austerity of the penitential season of Lent. But that life is indisputable, and it will burst forth on Easter as Christ coming forth from his tomb!

Three prominent ideas are proposed for our contemplation by the liturgy of Lent: the Passion and Resurrection of Christ, and our own conversion. Lent starts with Ash Wednesday either in the last half of February or the beginning of March. We begin our journey to the cross by receiving ashes. The liturgical color for Lent is purple = a symbol of penance, mortification and the sorrow of a contrite heart. We reflect on our mortality "Remember man, you are dust" and the shortness of life "and to dust you will return." We listen to the call, "Now is the acceptable time, now is "the day of salvation (2 Corinthians 6:2)."

Just like Our Lord's earthly life - every moment of our lives is leading up to the last moment - when for eternity we will either go to God or suffer the fires of hell.

The Solemnity of the Annunciation comes during Lent; a pure white flower in the purple Lenten landscape. It seems to be, at first glance, a Christmas feast, but upon reflection we grasp that the feast is intimately linked to the Paschal mystery. For what Christ inaugurated at His incarnation in accepting to offer himself for the human race, he will complete in his sacrifice on the cross.

As the weeks of Lent progress we exert extra effort to do good works and penance, but continue with the enthusiasm of the catechumens on their way to Easter and Baptism. Our Lenten observance can be a joyful journey — and not a forced march. As a good work we can pray for a person whose behavior irritates us. If as a penance we give up special treats during the 40 Days of Lent we need to fill that vacuum with acts of charity. When it becomes difficult we turn to Christ, who reminds us, "My grace is sufficient for you, for My power is made perfect in weakness." (2 Corinthians 12:9)

Stations of the Cross

- ❖ 1. Jesus is condemned to death.
- ❖ 2. Jesus bears His cross.
- ❖ 3. Jesus falls the first time.
- ❖ 4. Jesus meets his Mother.
- ❖ 5. Jesus is helped by Simon.
- ❖ 6. Jesus is comforted by Veronica.
- ❖ 7. Jesus falls the second time.
- ❖ 8. Jesus speaks to the weeping women.
- ❖ 9. Jesus falls the third time.
- ❖ 10. Jesus is stripped of his garments.
- ❖ 11. Jesus is nailed to the cross.
- ❖ 12. Jesus dies on the cross.
- ❖ 13. Jesus is taken down from the cross.
- ❖ 14. Jesus is laid in the sepulchre.

March   Self-Control

Polish–American Recipe = *Paczki:* Fried Doughnuts

1 cup rich sour milk = Two tablespoons sour cream in a measuring cup add milk or Half N' Half to the one
    cup line pour into a glass jar, shake and set in refrigerator over night.
1 teaspoon baking soda
1 egg well beaten
1cup sugar
1/2 teaspoon salt
1/2 teaspoon cinnamon
1/2 teaspoon nutmeg
1 Tablespoon melted Butter (cooled but still liquefied) or clarified butter

2 cups Flour plus 1/2 cup for dusting tortilla press
Into a medium sized bowl, sift together 2 cups Flour, 1 teaspoon baking soda, 1/2 teaspoon salt, 1/2
    teaspoon cinnamon, and 1/2 teaspoon nutmeg and set aside.
Into a large bowl, in this order, use a hand mixer to combine beaten egg, sour milk, butter, and sugar.

Add gradually the dry ingredients that have been sifted together.
This will make a "soft roll of dough" –
Chill in the refrigerator overnight if possible.

I placed balls of soft dough in each cup of a plastic egg carton.
I dusted the ball lightly with flour before placing it in each egg cup.
I closed the egg carton and placed it to chill in the refrigerator overnight.

1. Ball of soft dough in each cup of a plastic egg carton   2. Ready for frying

Use a Tortilla Press or roll out each ball to approximately 1/2 inch thick circles and poke the middle with
    the tip of a teaspoon to make a small hole in each fried cake. When this worked, my Husband cut
    a smooth, plastic rod for poking the hole in the middle – this worked much better.

Fry in at least three inches, deep pan in corn oil with up to 1/2 of a cup of butter added to each 2 cups of
    corn oil at 365º F. This will mixture will produce golden brown fried cakes.

Fry on first side until the edges are golden brown and small bubbles form on the surface of each Paczki.

3. Ready to flip over

4. Flip them over and fry for half of the time that they were fried on the first side.

I fry only four or five at a time, after preparing all of them and setting them on a plate.
The timing for each batch could vary with the temperature of the oil.
Drain on paper towel and sprinkle with powdered sugar.

5. Yes, I ate one before taking this picture.

Prepare "Prune Jam" to spread on each cut fried cake.
Traditional Polish Paczki are filled with "Prune Jam" –
American Paczki are often filled with berry jams; also flavored custards like lemon and chocolate.

Recipe for "Prune Jam" = Polish ingredients =
    2 cup dried pitted prunes, small prunes cut in half;
    1 tablespoon lemon juice, fresh squeezed about half of one lemon;
    1 tablespoon light brown sugar

1. Place prunes in small kettle and cover with purified water.
2. Bring to boiling, cover, remove from heat, and let stand for twenty (20) minutes.
3. Add lemon juice and sugar and simmer until almost all liquid is gone.
4. Instead of filling my Paczki, I slice my Paczki and spread the jam or custard on each piece.

March   Self-Control

Polish–American Activity = Palm Weaving

This Crucifix hangs in my bedroom, and it has some Palm Representations that I wove back in 2010 when my fingers were nimble. For the next three years, when we brought home our palms we only brought one or two, and the next year we would take those dry palms back to Church where they are collected and burned in a ceremony to produce the "ashes" for Ash Wednesday.

Crucifix - Palms 2010   Five Ways to Weave Palms 2014   Dried Palms 2014

Five Ways to Weave Palms 2014 -- REPRESENTATIONS

Left to right = 1. Nail - 2. Whip end curled and Whip end folded - 3. Spear

4. Crown of Thorns - lower right

When I started this book, I was sure that I would have to use the dry palms from 2010 and skip the instructions for weaving the representations. Once the Palms dry they are too brittle to weave. My body was not cooperating with my desires, and I could not even attend Mass on Palm Sunday, again this year. When my husband brought the Blest Palms home after Mass on Palm Sunday, I placed them in a vase with purified water and prayed that at least my hands would improve. Only through the grace of God, my hands were a little bit better, so I was determined to find a way to weave the fresh palms. So, I turned on Easter Sunday Mass on the Catholic Channel on Television, sat on the couch and prayed my way through each representation that I wove.

I started with the most difficult one, the Nail, and I only managed to succeed at weaving one, so I just took a few pictures of that one for this book. The other representations are much easier and usually even young children were able to share in this activity. I know that I was weaving palms before I received my First Communion at seven years young.

Three Nails One for Each Hand and One for Crossed Feet

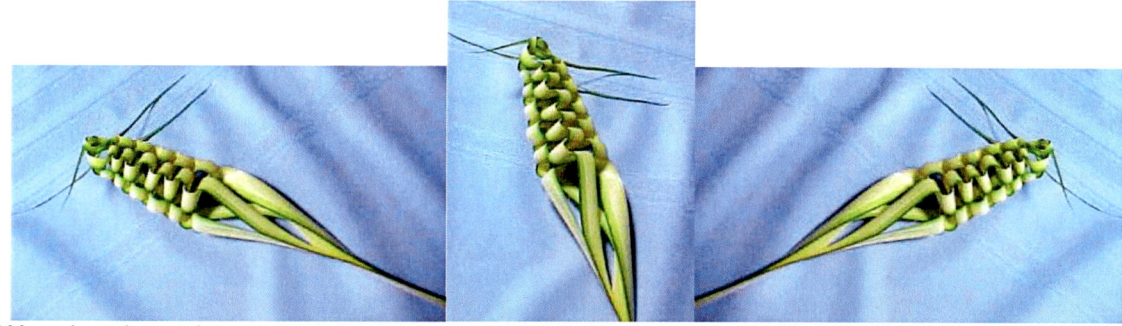

Weaving the palms to represent the nails that were used to crucify Jesus is the most intricate one. Since movement of my fingers, and holding the palms are limited, I am demonstrating the methods I used at this time of my life.

Fan Palm leaves are used for weaving these representations.

Picture A = Step 4.   Picture B = Step 6.   Picture C = Step 7.

Step 1.
   Take two leaves that are at least one inch wide and three feet long. If the leaves are still grown together, separate them from each other, leaving about eight to ten inches for a stem.
I used a small rubber band to hold the leaves securely together, and to a small bud vase, because my fingers are not as nimble as when I was younger.
Step 2.
   Slit each leaf in half down to just above the spot where the leaves are joined to each other. Bend the two halves of one leaf at right angles to each other, and bend/fold one half over the other half.
Step 3.
   Place one side of the second leaf at right angle to the top half that is already folded, and bend/fold the half-leaf on top.
Step 4.
   This step is most important. Take the last half-leaf and place on top of the third half-leaf, and slide the tip of the fourth half-leaf under the fold of the first half-leaf, and pull tips to tighten.
After doing these first four steps your palm nail base should look like the palm weave in Picture A.
Step 5.
   Start with the last half-leaf and fold it back over the half-leaf under which it was tucked. Always fold toward the center of the nail, so take the half-leaf that is outside this one, and bend/fold over as you did with the first set of four bends/folds.
Step 6.
   When you get to the fourth half-leaf tuck it under the first half-leaf of this layer.
Continue these steps are three or four sets the nail will start taking shape, as the palm leaf is narrower at the top, and the nail should look similar to the one in Picture B.

Step 7.
Continue until most of the palm leaves are securely woven into this shape.
Take one of the tips of the half-palm and tie it once to the tip on the opposite side.
Take the other loose tip and tie it to the last tip. Then slip the tips under the nearest fold to secure them.
The finished Nail Representation will look similar to the palm Nail in Picture C. The three at the beginning are this same nail. Each nail will be slightly different. After the palm nail dries they will keep for years.

The Representations of the Whips

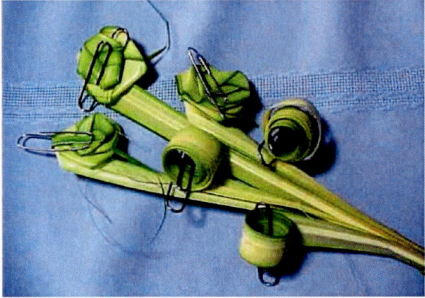
3 Curl Whips and 3 Fold Whips

Start at the tip and roll a tight curl, paper clip, let dry 24 hours, and unclip.

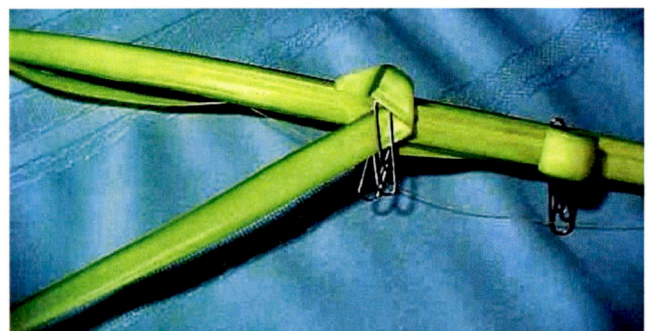
Fold one leaf at right angles to itself to make layers.

Loosen the folds to make tiers, paper clip, let dry 24 hours, and unclip.

The Representation of the Crown of Thorns

Take one leaf and split down the middle.
Do not split four inches; save for a stem.
Fold one half-leaf over the other.
Leave three inches to tie the ends together.

After tying the two half-leaves together;
tie them to the stem by pulling one tip
between the bottom fold and tie to the other
tip and tie again for a double not.
Use a paper clip to hold the ends until dry.

The Representation of the Spear that Pierced the Side of Jesus

Weaving the palms to represent the spear that was used to pierce the side of Jesus is quite easy to weave. Fan Palm leaves are used for weaving all of these representations.

Step 1.
Take two leaves that are at least one inch wide and three feet long. If the leaves are still grown together, separate them from each other, leaving about ten to twelve inches for a stem. Bend/fold both leaves and insert one inside the other. Picture A.

Step 2.
Continue pushing the loops through each other. After each insertion, gently tighten each loop, as shown in Picture B.

  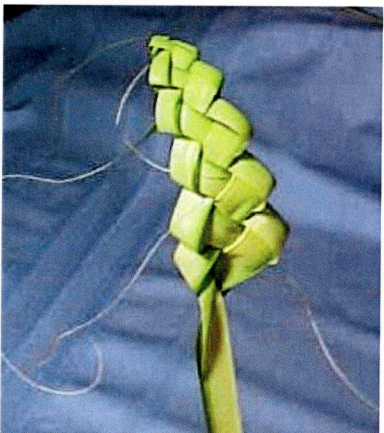

Picture A = Step 1.   Picture B = Step 2.   Picture C = Step 3.

Step 3.
Continue the first two steps until a "point" forms at the top resembling the head of a spear, similar to the one in Picture C. Tie the thin ends of the palm leaves together, and push the thin ends through one of the loops and pull gently and firmly in place.
After the palm spear dries the ends might break off or can be trimmed.
Every spear will be slightly different.

March   Self-Control

People of Polish Heritage = Uncle Steve and Aunt Irene

October 1941, my Uncle Steve Lukasavitz was stationed in Hawaii and sent these "Grass Skirts, Leis, and wrist bands" to my sister Barbara and Me. My Grass Skirt is in my Cedar Chest together with my Lei and a wrist band, also the locket that Aunt Irene and Uncle Steve gave to me.

In the July Chapter of this book, there are newspaper articles about my Uncle Steve, who was on the USSA Arizona Ship when it was bombed by the Japanese in Pearl Harbor on December 7, 1941.

On my First Holy Communion, May 1944, my Aunt Irene and Uncle Steve gave me a locket with their Wedding Picture inside.   Aunt Irene said, "This is a picture of us on our happiest day on your happiest day – so far. May the Good Lord bless You with many more happy days."   Aunt Irene died in childbirth along with her Baby girl. The Priest at the Mass of the Resurrection for Aunt Irene and her Baby said, "Irene took her Baby Girl and personally returned her to God her creator."

Throughout the turmoil of World War II both Irene and Steve displayed the loving Fruit of the Holy Spirit -- Self Control

April Faithfulness

Iris close-up in MY Backyard

Fruit of the Holy Spirit = Faithfulness

Liturgical Calendar = The Holy Spirit

Devotions = Divine Mercy

Celebrations = Easter and Basket for Easter Breakfast

Polish–American Recipe = *Zupa z Sliwek*: Prune Soup

Polish–American Activity = Wycinanki – Kwiat - Flower

People of Polish Heritage = My Mother's side of My Family

April Faithfulness

Fruit of the Holy Spirit = Faithfulness

Prayer:

    Creator Spirit, graciously impart to us the fruit of fidelity that we may rely with assured confidence on the Word of God.

Faithfulness = being upright in dealing with others.

Faith is the assurance of things hoped for, the conviction of things not seen, our firm belief in God and all that He has revealed to us through Holy Mother Church. (Hebrews 11: 1)

Thy steadfast love, O Lord, extends to the heavens, thy faithfulness to the clouds. (Psalm 36: 4-6)

For the Lord is good; his steadfast love endures for ever, and his faithfulness to all generations. (Psalm 100: 4-5)

The Lord's acts of mercy are inexhaustible, his compassion is endless. They are renewed each morning — great is your faithfulness! (Lamentations 3: 22-23)

But the fruit of the Holy Spirit is love, joy, peace, patience, kindness, goodness, faithfulness, gentleness, self-control, against such there is no law. (Galatians 5: 21-24)

"When you received the word of God which you heard from us, you accepted it not as the word of men but as what it really is, the word of God." (1 Thessalonians 2: 13)

The apostle Thomas gave Jesus three years of faithful service, but we remember him for his one moment of doubt.

Faith resides in our intellect; we believe because God is all-knowing and cannot be deceived.

Faith resides in our intellect; we believe because God is all-good and cannot deceive.

What Jesus tells us is infallibly true so our faith must be constant.

Our faith must be complete. We need to strive to submit our intellect and will to God.

Our faith therefore must illuminate our daily life.

April Faithfulness

Liturgical Calendar = The Holy Spirit

Litany to the Holy Spirit

LEADER PRAYS.	**FAITHFUL RESPOND.**
Lord, have mercy on us.	*Lord, have mercy on us.*
God the Father of Heaven,	*Have mercy on us.*
God the Son, Redeemer of the world,	*Have mercy on us.*
God the Holy Spirit,	*Have mercy on us.*
Holy Trinity, One God,	*Have mercy on us.*
Divine Essence, one true God,	*Have mercy on us*
Spirit of truth and wisdom,	*Have mercy on us*
Spirit of holiness and justice,	*Have mercy on us*
Spirit of understanding and counsel,	*Have mercy on us*
Spirit of love and joy,	*Have mercy on us*
Spirit of peace and patience,	*Have mercy on us*
Spirit of meekness,	*Have mercy on us*
Spirit of goodness,	*Have mercy on us*
Love substantial of the Father and the Son,	*Have mercy on us*
Love and life of saintly souls,	*Have mercy on us*
Fire ever burning,	*Have mercy on us*
Living water to quench the thirst of hearts,	*Have mercy on us*
From all evil,	*Deliver us, O Holy Spirit.*
From all impurity of soul and body,	*Deliver us, O Holy Spirit.*
From all gluttony and sensuality,	*Deliver us, O Holy Spirit.*
From all attachments to the things of the earth,	*Deliver us, O Holy Spirit.*
From all hypocrisy and pretense,	*Deliver us, O Holy Spirit.*
From all imperfections and deliberate faults,	*Deliver us, O Holy Spirit.*
From our own will,	*Deliver us, O Holy Spirit.*
From slander,	*Deliver us, O Holy Spirit.*
From deceiving our neighbors,	*Deliver us, O Holy Spirit.*
From our passions and disorderly appetites,	*Deliver us, O Holy Spirit.*
From our inattentiveness to Thy holy inspirations,	*Deliver us, O Holy Spirit.*
From despising little things,	*Deliver us, O Holy Spirit.*
From malice,	*Deliver us, O Holy Spirit.*
From love of comfort and luxury,	*Deliver us, O Holy Spirit.*
From wishing to seek or desire anything other than Thee,	*Deliver us, O Holy Spirit.*
From everything that displeases Thee,	*Deliver us, O Holy Spirit.*
Most loving Father,	*forgive us.*
Divine Word,	*have pity on us.*

Holy and divine Spirit, *leave us not until we are in possession of the Divine Essence, Heaven of heavens.*

Lamb of God, Who takes away the sins of the world,	*Send us the divine Consoler.*
Lamb of God, Who takes away the sins of the world,	*Fill us with the gifts of Thy Spirit.*
Lamb of God, Who takes away the sins of the world,	*Make the fruits of the Holy Spirit increase within us.*
Come, O Holy Spirit, fill the hearts of Thy faithful,	*And enkindle in them the fire of Thy love.*
Send forth Thy Spirit and they shall be created,	*And thou shalt renew the face of the earth*

Let us Pray:
God, Who by the light of the Holy Spirit instructed the hearts of the faithful, grant us by the same Spirit to be truly wise and ever to rejoice in His consolation, through Jesus Christ Our Lord. Amen.

Litany to the Holy Spirit – For Private use only

LEADER PRAYS.	**FAITHFUL RESPOND.**
Lord, have mercy on us.	Lord, have mercy on us.
Christ, have mercy on us.	Christ, have mercy on us.
Lord, have mercy on us.	Lord, have mercy on us.
Father all-powerful,	have mercy on us.
Jesus, Eternal Son of the Father, Redeemer of the world,	save us.
Spirit of the Father and the Son, boundless life of both,	sanctify us.
Holy Trinity,	hear us.
Holy Spirit, Who comes from the Father and the Son,	enter our hearts.
Holy Spirit, Who art equal to the Father and the Son,	enter our hearts.
Promise of God the Father,	have mercy on us.
Ray of heavenly light,	have mercy on us.
Author of all good,	have mercy on us.
Source of heavenly water Consuming fire,	have mercy on us.
Ardent charity,	have mercy on us.
Spiritual unction,	have mercy on us.
Spirit of love and truth,	have mercy on us.
Spirit of wisdom and understanding,	have mercy on us.
Spirit of counsel and fortitude,	have mercy on us.
Spirit of knowledge and piety,	have mercy on us.
Spirit of the fear of the Lord,	have mercy on us.
Spirit of grace and prayer,	have mercy on us.
Spirit of peace and meekness,	have mercy on us.
Spirit of modesty and innocence,	have mercy on us.
Holy Spirit, the Comforter,	have mercy on us.
Holy Spirit, the Sanctifier,	have mercy on us.
Holy Spirit, Who governs the Church,	have mercy on us.
Gift of God, the Most High,	have mercy on us.
Spirit Who fills the universe,	have mercy on us.
Spirit of the adoption of the children of God,	have mercy on us.
Holy Spirit,	inspire us with horror of sin.
Holy Spirit,	come and renew the face of the earth.
Holy Spirit,	shed Thy light in our souls.
Holy Spirit,	engrave Thy law in our hearts.
Holy Spirit,	inflame us with the flame of Thy love.
Holy Spirit,	open to us the treasures of Thy graces.
Holy Spirit,	teach us to pray well.
Holy Spirit,	enlighten us with Thy heavenly inspirations.
Holy Spirit,	lead us in the way of salvation.
Holy Spirit,	grant us the only necessary knowledge.
Holy Spirit,	inspire in us the practice of good.
Holy Spirit,	grant us the merits of all virtues.
Holy Spirit,	make us persevere in justice.
Holy Spirit,	be Thou our everlasting reward.

Lamb of God, Who takest away the sins of the world, send us Thy Holy Spirit.
Lamb of God, Who takest away the sins of the world, pour down into our souls the gifts of the Holy Spirit.
Lamb of God, Who takest away the sins of the world, grant us the Spirit of wisdom and piety.
Come, Holy Spirit! Fill the hearts of Thy faithful, enkindle in them the fire of Thy love.

Let us pray.

Grant, O merciful Father, that Thy Divine Spirit may enlighten, inflame and purify us, that He may penetrate us with His heavenly dew and make us fruitful in good works, through Our Lord Jesus Christ, Thy Son, Who with Thee, in the unity of the same Spirit, liveth and reigneth, one God, forever and ever. Amen.

Holy Spirit Novena

Dearest Holy Spirit, confiding in Your deep, personal love for me, I am making this novena for the following request, if it be Your Holy Will to grant it: *(mention your request)*

Teach me, Divine Spirit, to know and seek my last end; grant me the holy fear of God; grant me true contrition and patience. Do not let me fall into sin. Give me an increase of faith, hope and charity, and bring forth in my soul all the virtues proper to my state in life.

Make me a faithful disciple of Jesus and an obedient child of the Church. Give me efficacious grace sufficient to keep the Commandments and to receive the Sacraments worthily.
Give me the four Cardinal Virtues, Your Seven Gifts, Your Twelve Fruits.

Raise me to perfection in the state of life to which You have called me and lead me through a happy death to everlasting life. I ask this through Christ our Lord, Amen.

The month of April is dedicated to The Holy Spirit. Some days in April may fall during the season of Lent, which is represented by the liturgical color purple — a symbol of penance, mortification and the sorrow of a contrite heart. The rest of April usually is in the Easter season in which white, the color of light, a symbol of joy, purity, and innocence, is the liturgical color.

As our Lenten journey comes to a close we prepare to follow Christ all the way to the cross and to witness His glorious Resurrection. We have made the effort to sacrifice and pray so that we are now able to more fully reap the fruits of a well spent Lent. After our solemn commemoration of the last days and death of Our Lord we will spend the remainder of the month of April celebrating. As Spring breaks forth even nature will join us as buds and blooms begin to surface and we spend this month basking in the joy of the Resurrection. We continue throughout the entire month our cry.

"Christ is risen! Christ is truly risen! Alleluia"

April boasts the most solemn and sublime event of human history: the Resurrection of Jesus Christ – the Paschal mystery. Though the way to the Resurrection was the Via Cruce, the Sacrificial Lamb of God is now and forever Christ our Light, the Eternal high priest of the New Covenant. His sorrowful mother, the Stabat Mater of Good Friday, is now the jubilant Mother of the Regina Caeli.

We the members of Christ's Mystical Body exalt in the mystery by which we were redeemed. If in Baptism we were buried with Christ, so also will we share in his resurrection.

By his death we were reborn; "by his stripes we were healed." (Is 53:5)
Easter, the epicenter of time, is the event that links time and eternity.
It is indeed "the day the Lord has made; let us be glad and rejoice in it." (Ps 118:24)

"Christ is risen! Christ is truly risen! Alleluia!"

Novena in honor of the Holy Spirit

The novena in honor of the Holy Spirit is the oldest of all novenas since it was first made at the direction of Our Lord Jesus Christ when He sent His apostles back to Jerusalem to await the coming of the Holy Spirit on the first Pentecost. It is still the only novena officially prescribed by the Catholic Church. Addressed to the Third Person of the Blessed Trinity, it is a powerful plea for the light and strength and love so sorely needed by every Christian.

When I was growing up, the Solemnity of the Ascension was celebrated on Thursday of the 6th Week of Easter, so this Novena was started on the following Friday. Words like thee, helpeth, blest, vouchsafed, and even some Latin and Greek words were familiar to the very youngest children until the mid 1960's. Children attended All Sunday and special Holy Day Church services with their parents and Traditional prayers were "not dummied down" for them. At the "Children's Mass" on Sunday and some week days the Priest would use simpler terms to explain the Gospel lessons for the children.

ACT OF CONSECRATION TO THE HOLY SPIRIT
To be recited daily during the Novena.

On my knees before the great multitude of heavenly witnesses I offer myself, soul and body to You, Eternal Spirit of God. I adore the brightness of Your purity, the unerring keenness of Your justice, and the might of Your love. You are the Strength and Light of my soul. In You I live and move and am. I desire never to grieve You by unfaithfulness to grace and I pray with all my heart to be kept from the smallest sin against You. Mercifully guard my every thought and grant that I may always watch for Your light, and listen to Your voice, and follow Your gracious inspirations. I cling to You and give myself to You and ask You, by Your compassion to watch over me in my weakness. Holding the pierced Feet of Jesus and looking at His Five Wounds, and trusting in His Precious Blood and adoring His opened Side and stricken Heart, I implore You, Adorable Spirit, Helper of my infirmity, to keep me in Your grace that I may never sin against You. Give me grace O Holy Spirit, Spirit of the Father and the Son to say to You always and everywhere, "Speak Lord for Your servant heareth." Amen.

PRAYER FOR THE SEVEN GIFTS OF THE HOLY SPIRIT
To be recited daily during the Novena.

O Lord Jesus Christ Who, before ascending into heaven did promise to send the Holy Spirit to finish Your work in the souls of Your Apostles and Disciples, deign to grant the same Holy Spirit to me that He may perfect in my soul, the work of Your grace and Your love. Grant me the Spirit of Wisdom that I may despise the perishable things of this world and aspire only after the things that are eternal, the Spirit of Understanding to enlighten my mind with the light of Your divine truth, the Spirit on Counsel that I may ever choose the surest way of pleasing God and gaining heaven, the Spirit of Fortitude that I may bear my cross with You and that I may overcome with courage all the obstacles that oppose my salvation, the Spirit of Knowledge that I may know God and know myself and grow perfect in the science of the Saints, the Spirit of Piety that I may find the service of God sweet and amiable, and the Spirit of Fear that I may be filled with a loving reverence towards God and may dread in any way to displease Him. Mark me, dear Lord with the sign of Your true disciples, and animate me in all things with Your Spirit. Amen.

First Day (Friday after Ascension or Friday of 6th Week of Easter)
Holy Spirit! Lord of Light! From Your clear celestial height. Your pure beaming radiance give!

The Holy Spirit
Only one thing is important -- eternal salvation. Only one thing, therefore, is to be feared--sin? Sin is the result of ignorance, weakness, and indifference. The Holy Spirit is the Spirit of Light, of Strength, and of Love. With His sevenfold gifts He enlightens the mind, strengthens the will, and inflames the heart with love of God. To ensure our salvation we ought to invoke the Divine Spirit daily, for "The Spirit helpeth our infirmity. We know not what we should pray for as we ought. But the Spirit Himself asketh for us."

Prayer
Almighty and eternal God, Who hast vouchsafed to regenerate us by water and the Holy Spirit, and hast given us forgiveness of all sins, vouchsafe to send forth from heaven upon us your sevenfold Spirit, the Spirit of Wisdom and Understanding, the Spirit of Counsel and Fortitude, the Spirit of Knowledge and Piety, and fill us with the Spirit of Holy Fear. Amen.
Say the Our Father and Hail Mary once, Glory be to the Father seven times.
Add the Act of Consecration and Prayer for the Seven Gifts

Second Day (Saturday of 6th Week of Easter)

Come Father of the poor. Come, treasures which endure; Come, Light of all that live!

The Gift of Fear

The gift of Fear fills us with a sovereign respect for God, and makes us dread nothing so much as to offend Him by sin. It is a fear that arises, not from the thought of hell, but from sentiments of reverence and filial submission to our heavenly Father. It is the fear that is the beginning of wisdom, detaching us from worldly pleasures that could in any way separate us from God. "They that fear the Lord will prepare their hearts, and in His sight will sanctify their souls."

Prayer

Come, O blessed Spirit of Holy Fear, penetrate my inmost heart, that I may set you, my Lord and God, before my face forever, help me to shun all things that can offend You. Make me worthy to appear before the pure eyes of Your Divine Majesty in heaven, where You live and reign in the unity of the ever Blessed Trinity, God world without end. Amen.

Say the Our Father and Hail Mary once, Glory be to the Father seven times.
Add the Act of Consecration and Prayer for the Seven Gifts

Third Day (7th Sunday of Easter or transferred Ascension)

Thou, of all consolers best, visiting the troubled breast, dost refreshing peace bestow.

The Gift of Piety

The gift of Piety begets in our hearts a filial affection for God as our most loving Father. It inspires us to love and respect for His sake persons and things consecrated to Him, as well as those who are vested with His authority, His Blessed Mother and the Saints, the Church and its visible Head, our parents and superiors, our country and its rulers. He who is filled with the gift of Piety finds the practice of his religion, not a burdensome duty, but a delightful service. Where there is love, there is no labor.

Prayer

Come, O Blessed Spirit of Piety, possess my heart. Enkindle therein such a love for God, that I may find satisfaction only in His service, and for His sake lovingly submit to all legitimate authority. Amen.

Say the Our Father and Hail Mary once, Glory be to the Father seven times.
Add the Act of Consecration and Prayer for the Seven Gifts

Fourth Day (Monday, 7th Week of Easter)

Thou in toil art comfort sweet, pleasant coolness in the heat, solace in the midst of woe.

The Gift of Fortitude

By the gift of Fortitude the soul is strengthened against natural fear, and supported to the end in the performance of duty. Fortitude imparts to the will an impulse and energy which move it to under take without hesitancy the most arduous tasks, to face dangers, to trample under foot human respect, and to endure without complaint the slow martyrdom of even lifelong tribulation. "He that shall persevere unto the end, he shall be saved."

Prayer

Come, O Blessed Spirit of Fortitude, uphold my soul in time of trouble and adversity, sustain my efforts after holiness, strengthen my weakness, give me courage against all the assaults of my enemies, that I may never be overcome and separated from Thee, my God and greatest Good. Amen.

Say the Our Father and Hail Mary once, Glory be to the Father seven times.
Add the Act of Consecration and Prayer for the Seven Gifts

Fifth Day (Tuesday, 7th Week of Easter)
Light immortal! Light Divine! Visit Thou these hearts of Thine, and our inmost being fill!

The Gift of Knowledge
 The gift of Knowledge enables the soul to evaluate created things at their true worth - in their relation to God. Knowledge unmasks the pretense of creatures, reveals their emptiness, and points out their only true purpose as instruments in the service of God. It shows us the loving care of God even in adversity, and directs us to glorify Him in every circumstance of life. Guided by its light, we put first things first, and prize the friendship of God beyond all else. "Knowledge is a fountain of life to him that possesseth it."

Prayer
 Come, O Blessed Spirit of Knowledge, and grant that I may perceive the will of the Father; show me the nothingness of earthly things, that I may realize their vanity and use them only for Thy glory and my own salvation, looking ever beyond them to Thee, and Thy eternal rewards. Amen.
 Say the Our Father and Hail Mary once, Glory be to the Father seven times.
 Add the Act of Consecration and Prayer for the Seven Gifts

Sixth Day (Wednesday, 7th Week of Easter)
If Thou take Thy grace away, nothing pure in man will stay - All his good is turned to ill.

The Gift of Understanding
 Understanding, as a gift of the Holy Spirit, helps us to grasp the meaning of the truths of our holy religion by Faith we know them, but by Understanding we learn to appreciate and relish them. It enables us to penetrate the inner meaning of revealed truths and through them to be quickened to newness of life. Our faith ceases to be sterile and inactive, but inspires a mode of life that bears eloquent testimony to the faith that is in us; we begin to "walk worthy of God in all things pleasing, and increasing in the knowledge of God."

Prayer
 Come, O Spirit of Understanding, and enlighten our minds, that we may know and believe all the mysteries of salvation; and may merit at last to see the eternal light in Thy Light; and in the light of glory to have a clear vision of Thee and the Father and the Son. Amen.
 Say the Our Father and Hail Mary once, Glory be to the Father seven times.
 Add the Act of Consecration and Prayer for the Seven Gifts

Seventh Day (Thursday, 7th Week of Easter)
Heal our wounds--our strength renew. On our dryness pour Thy dew. Wash the stains of guilt away.

The Gift of Counsel
 The gift of Counsel endows the soul with supernatural prudence, enabling it to judge promptly and rightly what must be done, especially in difficult circumstances. Counsel applies the principles furnished by Knowledge and Understanding to the innumerable concrete cases that confront us in the course of our daily duty as parents, teachers, public servants, and Christian citizens. Counsel is supernatural common sense, a priceless treasure in the quest of salvation. "Above all these things, pray to the Most High, that He may direct thy way in truth."

Prayer
 Come, O Spirit of Counsel, help and guide me in all my ways, that I may always do Thy holy will. Incline my heart to that which is good; turn it away from all that is evil, and direct me by the straight path of Thy commandments to that goal of eternal life for which I long.
 Say the Our Father and Hail Mary once, Glory be to the Father seven times.
 Add the Act of Consecration and Prayer for the Seven Gifts.

Eighth Day (Friday, 7th Week of Easter)

Bend the stubborn heart and will, melt the frozen - warm the chill. Guide the steps that go astray!

The Gift of Wisdom

Embodying all the other gifts, as Charity embraces all the other virtues, Wisdom is the most perfect of the gifts. Of wisdom it is written "all good things came to me with her, and innumerable riches through her hands." It is the gift of Wisdom that strengthens our faith, fortifies hope, perfects charity, and promotes the practice of virtue in the highest degree. Wisdom enlightens the mind to discern and relish things divine, in the appreciation of which earthly joys lose their savor, whilst the Cross of Christ yields a divine sweetness according to the words of the Saviour: "Take up thy cross and follow me, for my yoke is sweet and my burden light.

Prayer

Come, O Spirit of Wisdom, and reveal to my soul the mysteries of heavenly things, their exceeding greatness, power and beauty. Teach me to love them above and beyond all the passing joys and satisfactions of earth. Help me to attain them and possess them for ever. Amen.

Say the Our Father and Hail Mary once, Glory be to the Father seven times.
Add the Act of Consecration and Prayer for the Seven Gifts

Ninth Day (Saturday, Vigil of Pentecost)

Thou, on those who evermore Thee confess and Thee Adore, in Thy sevenfold gifts, descend. Give Them Comfort when they die; Give them Life with Thee on high; Give them joys which never end. Amen

The Fruits of the Holy Spirit

The gifts of the Holy Spirit perfect the supernatural virtues by enabling us to practice them with greater docility to divine inspiration. As we grow in the knowledge and love of God under the direction of the Holy Spirit, our service becomes more sincere and generous, the practice of virtue more perfect. Such acts of virtue leave the heart filled with joy and consolation and are known as Fruits of the Holy Spirit. These Fruits in turn render the practice of virtue more attractive and become a powerful incentive for still greater efforts in the service of God.

Prayer

Come, O Divine Spirit, fill my heart with Thy heavenly fruits, Thy charity, joy, peace, patience, benignity, goodness, faith, mildness, and temperance, that I may never weary in the service of God, but by continued faithful submission to Thy inspiration may merit to be united eternally with Thee in the love of the Father and the Son. Amen.

Say the Our Father and Hail Mary once, Glory be to the Father seven times.
Add the Act of Consecration and Prayer for the Seven Gifts

April Faithfulness

Devotions and Celebrations Divine Mercy

A personal relationship with Jesus is the primary goal so the Polish Traditions are secondary in this book. The devotions/prayers are presented first and other optional practices are not necessarily in sequential order.

JEZU UFAM TOBIE

This is a recent photograph of the "Jesus I trust in You" – print that hung on the wall in the home of my Mother's Parents. I don't know what year it was originally hung there. I do know that it was there in 1943 because I received my First Holy Communion in May 1944 and at that time my Busia explained to me that the Polish words could be translated into English,
"Jesus in You I place my trust."

Using this image as a reminder of God's Mercy was mainly a Polish Tradition for many years. In the year 2000, Pope John Paul II canonized Saint Faustina and – dedicated the Sunday after Easter - Divine Mercy Sunday, bringing this devotion to the world.

Similar images now have the words, "Jesus I trust in You," printed on the bottom of each print. The English translation from my Busia places the emphasis on Jesus being worthy of our trust. The common translation shifts attention to our trust in Jesus.

Divine Mercy Litany
From Saint Faustina Kowalska's Diary

Divine Mercy, gushing forth from the bosom of the Father,	*I trust in You*
Divine Mercy, greatest attribute of God,	*I trust in You*
Divine Mercy, incomprehensible mystery,	*I trust in You*
Divine Mercy, fountain gushing forth from the mystery of the Most Blessed Trinity,	*I trust in You*
Divine Mercy, unfathomed by any intellect, human or angelic,	*I trust in You*
Divine Mercy, from which wells forth all life and happiness,	*I trust in You*
Divine Mercy, better than the heavens,	*I trust in You*
Divine Mercy, source of miracles and wonders,	*I trust in You*
Divine Mercy, encompassing the whole universe,	*I trust in You*
Divine Mercy, descending to earth in the Person of the Incarnate Word,	*I trust in You*

Divine Mercy, which flowed out from the open wound of the Heart of Jesus,	*I trust in You*
Divine Mercy, enclosed in the Heart of Jesus for us, and especially for sinners,	*I trust in You*
Divine Mercy, unfathomed in the institution of the Sacred Host,	*I trust in You*
Divine Mercy, in the founding of the Holy Church,	*I trust in You*
Divine Mercy, in the Sacrament of Holy Baptism,	*I trust in You*
Divine Mercy, in our justification through Jesus Christ,	*I trust in You*
Divine Mercy, accompanying us through our whole life,	*I trust in You*
Divine Mercy, embracing us especially at the hour of death,	*I trust in You*
Divine Mercy, endowing us with immortal life,	*I trust in You*
Divine Mercy, accompanying us every moment of our life,	*I trust in You*
Divine Mercy, shielding us from the fire of hell,	*I trust in You*
Divine Mercy, in the conversion of hardened sinners,	*I trust in You*
Divine Mercy, astonishment for Angels, incomprehensible to Saints,	*I trust in You*
Divine Mercy, unfathomed in all the mysteries of God,	*I trust in You*
Divine Mercy, lifting us out of every misery,	*I trust in You*
Divine Mercy, source of our happiness and joy,	*I trust in You*
Divine Mercy, in calling us forth from nothingness to existence,	*I trust in You*
Divine Mercy, embracing all the works of His hands,	*I trust in You*
Divine Mercy, crown of all God's handiwork,	*I trust in You*
Divine Mercy, in which we are all immersed,	*I trust in You*
Divine Mercy, sweet relief for anguished hearts,	*I trust in You*
Divine Mercy, only hope of despairing souls,	*I trust in You*
Divine Mercy, repose of hearts, peace amidst fear,	*I trust in You*
Divine Mercy, delight and ecstasy of holy souls,	*I trust in You*
Divine Mercy, inspiring hope against all hope,	*I trust in You*

Prayer

Eternal God, in whom mercy is endless and the treasury of compassion inexhaustible, look kindly upon us and increase Your mercy in us, that in difficult moments we might not despair nor become despondent, but with great confidence submit ourselves to Your holy will, which is Love and Mercy itself.

Divine Mercy Novena

I fly to Your Mercy, Compassionate God, Who alone are good. Although my misery is great and my offenses are many, I trust in Your Mercy because You are the God of Mercy, and it has never been heard of in all ages, nor do Heaven or Earth remember, that a soul trusting in Your Mercy has been disappointed. *(State your intentions)*

Jesus, Friend of a lonely heart, You are my haven.
    You are my peace.
    You are my salvation.
    You are my serenity in moments of struggle and amidst an ocean of doubts.
    Amen

Jesus asked that the Feast of the Divine Mercy be preceded by a Novena to the Divine Mercy which would begin on Good Friday. He gave St. Faustina an intention to pray for on each day of the Novena, saving for the last day the most difficult intention of all, the lukewarm and indifferent of whom Jesus said: "These souls cause Me more suffering than any others; it was from such souls that My soul felt the most revulsion in the Garden of Olives. It was on their account that I said: 'My Father, if it is possible, let this cup pass Me by.' The last hope of salvation for them is to flee to My Mercy."

In her diary, St. Faustina wrote that Jesus told her: "On each day of the novena you will bring to My heart a different group of souls and you will immerse them in this ocean of My mercy
Jesus requested "... On each day you will beg My Father, on the strength of My passion, for the graces for these souls."

The different souls prayed for on each day of the Divine Mercy Novena are:

First Day – Good Friday
 Today bring to Me all mankind, especially all sinners.

Second Day – Holy Saturday
 Today bring to Me the Souls of Priests and Religious.

Third Day – Easter Sunday
 Today bring to Me all Devout and Faithful Souls.

Fourth Day – Easter Monday
 Today bring to Me those who do not believe in God and those who do not know Me.

Fifth Day – Easter Tuesday
 Today bring to Me the Souls of those who have separated themselves from My Church.

Sixth Day – Easter Wednesday
 Today bring to Me the Meek and Humble Souls and the Souls of Little Children.

Seventh Day – Easter Thursday
 Today bring to Me the Souls who especially venerate and glorify My Mercy.

Eighth Day – Easter Friday
 Today bring to Me the Souls who are in the prison of Purgatory.

Ninth Day – Easter Saturday
 Today bring to Me the Souls who have become Lukewarm.

 Many versions of prayers and meditations in pamphlets and booklets are available or a person can just say the Chaplet of Divine Mercy each day for the intentions of the specific groups of people.

Chaplet of Divine Mercy

During the Solemn Novena leading to Divine Mercy Sunday, the Chaplet of Divine Mercy should be offered each day for the day's intentions.

Rosary Beads are used to count the short prayers.

1. Begin with the Sign of the Cross, 1 Our Father, 1 Hail Mary and The Apostles Creed.
2. Then on the large Beads say the following:
    Eternal Father, I offer You the Body and Blood, Soul and Divinity of Your dearly beloved Son, Our Lord Jesus Christ, in atonement for our sins and those of the whole world.
3. On the ten smaller Beads say the following:
    For the sake of His sorrowful Passion, have mercy on us and on the whole world.

(Repeat step 2 and 3 for all five decades).

4. Conclude with - Holy God, Holy Mighty One, Holy Immortal One,
    have mercy on us and on the whole world.   *(Repeat three (3) times.)*

 Praying for the souls of the sick and dying are recited or sung at the 3:00 hour of Divine Mercy every day by members of a group called, Apostles of Divine Mercy.

April Faithfulness

Basket for Easter Breakfast -- "Food Blessing/Swieconka"

Swieconka is one of the most enduring and beloved Polish traditions.

On the Saturday before Easter, people take decorated baskets to Catholic Churches containing a sampling of traditional food to be blest.

Each food has a symbolic meaning, for example:

Eggs (Hard boiled) – symbolize life and Christ's resurrection,

Bread – symbolic of Jesus, the Bread of Life,

Butter Lamb – represents Christ, the Lamb of God,

Salt – represents purification,

Sour Fruit Sauce (Cranberries or Tart Cherries) – symbolic of the bitter sacrifice of Christ, Polish Tradition = Horseradish,

Ham or sausage or both – symbolic of great joy and abundance,

Coffee Cake (Cupcakes) – symbolic of our hope of salvation

The food blest in Church remains untouched until Easter Sunday morning, breakfast. The food that needs refrigeration is put in small containers in the "Frigidaire."

Polish was my first language, and I learned that the "box in our kitchen that kept food cold" was a "Frigidaire." That was the name on the outside of the "Frigidaire." I did not learn the generic term "refrigerator" until I was getting married in 1958. My Mother gave me the "Owners Manual that came with her "Frigidaire" - The word "refrigerator" was not in the book.
The difference between Brand names and the generic names of appliances and other products were not taught in schools or at home. I had to learn these lessons through many embarrassing conversations and life experiences. For example, June 1958, Ronald and I were shopping for appliances and part of the conversation went like this:

Jean Marie: We need a "Frigidaire" -

Ronald: Why not a "Kenmore" -

Jean Marie: Because I already have a sewing machine.

The box in Busia's kitchen that kept food cold was an "Ice Box" in which a large block of ice was placed in the top cabinet, and the food was in the cabinet below. The drippings from the melting ice were collected and used to water her house plants.

April   Faithfulness

Polish–American Recipe = *Zupa z Sliwek*: Prune Soup

These are the smallest portions that I prepare. Keep the proportions about the same. The order of adding ingredients is important for the textures and flavors to blend.

<u>Ingredients are underlined.</u>

1. Use the shank bone from the Easter ham, place the fully baked shank bone in a "Crockpot," slow cooker, or large kettle, cover with purified water and simmer on low heat for three hours to pull all of the good nutrients out of the bone. Make sure to remove all bones and skin pieces from the broth. Use this broth by placing it in a two (2) quart kettle; add purified bottled water to about half full, even for a small batch, because you will be adding vegetables, fruits, and pasta with additional water. Refrigerate over night. skim off fat and reheat to simmer before going to Step 2.

2. Chop into bite-sized pieces, one (1) cup full of "Organic Baby <u>Carrots</u>" and put them into a second kettle with purified water. I used "Match stick carrots" for this recipe – provided the flavor but very little texture and visual evidence.

3. In a "Tea Ball" place six (6) "<u>Whole Allspice</u>" and one large or two small <u>bay leaves</u>, broken in pieces to release the flavor and big enough to stay safely in the tea ball.

4. Bring these ingredients to a simmering boil, and cook for ten (10) minutes or longer.

5. In the meantime, chop into smaller than bite-sized pieces, one (1) cup of <u>onions</u>, salt lightly, add about one tablespoon butter, "stir-fry" them in a medium sized frying pan until onions are translucent.

6. Also chop into smaller than bite-sized pieces, one (1) cup of underline{celery}, salt lightly, and add them to the onions in the frying pan and continue to cook them on a low heat.

7. Put one (1) cup boiling water in a small kettle or bowl, and add one (1) cup of raisins to the water and just let them set in the boiling water to soften the skins.

8. Buy "Pitted Dried Plums" (Prunes), not canned or in a jar. I buy the small ones and cut them in half. If you buy the larger ones cut them into quarters. Prepare enough prunes to fill one (1) cup, and add the prunes to the container of raisins and stir them together and let them sit, while adding the other vegetables.

9. Add the onions and celery to the carrots and other ingredients in the kettle with just water, and cook on the low simmering boil for ten (10) more minutes.

10. Add the raisins and prunes and all the water that may be left in the container to the soup and simmer for ten (10) more minutes.

11. Add ALL Ingredients to the large kettle of ham broth and simmer for twenty (20 minutes.

12. Prepare one (1) cup of small elbow macaroni according to the package directions. I cook them about two minutes less than the directions before adding them, water and all to the soup, and continue to simmer for at least another ten (10) minutes.

13. When I am planning on freezing the prune soup, I do not add the macaroni to the soup. Instead I prepare it on the side fresh each time I thaw out a container of prune soup, and the amount of macaroni can be added by each person as desired.

For Vegetarian Prune Soup start with just water rather than the broth.
    The flavors from the remaining ingredients will blend into a tasty soup.

April Faithfulness

Polish–American Activity = Wycinanki – Kwiat - Flower

1. General placement

2. Leaves assembling

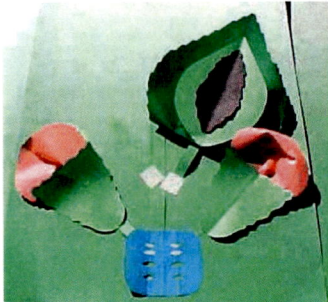
3. Small flowers & vase

4. Placing leaves

5. Large flower layers next to placement sheet

6. Flower secured on top of one leaf flower.

7. One layer of leaf tucked under.

    The Flower Wycinanki offers endless possibilities for creativity to be expressed: size, shape, colors, textures, quantity, realistic and fantastic. All of the pieces were secured to each other and the placement sheet with "Photo Splits" = small tabs with adhesive on both sides. Glue or paste was used when I was learning this Polish Folk Art sitting at my Busia's dining room table. When I was young I used only a small pair of sewing scissors; later when my hands were bigger, I used Busia' "Pinking Sheers." Craft scissors with different designs were the American Addition for these beautiful flowers.

April Faithfulness

People of Polish Heritage = My Mother's side of My Family

1. and 2. 3. My Grandparents home. I am standing on the porch.

1. Front and right side of my Mother's parents home on Industrial Avenue.
2. Left side and back of their home that shows the large "shoonka" = mud room.
3. My Grandparents home. Busia is standing on the porch scolding the person who is taking the picture because he was standing in the street. He was one of the older Uncles.
   I am standing on the porch. My sister Barbara and Uncle Danny are sitting on the stoops.

4. 5. 6.

4. Uncle Johnny, Aunt Janet, and Uncle Albin; Uncle was easier to say than Wujek.
   Uncle Albin, my Mother's elder brother, shortened his last name when he went into business.
5. Uncle Albin, Aunt Janet and their four daughters, Terry, Valley, Laney, and Patsy, lived in a large home in Lake Orion, Michigan.
6. Left to right: Madeline, my best friend, my cousin Hania, Me, and Sister Mary Anastasia.

7. Uncle Albin, Aunt Janet, and their four daughters' home was at the top of a hill and their private lake access was across a paved road.. This picture was taken when the hill was covered with soft grass.

7..   8..   9..

8. My Mother's four younger brothers John, Bernard, Daniel, and Benedict. Bernard and Benny are twins. Daniel was eighteen years younger than my Mother.
9. Busia Helen on her 90th Birthday.

More time was spent at my Mother's parents' house because it was right across the street from All Saints Catholic Church and one block from the school. The school did not provide lunches for the students so the children usually went home, to their grandparents' homes, or to a friend's home to eat their lunches. On nice days I ran home for lunch which was almost one mile from school. On cold or rainy days I went to Busia Helen's house.

. My sister went to the homes of her classmates. Several of my friends lived only one or two blocks away from the school and their Mothers would invite me to lunch. We would eat and still have time to play games like Jump Rope, Hop Scotch, Dodge Ball, Jacks, and even Baseball with no coaches or parents to interfere. We had learned the rules from watching the bigger children play Baseball Games.

I was only around six years old when I used to play Baseball with the bigger boys. I played "Out Field, all three positions," because I could run fast to catch and retrieve balls. My Uncle Danny earned an Athletic Scholarship to Michigan State University, and later became a Scout for New Players for the San Diego Padres.

I vividly remember a Double Header Tigers Game in Detroit, Michigan. My Uncle Benny took me and my cousin Val Joan. When he brought me home My Mother asked if I behaved myself. Uncle Benny said, "Yes ... and she didn't have to go pee." Imagine a teenaged young man having to figure out how to take his little nieces to the bathroom in a big Baseball Stadium. After the games he took us to the White Tower for special hamburgers with small onion pieces fried on them. More details about this game are told in my book, Christmas in the Living room.

Frequently our family, My Daddy, My Mother, and one or more Uncles would visit Uncle Albin, Aunt Janet, Terry, Val Joan, Laney, and Patsy at their home in Lake Orion, Michigan. It was fantastic because the cousins shared a big room that was upstairs. I don't remember if there were extra beds for me and my sister. Windows with screens were on three sides of the room and overlooked Lake Orion. They had private access to the Lake, just down one hill, cross the road, another smaller hill, and beautiful light brown sugar sand on the beach. The water was pristine and shallow for quite a long distance.
I do not recall any "drop-offs" or other dangerous obstacles. The fun times are still fresh in my memory.

All these people were faithful to their Faith, Family, and Friends.

May   Modesty

My painting of Pink Flowers
I had sketched it out when we were living in CA.
I completed it from memory in 2012.
Actual size is 30 inches wide by 20 inches high.

Fruit of the Holy Spirit = Modesty

Liturgical Calendar = The Blessed Virgin Mary

Devotions and Celebrations = First Communions,
Wianek – Children of Mary & Young Ladies Sodality

Polish–American Recipe = *Ciasto Szybki*: Quick Cake and Variations

Polish–American Activity = Garden Flowers

People of Polish Heritage = My Mother

May Modesty

Fruit of the Holy Spirit = Modesty

Prayer:

    Holy Spirit, eternal Love of the Father and the Son, kindly bestow on us the fruit of modesty, that we may order our exterior life regularly. Grant us the graces to exhibit modesty by being pure in our thoughts, words, and dress.

Modesty is grounded in humility, which reminds us of our true worth before God.

Those parts of the body which we think less honorable we invest with the greater honor, and our unpresentable parts are treated with greater modesty. (Corinthians 12: 22-24)

Yet woman will be saved through bearing children, if she continues in faith and love and holiness, with modesty. (1Timothy 2: 14-15)

Lightning speeds before the thunder, and approval precedes a modest man. (Sirach 32: 9-11)

May   Modesty

Liturgical Calendar = The Blessed Virgin Mary

My current Blessed Virgin Mary corner in my bedroom

Litany of the Blessed Virgin Mary

This litany to the Blessed Virgin Mary was composed during the Middle Ages. The place of honor it now holds in the life of the Church is due to its faithful use at the shrine of the Holy House at Loreto. It was definitely approved by Sixtus V in 1587, and all other Marian litanies were suppressed, at least for public use for several decades. Its titles and invocations set before us Mary's exalted privileges, her holiness of life, her amiability and power, her motherly spirit and queenly majesty.

LEADER PRAYS.	**FAITHFUL RESPOND.**
Lord, have mercy on us.	Lord, have mercy on us.
Christ have mercy on us.	Christ have mercy on us.
Lord, have mercy on us.	Lord, have mercy on us.
Christ, hear us.	Christ graciously hear us.
God the Father of Heaven,	have mercy on us.
God the Son, Redeemer of the world,	have mercy on us.
God the Holy Spirit,	have mercy on us.
Holy Trinity, One God,	have mercy on us.
Holy Mary,	pray for us.
Holy Mother of God,	pray for us.
Holy Virgin of virgins,	pray for us.

Mother of Christ, pray for us.	pray for us.
Mother of divine grace,	pray for us.
Mother most pure,	pray for us.
Mother most chaste,	pray for us.
Mother inviolate,	pray for us.
Mother undefiled,	pray for us.
Mother most amiable,	pray for us.
Mother most admirable,	pray for us.
Mother of good counsel,	pray for us.
Mother of our Creator,	pray for us.
Mother of our Savior,	pray for us.
Mother of the Church,	pray for us.
Virgin most prudent,	pray for us.
Virgin most venerable,	pray for us.
Virgin most renowned,	pray for us.
Virgin most powerful,	pray for us.
Virgin most merciful,	pray for us.
Virgin most faithful,	pray for us.
Mirror of justice,	pray for us.
Seat of wisdom,	pray for us.
Cause of our joy,	pray for us.
Spiritual vessel,	pray for us.
Vessel of honor,	pray for us.
Singular vessel of devotion,	pray for us.
Mystical rose,	pray for us.
Tower of David,	pray for us.
Tower of ivory,	pray for us.
House of gold,	pray for us.
Ark of the covenant,	pray for us.
Gate of Heaven,	pray for us.
Morning star,	pray for us.
Health of the sick,	pray for us.
Refuge of sinners,	pray for us.
Comforter of the afflicted,	pray for us.
Help of Christians,	pray for us.
Queen of angels,	pray for us.
Queen of patriarchs,	pray for us.
Queen of prophets,	pray for us.
Queen of apostles,	pray for us.
Queen of martyrs,	pray for us.
Queen of confessors,	pray for us.
Queen of virgins,	pray for us.
Queen of all saints,	pray for us.
Queen conceived without Original Sin,	pray for us.
Queen assumed into Heaven,	pray for us.
Queen of the holy Rosary,	pray for us.
Queen of families,	pray for us.
Queen of peace,	pray for us.

Lamb of God, Who takest away the sins of the world,	spare us, O Lord.
Lamb of God, Who takest away the sins of the world,	graciously spare us, O Lord.
Lamb of God, Who takest away the sins of the world,	have mercy on us.

Pray for us, O holy Mother of God, that we may be made worthy of the promises of Christ.

General Prayers:

Let us pray- Grant, we beseech Thee, O Lord God, that we Thy servants may enjoy perpetual health of mind and body, and by the glorious intercession of the Blessed Mary, ever Virgin, be delivered from present sorrow and enjoy everlasting happiness. Through Christ Our Lord. Amen

Let us pray - O God, you willed that, at the message of an angel, your word should take flesh in the womb of the Blessed Virgin Mary; grant to your suppliant people, that we, who believe her to be truly the Mother of God, may be helped by her intercession with you. Through the same Christ Our Lord. Amen.

Let us pray - O God, by the fruitful virginity of Blessed Mary, you bestowed upon the human race the rewards of eternal salvation; grant, we beg you, that we may feel the power of her intercession, through whom we have been made worthy to receive the Author of life, our Lord Jesus Christ your Son, who lives and reigns with you forever and ever. Amen.

Let us pray - O God, who by the Resurrection of your Son, our Lord Jesus Christ, granted joy to the whole world, grant, we beg you, that through the intercession of the Virgin Mary, his Mother, we may attain the joys of eternal life. Through the same Christ our Lord. Amen.

Novena to Our Lady of Hope

Devotion to Our Lady of Hope is one of the oldest Marian devotions. The first shrine bearing that title was erected at Mezieres in the year 930.

On January 17, 1871, Our Lady of Hope appeared in the French village of Pontmain. There she reveals herself as the "Madonna of the Crucifix" and gave the world her message of hope through prayer and the cross. The basilica built at Pontmain by the Oblates of Mary Immaculate is one of the great French pilgrimage places, noted for its miracles of grace.

The Oblate Fathers introduced the devotion to Europe including Poland, and finally to America in 1952. Novena devotions are still maintained at the Shrine of Our Lady of Hope, Oblate Fathers' Novitiate and Infirmary, Tewksbury, Massachusetts.

I am the mother of fair love, of fear, of knowledge, and of holy hope. In me is all grace of the way and of the truth; in me is all hope of life and of virtue. Come to me all that desire me and be filled with my fruits. (Sirach 24: 24-26)

Let Us Pray:

O God, who by the marvellous protection of the Blessed Virgin Mary has strengthened us firmly in hope, grant we beseech You; that by persevering in prayer at her admonition, we may obtain the favors we devoutly implore. Through Christ Our Lord. Amen.

Prayer to Our Lady of Hope

O Blessed Virgin Mary, Mother of Grace, Hope of the world. Hear us, your children, who cry to you. O Mary, my Mother, I kneel before you with heavy heart. The burden of my sins oppresses me. The knowledge of my weakness discourages me. I am beset by fears and temptations of every sort. Yet I am so attached to the things of this world that instead of longing for Heaven I am filled with dread at the thought of death.

O Mother of Mercy, have pity on me in my distress. You are all-powerful with your Divine Son. He can refuse no request of your Immaculate Heart. Show yourself a true Mother to me by being my advocate before His throne. O Refuge of Sinners and Hope of the Hopeless, to whom shall I turn if not you?

Obtain for me, then, O Mother of Hope, the grace of true sorrow for my sins, the gift of perfect resignation to God's Holy Will, and the courage to take up my cross and follow Jesus. Beg of His Sacred Heart the special favor that I ask in this novena. (Make your request.)

But above all I pray, O dearest Mother, that through your most powerful intercession my heart may be filled with Holy Hope, so that in life's darkest hour I may never fail to trust in God my Savior, but by walking in the way of His commandments I may merit to be united with Him, and with you in the eternal joys of Heaven. Amen.

Mary, our Hope, have pity on us. Hope of the Hopeless, pray for us.
Say the Hail Mary three (3) times.

The month of May is dedicated to The Blessed Virgin Mary. May usually falls within the liturgical season of Easter. The liturgical color is white - the color of light, a symbol of joy, purity and innocence, absolute or restored.

The world is resplendent with Spring's increased light and new growth. It is Mary's month in the Easter season and all of nature rejoices with the Queen of Heaven at the Resurrection of Her Son during the remainder of Easter time.

As Spring blossoms forth and we are surrounded by new life, the time is full of the joy of our Easter celebration and in anticipation of the coming of the Holy Spirit, our Consoler and Advocate.

The Solemnity of the Ascension of Jesus is celebrated on Sunday in most dioceses in the United States. When I was young, the Solemnity of the Ascension of Jesus was celebrated on Thursday.

In the hierarchy of holiness it is precisely the 'woman', Mary of Nazareth, who is the 'figure' of the Church. She 'precedes' everyone on the path to holiness; in her person 'the Church has already reached that perfection whereby she exists without spot or wrinkle.'
John Paul II - Mulieris Dignitatem, 1988

Two feast days dedicated to Mary are currently celebrated in the month of May:
Our Lady of Fatima on May 13, and the Visitation of Mary to her cousin Elizabeth on May 31.

May   Modesty

Devotions and Celebrations = First Communions
Wianek – Children of Mary

My sister, Barbara, First Communion

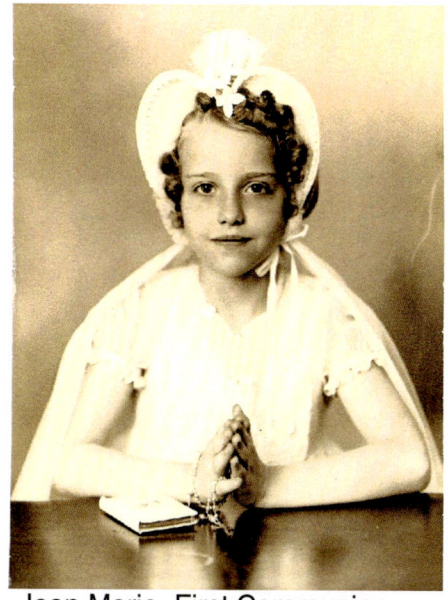

Jean Marie, First Communion

My Teachers at All Saints School =
Sister Mary Ludgera, Kindergarten
Sister Mary Anastasia, Second Grade
Sister Mary Domitilla, First Grade

My First Holy Communion was May 21, 1944.
My Heart shaped veil was my choice.
Each child received a framed certificate.
My little prayer book and other memorabilia
are in my Cedar Chest.

Wianek – Garland – Children of Mary

      Wianek means Garland or wreath in English. In my prayer book, Catholic Girls Guide, the virtues we are taught are presented as "flowers" to be placed before the Lord in response to graces that have been bestowed on us by God. Polish girls joined the Wianek in Kindergarten and after we made our First Communion we were given a copy of The Catholic Girls Guide 1937 Edition. It was only four inches wide and six inches high and had seven-hundred-eighty pages, making it difficult for our little hands to handle.

      In Kindergarten, I remember big pages with flowers on them that we could color and a summary of each lesson and a To Do List of three actions. The first "To Do" was to pray for the Virtue the other two were age appropriate. One example I do remember is: Carnation – Obedience. We were taught the Ten Commandments with emphasis on "Honor your Father and your Mother" with the promise of a long life. They did say that it meant living for eternity with God. For six years we were taught using The Catholic Girls Guide as an outline. At each grade level, more age appropriate practical applications were introduced to encourage our spiritual development.

The virgin thinks on things of the Lord: that she may be holy in body and in spirit. (1 Corinthians 3: 34)

Be thou an example of the faithful, in word, in conversation, in charity, in faith, in purity. (1Timothy 42)

The Children of Mary Table of Contents included the following:

First – The Maiden's Wreath
    1. Sunflower – Faith
    2. Ivy – Hope
    3. Peony – Love of God
    4. Rose – Love of Our Neighbor
    5. Carnation – Obedience
    6. Forget-me-not – Piety
    7. Violet – Humility
    8. Daffodil – Industry
    9. Narcissus – Truthfulness

    Second – Wreath of Lilies – Purity
      These lessons stressed purity in thoughts, words, and deeds, both alone and with others.

      In some ways, Wianek could be compared to other girls' organizations; we played games learned crafts, embroidering, sewing, and cooking skills. The big difference is Spiritual development is top priority in the Wianek organization.

Young Ladies Sodality

"By their fruits you will know them." The Twelve Fruits of the Holy Spirit are basically character traits of a good person. In the Children of Mary Organization and the Young Ladies Sodality at All Saints Catholic School, I learned to call these Twelve Fruits of the Holy Spirit, Virtues.

The Catholic Girls Guide contains Counsels and Devotions for Girls in the ordinary walks of Life; in particular for The Children of Mary and Young Ladies in the Sodality. The Catholic Girls Guide is written to inspire young girls with a love of virtues and to encourage them to pursue virtuous lives by applying the counsels to themselves and not to others. The fact that virtue and piety do not interfere with enjoyment of life was emphasized. Fun in sports, active games, and moderate participation in harmless amusements were encouraged to lead balanced lives.

The Sodality of the Blessed Virgin Mary

The last section of the Catholic Girls Guide is devoted to the formalities for the Solemn Reception of new members, along with the obligations, pious exercises, and prayers for meetings. The last section includes Devotions and Meditations on the Life of the Blessed Virgin Mary – one for every day in the month of May.

At sixteen years of age, I attended the 1953 Summer School of Catholic Action and became a "Free Lance Contributor" to a National Catholic Magazine, The Queen's Work. This magazine was written for high school and college students both young men and young women. Two of my articles were published. The first one I wrote was titled, "My Sister Barbara – Others First." The magazine included a picture of my sister and my article in which I wrote about many of the extra nice things that my sister did for the Church, our family, friends, and neighbors.

The second article that I wrote was published as a two-page center-fold in the National Catholic Magazine, The Queen's Work. It included detailed information about the annual, "Be Modern and Modest" style show that was presented at All Saints High School, to encourage the young ladies to dress modestly. For my Senior Prom I designed my formal and went with one of my good friends, Steven Gresock. We are standing in front of the Holy Reminders to be virtuous even at Proms.

The 1953 Summer School of Catholic Action was a life changing experience for me. There I Spiritually matured and discovered my God given talents for writing and teaching. It was the first time I was miles away from home in a different City and State in a big Hotel without a family member. That Summer School of Catholic Action was led by Father Daniel Lord S. J. There were hundreds of young people between the age of sixteen and twenty five. Our day started with morning Mass and a light breakfast and we attended different Workshops and had lunch between 11:00 am and 1:00 pm. There were more workshops later in the day. We were expected to dress in our Sunday best clothes for Dinner in the elegant Hotel Dining Room.

The evenings were for socializing and three evenings stand out. The first was a Talent Show in which I didn't participate because I was very reserved at the time. I was not shy in that I fully participated in the Workshops. I attended with two young men and one young lady from Charleston, West Virginia. One of the young men was dating the young lady and the other young man asked if I would go with him to an evening Roller Skating Party the next day when I told him that it would be my seventeenth Birthday.

The reason I agreed was that Father O. H. Walker would be the chaperone. We had special permission to stay out one hour later than curfew. On the last night there was a semi-formal dance to which I went alone and still had several male dance partners keeping me dancing most of the night. At midnight Father Daniel Lord said, "Time for our night prayers." and right there all of the hundreds of young people knelt down on the dance floor and we prayed together. Most of us went straight to our rooms because we intended to go to Mass in the morning. Fasting from food from midnight was a Church regulation before receiving the Holy Eucharist the next morning. The requirement has been changed to only one hour so people who work the different shifts can eat to maintain their good health.
.

At my sister Barbara's wedding to Gerald Edel in 1956, I was her Maid-of-Honor.
Jean Marie is next to the Bride.

May Modesty

Polish–American Recipe = *Ciasto Szybki*: Quick Cake and Variations

Quick Cake Basic Recipe

Recipe with directions: Preheat oven to 400º degrees.
1. Place ¾ cup of granulated sugar in the two quart bowl.
2. Add ¼ cup of butter softened to room temperature.
3. Cream together with mixing spoon.
4. Crack open one (1) large egg into the one quart bowl.
5. Mix with hand mixer for about two minutes until creamy and small bubbles form on top.
6. Add ½ cup of whole milk to the beaten egg and beat again until small bubbles form.
7. Pour the egg and milk mixture into the sugar and butter mixture and beat well.
8. Place one (1) cup of flour in a sifter 1/3 of a cup at a time.
9. After each 1/3 cup of flour add ½ teaspoon of Baking Powder.
10. Sift about 1/3 third of the dry ingredients onto a paper plate and pour into the egg and milk mixture.
11. Stir this together and beat with the mixer until well blended.
12. Continue steps 9 and 10 - two more times.
13. Grease and lightly flour a 9 inch by 9 inch oven proof glass baking dish.
14. Pour cake batter into the dish.
15. Sprinkle top with 1 teaspoon cinnamon and 2 teaspoons granulated sugar mixture.
16. Bake for twenty (20) to twenty-five minutes (25).
17. Shut off oven and open the oven door a crack to allow cake to cool. This reduces the chances of the middle of the cake dropping down.
18. Store in the baking dish with a parchment paper cover or a "vented aluminum" cover.
19. Cut as needed. Spread with butter and serve warm. Cake will keep well at room temperature for three days. In the remote possibility that there is some cake left on the third day, place left over pieces in a smaller container and refrigerate.

Coffee Cake Variations = Pineapple Upside Down Cake

Utensils: two medium sized bowls (one quart and two quarts), hand mixer, measuring spoons, mixing spoon, table knife, and 9 inch by 9 inch oven proof glass baking dish.

Recipe with directions: Preheat oven to 375º degrees.

Spread a mixture of 4 tablespoons of melted butter and half cup light brown sugar that has been stirred together inside the bottom of the 9 inch by 9 inch oven proof glass baking dish.
Place well drained pineapple pieces in a single layer on top of the butter and sugar mixture. Canned Pineapple – Tidbits were used for this recipe.

1. Place ¾ cup of granulated sugar in the two quart bowl.
2. Add ¼ cup of butter softened to room temperature.
3. Cream together with mixing spoon.
4. Crack open one (1) large egg into the one quart bowl.
5. Mix with hand mixer for about two minutes until creamy and small bubbles form on top.
6. Add ½ cup of whole milk to the beaten egg and beat again until small bubbles form.
7. Pour the egg and milk mixture into the sugar and butter mixture and beat well.
8. Place one (1) cup of flour in a sifter 1/3 of a cup at a time.
9. After each 1/3 cup of flour add ½ teaspoon of Baking Powder.
10. Sift about 1/3 third of the dry ingredients onto a paper plate and pour into the egg and milk mixture.
11. Stir this together and beat with the mixer until well blended.
12. Continue steps 9 and 10 two more times.
13. Carefully spoon cake batter over the pineapple and brown sugar base.
14. Sprinkle top with 1 teaspoon cinnamon and 2 teaspoons granulated sugar mixture.
15. Bake in oven set at 375º for 30 to 35 minutes.
16. Cap with aluminum foil tent vented on two sides and set aside to cool.

12. Pineapple pieces on butter and sugar base.   13. Sprinkle top with cinnamon and sugar mixture.

Bake in oven set at 375º for 30 to 35 minutes.

All done = Cap with aluminum foil tent vented on two sides and set aside to cool. **Serve upside down.**

Coffee Cake Variations = Huckleberry Muffins

Recipe makes twelve medium sized muffins about 2 ½ inches in diameter.
Muffins: Wild Michigan Huckleberries were use for this example.
Add small pieces of chocolate, blueberries, pecan pieces, and small pieces of apples (peeled of course), to make other tasty treats.
Utensils: two medium sized bowls (one quart and two quarts), hand mixer, paper liners, measuring spoons, mixing spoon, table knife, and muffin tin.

Recipe with directions: Preheat oven to 400º degrees.

1. Place ¾ cup of granulated sugar in the two quart bowl.
2. Add ¼ cup of butter softened to room temperature.
3. Cream together with mixing spoon.
4. Crack open one (1) large egg into the one quart bowl.
5. Mix with hand mixer for about two minutes until creamy and small bubbles form on top.
6. Add ½ cup of whole milk to the beaten egg and beat again until small bubbles form.
7. Pour the egg and milk mixture into the sugar and butter mixture and beat well.
8. Place one (1) cup of flour in a sifter 1/3 of a cup at a time.
9. After each 1/3 cup of flour add ½ teaspoon of Baking Powder.
10. Sift1/3 third of the dry ingredients onto a paper plate and pour into the egg and milk mixture.
11. Stir this together and beat with the mixer until well blended.
12. Continue steps 9 and 10 two more times.
13. Spoon about two (2) tablespoons of cake batter into each muffin paper.
14. Sprinkle one (1) tablespoon of berries on top and lightly pat the berries into the batter.

Step 12 and 13

Step 14 and 15

15. Next place one (1) tablespoon batter on top of the berries and spread the batter to cover the berries.
16. Sprinkle a mixture of half granulated sugar to half cinnamon on top of each muffin.
17. Bake twenty (20) minutes at 400º degrees.

Step 17

Step 18

Enjoy!

18. Remove muffins from tin by placing a piece of parchment paper on top of the pan.
19. Tip the muffins out and quickly place them to cool on rack for about ten minutes.

Enjoy - any way you cut them or even take a big bite of deliciousness.

May   Modesty

Polish–American Activity = Garden Flowers

    Flowers were not growing in our gardens in Michigan during the month of May 2014, so these Day Lilies were picked in July when I started compiling this book.

    My Mother would Pick one pretty flower from our yard in Michigan starting in May, and place it in a beautiful glass bowl or vase, and put it on our dining room table. My Mother said, "Flowers belong in the garden, so that is the reason she didn't pick a full bouquet to bring into the house.

    We ate most of our weekly meals on the small table in the kitchen. Sunday breakfast after Mass and our main meals later in the day were eaten on the dining room table. Frequently we had our lunch meal as a picnic in the park or at relatives' and friends' homes. This continued on almost every warm day into Autumn. On the weekends when my Daddy went fishing, my Mother would continue these traditions, and serve smaller evening meals.

"Hollyhock Dolls"

    In May of 2004, my husband and I were moving back to Michigan to "retire" – I had planted Hollyhocks in our side yard in CA with hopes to make "Hollyhock Dolls" with my Granddaughter Brianna; she was only five years old at the time. That year God blest me with an early summer in California and the Hollyhocks were in full bloom in May instead of summer. All of our furniture was already on the way to Michigan. I and our son, Martin were sleeping on the floor in sleeping bags and finishing packing and cleaning the house. You guessed it I called up our daughter, Karen and asked if I could please, have Brianna visit with me one beautiful sunny day.

The following pictures tell the story of that delightful afternoon.

1.   2. & 3.

1. Brianna choosing and picking the buds and flowers for Hollyhock Dolls.
2. Buds and flowers for a pink Doll on first plate.
3. The three steps for making a red Hollyhock Doll on the second plate.

4. Hollyhock Dolls in various stages of progress.
5. Putting the finishing touches on Hollyhock Dolls.

Did we have fun?
One picture is worth a thousand words!

When Brianna was in middle school, her Math teacher asked, "When did each student first learn to understand Math concepts?" They were to write about it. Brianna wrote about making Hollyhock Dolls with her Grammy Jean Marie.

She had to find big buds for the head, one for each doll. She had to find two smaller buds, one for each hand on each doll. One full blooming flower was needed for each skirt. She had made ten dolls. Her own idea was to poke the edge of the blossom on the tooth pick with a bud for one of the hands to make the skirts look like the dolls were dancing.

Both of my BUSIAS made Hollyhock Dolls with me and I made them at my home, sometimes with my playmates. I don't think it was a Polish Tradition exclusively. I think rather making Hollyhock Dolls was and still is a Michigan past-time. In California Hollyhocks were considered weeds, so I had purchased my Hollyhock Seeds from a Michigan based company.

Most Polish women in Poland and the United States of America had beautiful flower gardens. Year-round they had house plants, and their nimble fingers also made flowers out of paper and ribbons.

May   Modesty

People of Polish Heritage = My Mother

1. My Mother is standing in front of her Parent's home on Industrial Avenue. Upper right hand corner of picture is All Saints Catholic Church.
2. Five Generations of Mothers: Busia Helen, Stefania my Mother, Jean Marie, Mary my second daughter is holding her daughter Crescentia.

Women all ages loved to dance in that era. Men started to get interested when Fred Astaire and Ginger Rogers were dancing in the movies. Even more men started dancing when Gene Kelly with his athletic style came to the Silver Screen. My Daddy was the exception. He learned to dance because he was attracted to My Mother and she loved to dance.

My Daddy liked to share this memory. He said that he only had learned to dance a Waltz and went to a dance to which he knew My Mother would be going. The women had little dance cards and "would-be-partners" would sign them. My Daddy very respectfully asked My Mother "Will you save the next waltz for me, Miss Urbanik?" She said yes, and the next waltz that was played was titled, "The Waltz You Saved for Me."

Just Mommy and Me and BABY MAKES THREE
OOPS and Jean Marie

1.

2. & 3.

4.

1. My parents rented their first home, 406 West Flint Park Boulevard,
2. My Sunday and visiting clothes were this light blue dress, white shoes and anklets and a ribbon in my hair. When my Mother took me to Busia Helen's home, I was usually dressed like this picture from a very young age.
3. My parents purchased their first and only house on Roberts Street in Flint, Michigan, when I was around three years old, and soon made it into Our Home. My Mother had high standards of cleanliness. No toys in the living room and kitchen. We had a small Playroom off the kitchen. It was probably meant to be a mud-room, similar to the one on the back of her parents' home.
4. This tea cup and saucer are only two inches high and from the Dining Car of a Railroad. A set of service for four was set on our dining room table on Christmas morning 1942, along with two doll high chairs that my Daddy made to fit our dolls from the previous year. My Mother woke up my sister Barbara and me early. She said that we had to clear off the dining room table before Mass. We were pleasantly surprised to open our sleepy eyes to Christmas Presents. You read January Chapter in this book – didn't you?

My Doll Collection and More

Even though My Aunt Olga started my doll collection, my Mother added to my collection right up to ten months before she died. Most of them were for special occasions. Growing up my Mother had only one doll. She made sure that I had lots of dolls.

1.

2.

3.

1. Jack and Jill had more bumps and bruises after I played with them.
    I received them for Christmas 1940.

2. The Mexican peasant girl doll was given to me in 1944 when I was very ill from the fumes from the cleaning fluids on my Daddy's work clothes.

3. I was fourteen when this roller skating doll joined my collection. My Mother had taken me to see the "Roller-Capades" at the I. M. A. Auditorium. I wanted the doll and my sister chose a Fully Illustrated Program. In my book, Christmas in the Living Room, I tell the story about my Daddy shopping for shoe skates during World War II when there was a leather shortage.

4.

5.

4. This bride doll, my Mother gave to me when I first learned, that a woman was dressed as "The Bride of Christ" when she took her final, Perpetual Vows at her investiture as a Sister/Nun. I wanted to go to the convent from an early age. I think I was four years old or even younger.

5. Last Visit – Mother's Gift to me December 1986.

   Christmas 1986, My Mother took me to the International Institute in Flint to see their new facility. When I was very young the Polish Choir members took their families and went to sing Kolendy during the Christmas Season; back then the International Institute was in a small two story house. Choirs composed of People from around the world came and sang familiar Carols in their own languages to the same melody. The beautiful blend of the voices flowed out into the streets.

   My mother-in-law died in 1986. Since both of my parents were still living, my husband made sure that I visited them. This was the last time I saw my mother when she was still able to drive.

   I learned to know my mother's ways of getting information in order to "surprise" me. When she took me into the Gift Shop and asked me which dolls did I like. I chose these two little dolls, two inches tall. I said, "I don't have any Japanese dolls made in Japan." We laughed because many Doll Collections were made in Japan and dressed in the native dress from other countries. We then went and viewed the other displays. When she excused herself to go to the restroom and didn't ask if I needed to go, I knew that she was going back to buy these dolls. She wrapped them and gave them to me on Christmas Day.

My Mother provided good examples of Modesty in clothing, language, and behavior.

The Wianek and the Young Ladies Sodality organizations contributed to the development of all Twelve Virtues and continue to influence my choices.

June Purity

Petunias in Neighbor's Yard

Fruit of the Holy Spirit = Purity

Liturgical Calendar = The Sacred Heart of Jesus

Devotions and Celebrations = Corpus Christi Procession

Polish–American Recipe = *Kapusniak*: Cabbage Side Dish

Polish–American Activity = Wycinanki – Wstazka = Ribbon Style

People of Polish Heritage = Sisters of Saint Joseph

June Purity

Fruit of the Holy Spirit = Purity

Prayer:

    Holy Spirit, eternal Love of the Father and the Son, kindly bestow on us the the fruits of Purity, that we may keep our bodies in such holiness as befits your temple, so that having by your assistance preserved our hearts pure on earth, we may merit in Jesus Christ, according to the words of the Gospel, to see God eternally in the glory of his kingdom.

We live the virtue of Purity when we use the gift of sexuality wisely, according to God's plan.

Purity helps one guard his/her senses so that they will not cause him/her to sin; it helps one regard his/her own body and those of others as temple of the Holy Spirit

He who loves purity of heart, and whose speech is gracious, will have the king as his friend. (Proverbs 22: 10-12)

Let no one despise your youth, but set the believers an example in speech and conduct, in love, in faith, in purity. (1Timothy 4: 11-13)

Blessed are the pure in heart, for they shall see God. (Matthew 5: 7-9)

So shun youthful passions and aim at righteousness, faith, love, and peace, along with those who call upon the Lord from a pure heart. (2 Timothy 2: 21-23)

June   Purity

Liturgical Calendar = The Sacred Heart of Jesus

Litany of the Sacred Heart of Jesus

In 1899 Pope Leo XIII approved this Litany of the Sacred Heart of Jesus for public use. This litany is actually a synthesis of several other litanies dating back to the 17th century. Father Croiset composed a litany in 1691 from which 17 invocations were used by Venerable Anne Madeleine Remuzat when she composed her litany in 1718 at Marseille. She joined an additional 10 invocations to those of Father Croiset, for a total of 27 invocations. Six more invocations written by Sister Madeleine Joly of Dijon in 1686 were added by the Sacred Congregation for Rites when it was approved for public use in 1899.

This makes a total of 33 invocations, one for each year of life of our Lord Jesus Christ.

LEADER PRAYS.	**FAITHFUL RESPOND.**
Lord, have mercy.	Lord, have mercy.
Christ, have mercy.	Christ, have mercy.
Lord, have mercy.	Lord, have mercy.
Christ, hear us.	Christ, graciously hear us.
God the Father of Heaven,	have mercy on us.
God the Son, Redeemer of the world,	have mercy on us.
God, the Holy Spirit,	have mercy on us.
Holy Trinity, One God,	have mercy on us.
Heart of Jesus, Son of the Eternal Father,	have mercy on us.
Heart of Jesus, formed by the Holy Spirit in the womb of the Virgin Mother,	have mercy on us.
Heart of Jesus, substantially united to the Word of God,	have mercy on us.
Heart of Jesus, of Infinite Majesty,	have mercy on us.
Heart of Jesus, Sacred Temple of God,	have mercy on us.
Heart of Jesus, Tabernacle of the Most High,	have mercy on us.
Heart of Jesus, House of God and Gate of Heaven,	have mercy on us.
Heart of Jesus, burning furnace of charity,	have mercy on us.
Heart of Jesus, abode of justice and love,	have mercy on us.
Heart of Jesus, full of goodness and love,	have mercy on us.
Heart of Jesus, abyss of all virtues,	have mercy on us.
Heart of Jesus, most worthy of all praise,	have mercy on us.
Heart of Jesus, king and center of all hearts,	have mercy on us.
Heart of Jesus, in whom are all treasures of wisdom and knowledge,	have mercy on us.
Heart of Jesus, in whom dwells the fullness of divinity,	have mercy on us.
Heart of Jesus, in whom the Father was well pleased,	have mercy on us.
Heart of Jesus, of whose fullness we have all received,	have mercy on us.
Heart of Jesus, desire of the everlasting hills,	have mercy on us.
Heart of Jesus, patient and most merciful,	have mercy on us.
Heart of Jesus, enriching all who invoke Thee,	have mercy on us.
Heart of Jesus, fountain of life and holiness,	have mercy on us.
Heart of Jesus, propitiation for our sins,	have mercy on us.
Heart of Jesus, loaded down with opprobrium,	have mercy on us.

Heart of Jesus, bruised for our offenses,	have mercy on us.
Heart of Jesus, obedient to death,	have mercy on us.
Heart of Jesus, pierced with a lance,	have mercy on us.
Heart of Jesus, source of all consolation,	have mercy on us.
Heart of Jesus, our life and resurrection,	have mercy on us.
Heart of Jesus, our peace and our reconciliation,	have mercy on us.
Heart of Jesus, victim for our sins,	have mercy on us.
Heart of Jesus, salvation of those who trust in Thee,	have mercy on us.
Heart of Jesus, hope of those who die in Thee,	have mercy on us.
Heart of Jesus, delight of all the Saints,	have mercy on us.
Lamb of God, who taketh away the sins of the world,	spare us, O Lord.
Lamb of God, who taketh away the sins of the world,	graciously hear us, O Lord.
Lamb of God, who taketh away the sins of the world,	have mercy on us, O Lord.
Jesus, meek and humble of heart,	make our hearts like unto thine.

Let us pray:

Almighty and eternal God, look upon the Heart of Thy most beloved Son and upon the praises and satisfaction which He offers Thee in the name of sinners; and to those who implore Thy mercy, in Thy great goodness, grant forgiveness in the name of the same Jesus Christ, Thy Son, who livest and reignest with Thee forever and ever. Amen.

Efficacious Novena to the Sacred Heart of Jesus

O my Jesus, you have said: "Truly I say to you, ask and you will receive, seek and you will find, knock and it will be opened to you." Behold I knock; I seek and ask for the grace of... (Here name your request)

Our Father....Hail Mary....Glory Be to the Father...

Sacred Heart of Jesus, I place all my trust in you.

O my Jesus, you have said: "Truly I say to you, if you ask anything of the Father in my name, he will give it to you." Behold, in your name, I ask the Father for the grace of...... (Here name your request)

Our Father...Hail Mary....Glory Be To the Father...

Sacred Heart of Jesus, I place all my trust in you.

O my Jesus, you have said: "Truly I say to you, heaven and earth will pass away but my words will not pass away." Encouraged by your infallible words I now ask for the grace of... (Here name your request)

Our Father....Hail Mary....Glory Be to the Father...

Sacred Heart of Jesus, I place all my trust in you.

O Sacred Heart of Jesus, for whom it is impossible not to have compassion on the afflicted, have pity on us miserable sinners and grant us the grace which we ask of you, through the Sorrowful and Immaculate Heart of Mary, your tender Mother and ours.

Say the Hail, Holy Queen and add: St. Joseph, foster father of Jesus, pray for us.
-- St. Margaret Mary Alacoque

The month of June is dedicated to The Sacred Heart of Jesus. The beginning of the month falls within the liturgical season of Easter, which is represented by the liturgical color white — the color of light, a symbol of joy, purity and innocence, absolute or restored through the Sacrament of Reconciliation. The remainder of the month falls within the liturgical season of Ordinary Time, which is represented by the liturgical color green. This symbol of hope is the color of the sprouting seed and arouses in the faithful the hope of reaping the eternal harvest of heaven, especially the hope of a glorious resurrection. It is used in the offices and Masses of Ordinary Time. The last portion of the liturgical year represents the time of our pilgrimage to heaven during which we hope to Love and Praise God for eternity.

Following Pentecost, the Church begins her slow descent from the great peaks of the Easter Season to the verdant pastures of Ordinary Time, the longest of the liturgical seasons. Like the lush June growth all around us, the green of the liturgical season points to the new life won for us by the Redemption of Jesus Christ, the new life of Charity. For Our Lord came to cast the fire of His love on the earth, and to that end, sent His Holy Spirit at Pentecost in the form of tongues of fire.

Ordinary Time is the hour to "go out to all the world and tell the good news." The feasts of June highlight this expansion of the Church. At least ten times, the Church vests in the red of the martyrs whose blood is the very seed of her growth.

The Special Holy Days Remembered in June

Ascension Sunday/7th Sunday of Easter
> Jesus tells the apostles to "Go and make disciples of all nations, baptizing them in the name of the Father and of the Son and of the Holy Spirit."

Pentecost Sunday
> In this Gospel Jesus gives the disciples the power to forgive sins.

Trinity Sunday
> This Gospel tells us that whoever believes in Jesus might not perish but might have eternal life.

Corpus Christi = Body and Blood of Christ
> "I am the living bread that came down from Heaven; whoever eats this bread will live forever."

Saints Peter and Paul
> In this Gospel Peter confesses that Jesus is the Christ the Son of God.

Sacred Heart of Jesus
> God is Love and the Sacred Heart of Jesus — present on earth in the Blessed Sacrament — is the human manifestation of God's Love for men.

Immaculate Heart of Mary

We too are called to be witnesses like the apostles and martyrs. May the Heart of Jesus inflame our hearts so that we may be worthy of our Baptismal call to holiness. Immaculate Heart of Mary, pray for us.

June   Purity

Devotions and Celebrations = Corpus Christi Procession

1.
2.

1. In this picture I am in first grade and third in line even though I am shorter than the Kindergarten girls in front.
2. My Bonnet and formal were worn when I was in Kindergarten and First Grade for all Processions. Please refer to the May Chapter in this book. In addition I wore them when I was Flower Girl for my Aunt Agnes' and Uncle Bob's wedding.

Corpus Christi Procession – 1979

Processions are a popular tradition among the Polish in the Catholic Church. It was natural that a beautiful, colorful procession began the ceremonies. Patricia Mroczek continues her coverage: Her article is printed (With permission.) here in its entirety because it presents the deep seated appreciation of the Polish culture by the Polish people in the United States of America.

> An altar boy, clad in an all-white long gown and carrying a tall golden cross, began the services by leading the procession down the middle aisle of the parish.
> Small children, carrying red and white gladiolas, the Polish colors, served as honor guards.
> Ninety-one-year-old Mrs. Frank Lerash of Kinde carried a portrait of Polish Pope John Paul II in the long processional line. The painting was blessed and will hang on display at the church, St. Mary of Czestochowa Church.
> Four teenaged girls then carried a special processional display of white linen to accent the portrait of the Black Madonna, Our Lady of Czestochowa and her Child.

Concluding the marchers were Parish Administrator Rev. Francis J. Murray (who relieved Rev. Ron Dombrowski) former pastor Rev. Stanley Surman of St. Mary's Parisville and former pastor Rev. Barney Janowicz of Holy Trinity, Bay City, who joined the monsignor.

As the procession began to move up the aisle, the organ played a prelude and the large congregation filled the church with the harmonious chorus of a Polish song.

Church member Ralph Majeski described the Polish choir interspersed in the crowd as "unbelievable."

"It made tears come to my eyes when the inside of our church filled with those Polish voices," Majeski said.

Peszkowski had credited Majeski with organizing the "historic event for Our Lady."

Majeski explained why he and a small committee planned the ceremonious services:

"I did it for the sake of the people who believe in St. Mary's of Czestochowa church ... for all the years they've come.

"I did it for the older people ... and for the younger people so they can get a feeling of what it's all about and continue with the tradition of Our Lady,"

Majeski said the services gave him "goose-bumps ... it was so beautiful."

"It taught me to be proud of your name, because your name will be with you forever," he added.

Peszkowski gave the sermon during the Mass. He told the large, quiet crowd that, fourteen days ago, he was at Jasna Gora, the high hill where the historic Black Madonna is on display near Czestochowa, Poland. While in Poland, Peszkowski spoke with part of the 27,000 people who walked the nine days from Warsaw to Czestochowa to pray before Our Lady, he said.

"I told those people about this parish and its fight to keep its identity."

"When you are talking of Our Lady of Czestochowa, we are talking of our heritage," Peszkowski added.

"We must be strong," Peszkowski said, stirring the crowd. "Every third Pole is out of Poland."

The monsignor said Poland and its people must "fight all the time for our identity ... it is necessary to fight all the time for our name."

"I beg of you. Use your imagination ... for the most precious things we have are our immortal souls and our names."
(Chominski, April 1, 1981)

At All Saints Church, the little girls in long dresses led the Processions, followed by the girls who had recently made their First Communion. Next, the boys in white suits who had recently made their First Communion followed. Acolytes of all ages were next in line. Following an Acolyte with the Crucifix are bell-ringers who alternate ringing high and low toned bells, then an incensor, and finally the Priest Celebrant with a large Host held high above his head for all to see. Catholics believe that the consecrated Host is the real presence of the body of Christ

June   Purity

Polish–American Recipe = *Kapusniak/Kapusta*: Cabbage Side Dish

       August 2014, my daughter Michelle brought me a quart jar of Organic Sauerkraut. I decided to add my Polish-American Recipe for Kapusta to this book. The word Kapusta simply means Cabbage. Growing up the following Recipe was called, Kapusta. The basic Ingredients are the Polish Recipe; the Process and spices are the ones I use – the American Addition.

1. 8 (eight) ounces of "Button" Mushrooms.
   My relatives used to grow their own mushrooms in the basement "cold storage room".
   Cut off stems, rinse and cut into small pieces.
   Rinse the "Button Caps" with cold water, and pat dry with paper towels.
   Slice the "Button Caps" into 1/4 inch slices as pictured and cut slices in half.
   Stir Fry Button Cap slices in about 1 (one) tablespoon of butter and set aside to add later.

1.   2.

2. Crockpot or other slow cooker. My relatives prepared this side dish on the stove in a big kettle. This way the ingredients have to be stirred about every five minutes or less.
   Place one quart of Sauerkraut in the crock pot and set on lowest heat.
   My relatives prepared their own Sauerkraut.
   I purchase Sauerkraut in a glass jar whenever possible.
   Add about one pound of shredded raw green cabbage.
   I purchase "shredded raw green cabbage" for salads.

If this product is used – place the shredded raw green cabbage in a bowl of cold water and with about one teaspoon salt. Stir and let set in the salt water for at least ten minutes. This kills most bacteria that may have been introduced in the processing plants.

Spin out all of the water from the shredded raw green cabbage, add to the Crockpot, stir together with the Sauerkraut, and simmer for one hour.

3. One large sweet onion. Peel and cut into fourths, and then cut each wedge into slices about one-third of an inch. Stir Fry onion slices in about 3 (three) tablespoons butter and seasonings (Salt and Poultry Seasoning to your taste, only about one-half teaspoon of each.), until "translucent" and tender but not "floppy." Remove onions from the frying pan and leave the butter and seasonings in the pan.

4. 6 (six) ribs of celery. Cut off both ends of each celery rib, break each rib in the middle carefully to remove the large "strings," then slice into about one-third of an inch pieces. Stir Fry celery pieces adding about 3 (three) tablespoons butter and seasonings (Salt and Poultry Seasoning to your taste only about one-half teaspoon of each.), until tender but still firm.

5.

7.

5. Stir onion slices and celery pieces together before adding to Crockpot. Yes, the onions and celery are Stir Fried separately because they have different cooking times.

6. Add the onions and celery to Crockpot and simmer on low for one more hour.

7. Add one half-cup of water (I use purified water for cooking.) to the fraying pan in which the onions and celery were cooked. Stir to remove all of the spices and drippings, add the mushroom pieces, heat back up to a slow simmer, then add to Crockpot. Turn the heat on the Crockpot to high for one hour more, and let cool. Kapusta made this way freezes well. Thaw and warm up on low heat on top of the stove.

Kapusta tastes great to me either warm or room temperature.
Serve with Polish Sausage on rye bread.

P. S. The recipe for **Kapusniak** is not included because it is the same as those found in other Polish cookbooks.

June   Purity

Polish–American Activity = Wycinanki – Wstazka = Ribbon Style

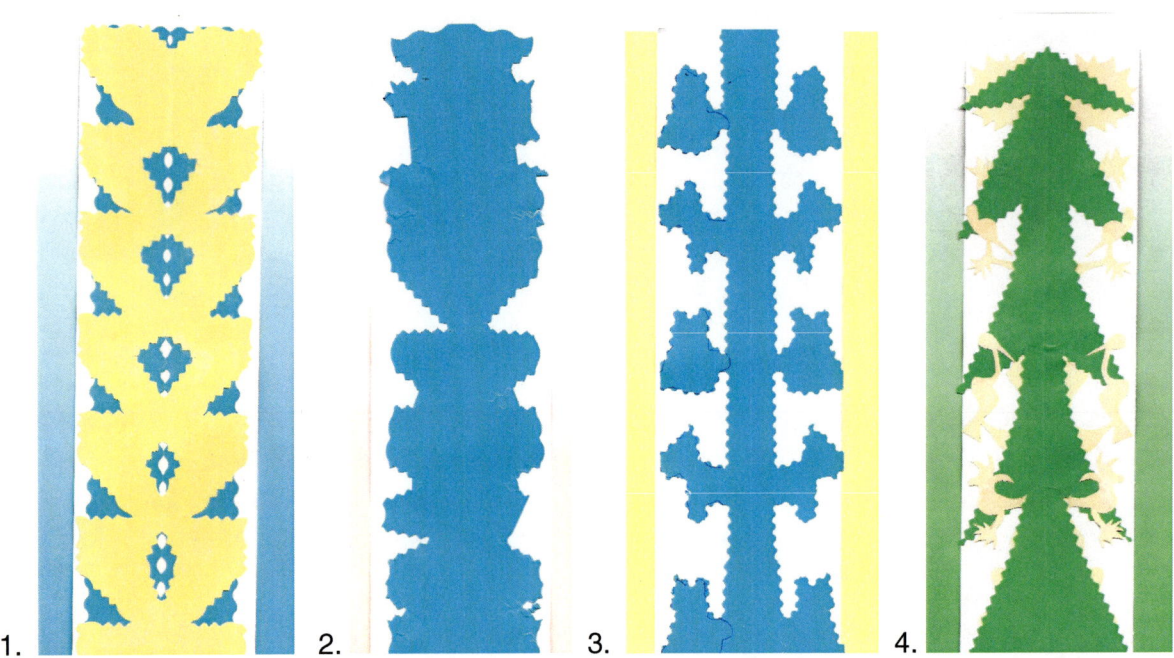

1.   2.   3.   4.

Ribbon Style Wycinanki are frequently integrated with other styles on greeting cards for borders and background colors, also for wrapping gifts as name tags and to secure bows to the packages. We even made Ribbon Style Wycinanki bookmarkers out of Greeting cards.

1. This repetitive design would make an easy border.

2. This abstract, free form design would provide an interesting, conversation starter, name tag. I suggest writing on the back.

3. Look closely at this Ribbon Wycinanki. Do you see what I see? From top down I see two little birds, two little puppies looking out, and this next set could be little kittens, baby bunnies, or even bear cubs.

4. At first glance this looks like just an evergreen tree. As you look closer you can identify different birds, and perhaps a set of storks. The pattern used to decorate the evergreen tree in 4 was hand drawn by our son, Matthew.

All of the designs in this book are original works of art. A big thank you needs to be extended to Matthew, his wife Jody and their three precocious children, who provided the Wycinanki examples for this book, Polish Traditions with American Additions. Crafting tools that were not available to me when I learned the art of paper cutting were added to pencils and scissors to create the exquisite art masterpieces.

June   Purity

People of Polish Heritage = Sisters of Saint Joseph

Unconditional Love from Sisters of Saint Joseph, Third Order of Saint Francis, was wrapped around me from the time I was three years young right up to my wedding day. After that periodically, I would visit some of them in their convents and for celebrations. To this day, I know that they still love me and pray for me; and I hold all of them in my heart and in my prayers.

1. At three years old I would visit the Convent.

2. Surprise Visit from My High School Friend

1. When I was "visiting" my Busia who lived across the street from the All Saints Church. Sister Mary Zita who baked bread for the Nuns, would "call" to my Grandmother, "Bread is out of the oven."
My Busia would take me by the hand across the street and Sister Mary Zita and I would "Skip" hand-in-hand to the back of the Church and go in the back-side door, which led to the kitchen of the Convent. The Sisters had the same kind of step-stool as my Grandmothers. She set me up to the table where four or more loaves of bread were cooling, and hand me a slice of fresh baked bread slathered in "home-churned" butter, and she ate one slice. She would say, "Just checking if it is good enough to serve or we might have to eat up all of it." She would laugh but not out loud. She would then take me to the small convent chapel to visit Jesus. When we walked back past their garden if some fruit or vegetable was ripe she would pick some and wrap them in a white cloth napkin to give to "Mine Busia." On my next visit to Sister Mary Zita, I would take the freshly laundered napkin back to the Convent.

2. Sisters of Saint Joseph Were Not Allowed to Pose for Pictures. They look like they are posing but the photographer didn't use the flash on the camera and I didn't know that this picture was taken until I went to the studio to choose the pictures that I wanted to purchase. Before their final vows Sisters of Saint Joseph can go home any time they wish. Some women go home and decide to stay home others go back to the convent. Sisters of Saint Joseph were not allowed to visit home until two years after their final/perpetual vows.

As a Postulant the women wear simple uniforms similar to our Catholic High Schools, just blue skirts and white blouses. We liked having uniforms for high school. Most of us were from low income families. Having uniforms for school left us money for street clothes and even prom dresses. School hours at All Saints in Flint, Michigan were from 8:00 am to 1:00 pm with one, half-hour study hall to do "Homework." Most of the students in their Junior and Senior years had part time jobs after school hours. I worked at S. S. Kresge Company for thirty-seven cents an hour.

Sisters of Saint Joseph – Polish Order

Oh how I loved being loved by the Nuns!

I knew and still love the Sisters of Saint Joseph and I know that they love ME.

1952 - Left to right: All Saints High School – Grades 9 – 12 and Adult Library,
Elementary School – Grades Kindergarten – 8 and Children's Library,
Auditorium with Stage in one corner and Costume Storage and Dressing Room below,
A Large Kitchen was adjacent to the Auditorium.
My sister Barbara and two of her friends are on the steps of All Saints High School.

Unconditional Love from
Sisters of Saint Joseph, Third Order of Saint Francis

In all the years that I was in the care of Sisters of Saint Joseph, I can remember hundreds of positive experiences and only five somewhat negative experiences.

We were taught to obey the Ten Commandments, to actively engage in the Corporal and Spiritual Works of Mercy, and to follow the beautiful teachings of Jesus.

For example we were taught:

The Silver rule is," Do unto others like you would like them to do to you."
The Golden Rule is, "Treat others as Jesus taught us to do."
Jesus said, "It is written, Thou shall not kill. I say to you, do not even be angry at others."

At All Saints School, our consciences were formed to follow the narrow path between scrupulosity and presumption. Scrupulous people see sin where there is no sin. Presumptuous people do not see the sin when sin is there.

On my First Communion Day, My Second Grade Teacher gave me a special Autograph Book with inspirational messages from all of the Sisters in the Convent at All Saints, at that time. Over the years other Sisters of Saint Joseph added their autographs. The Sisters that were still at All Saints when I graduated from High School in 1954, either added to their original autographs or added the date.
The book is filled with autographs from thirty-one (31) different Sisters of Saint Joseph.

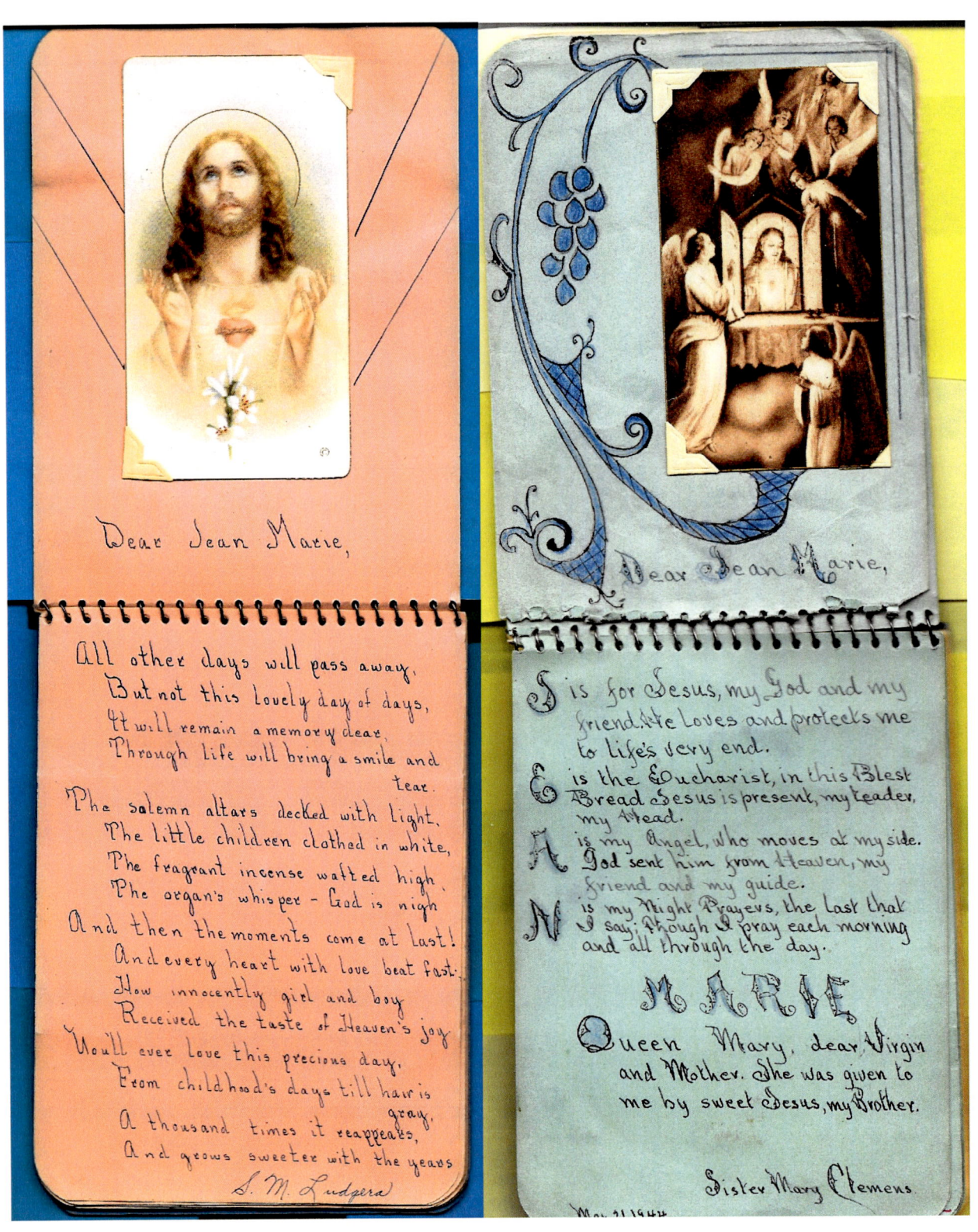

The Sisters of Saint Joseph, Third Order of Saint Francis are living examples in words and deeds of the Virtue of Purity which they taught.

July   Joy

Zinnias in Neighbor's Yard

Fruit of the Holy Spirit = Joy

Liturgical Calendar = The Precious Blood of Jesus

Devotions and Celebrations = Independence Day – God and Country

Polish–American Recipe = *Wieprzowa Przyjecie*: Pork Barbeque

Polish–American Activity = Patriotic – American Flags

People of Polish Heritage = My Daddy's Parents & Grandparents

July   Joy

Fruit of the Holy Spirit = Joy

Prayer:

    Holy Spirit, eternal Love of the Father and the Son, kindly bestow on us the fruit of joy, that we may be filled with holy consolation. May the God of hope fill you with all joy and peace in believing, so that by the power of the Holy Spirit you may abound in hope. (Romans 15: 12-14)

Joy - Keeps us happily aware of God's infinite goodness.

We live with joy when we recognize that true happiness comes, not from money or possessions, but from knowing and following Christ.

Joy is the sense aroused in higher faculties of the soul by the expectation or possession of some good.

Holy angels and virtuous human persons experience joy; its source is the rational will.

Joy differs from pleasure because pleasure may affect the human spirit but originates in body sensation.

In the Gospel according to Saint Luke there are three parables; each one ends with JOY.

When He, the Good Shepherd, finds His lost Sheep He, "lays it on His shoulders rejoicing." (Luke 15:5)

"And then when He got home, He called together His friends and neighbors, saying to them, "Rejoice with me, I have found my sheep that was lost." (Luke 15:6)

"And when she had found the lost coin, she called together her friends and neighbors, saying to them, "Rejoice with me, I have found the drachma that I lost." (Luke 15:9)

"But it was only right that we should celebrate and rejoice, because your brother here was dead and has come to life; he was lost and is found." said, by the Father of the prodigal son. (Luke 15:32)

"Just so, I tell you, there will be more joy in heaven over one sinner who repents than over ninety-nine righteous persons who need no repentance." (Luke 15:7)

Be glad in the Lord, and rejoice, O righteous, and shout for joy, all you upright in heart! (Psalm 32:10-11)

Then our mouth was filled with laughter, and our tongue with shouts of joy; then they said among the nations, "The Lord has done great things for them." (Psalm 126: 1-3)

These things I have spoken to you, that my joy may be in you, and that your joy may be complete. (John 15: 10-17)

And the disciples were filled with joy and with the Holy Spirit. (Acts 13: 51-52)

July   Joy

Liturgical Calendar = The Precious Blood of Jesus

LITANY OF THE PRECIOUS BLOOD OF JESUS

LEADER PRAYS.	**FAITHFUL RESPOND.**
Lord, have mercy.	Lord, have mercy.
Christ, have mercy.	Christ, have mercy.
Lord, have mercy.	Lord, have mercy.
Christ, hear us.	Christ, hear us.
Christ, graciously hear us.	Christ, graciously hear us.
God the Father of Heaven,	have mercy on us.
God the Son, Redeemer of the world,	have mercy on us.
God, the Holy Spirit,	have mercy on us.
Holy Trinity, One God,	have mercy on us.
Blood of Christ, only-begotten Son of the eternal Father,	save us.
Blood of Christ, Incarnate Word or God,	save us.
Blood of Christ, of the New and Eternal Testament,	save us.
Blood of Christ, falling upon the earth in Agony,	save us.
Blood of Christ, shed profusely in the Scourging,	save us.
Blood of Christ, flowing forth in the Crowning with Thorns,	save us.
Blood of Christ, poured out on the Cross,	save us.
Blood of Christ, price of our salvation,	save us.
Blood of Christ, without which there is no forgiveness,	save us.
Blood of Christ, Eucharistic drink and refreshment of souls,	save us.
Blood of Christ, stream of mercy,	save us.
Blood of Christ, victor over demons,	save us.
Blood of Christ, courage of Martyrs,	save us.
Blood of Christ, strength of Confessors,	save us.
Blood of Christ, bringing forth Virgins,	save us.
Blood of Christ, help of those in peril,	save us.
Blood of Christ, relief of the burdened,	save us.
Blood of Christ, solace in sorrow,	save us.
Blood of Christ, hope of the penitent,	save us.
Blood of Christ, consolation of the dying,	save us.
Blood of Christ, peace and tenderness of hearts,	save us.
Blood of Christ, pledge of eternal life,	save us.
Blood of Christ, freeing souls from purgatory,	save us.
Blood of Christ, most worthy of all glory and honor,	save us.
Lamb of God, who taketh away the sins of the world,	spare us, O Lord.
Lamb of God, who taketh away the sins of the world,	graciously hear us, O Lord.
Lamb of God, who taketh away the sins of the world,	have mercy on us, O Lord.

Thou hast redeemed us, O Lord, in Thy Blood, and made us, for our God, a kingdom.

    Almighty and eternal God, Thou hast appointed Thine only-begotten Son the Redeemer of the world and willed to be appeased by his blood. Grant, we beg of Thee, that we may worthily adore this price of our salvation and through its power be safeguarded from the evils of the present life so that we may rejoice in its fruits forever in heaven. Through the same Christ our Lord. Amen.

This Litany in honor of Jesus in His Most Precious Blood was drawn up by the Sacred Congregation of Rites and promulgated by Pope John XXIII on February 24, 1960. I couldn't find the earlier version. The devotion to Jesus in His most Precious Blood was first popularized by Saint Gaspar del Buffalo (1786-1837, feast Dec. 28) who founded the Missioners of the Most Precious Blood.

Our Lady of Mount Carmel Novena – July 7 – 15 – Feast Day July 16

Queen of Carmel Mother of God and of poor sinners; special protectress of all who wear thy holy scapular, I ask thee to obtain for me the pardon of my sins, amendment of my life, salvation of my soul, comfort in my suffering, and particularly the grace I now ask:
(Mention your request).

Prayers: Our Father, Hail Mary, Glory Be –

Blessed are the merciful for they shall obtain mercy. (Matthew 5: 7)

Jesus Christ taught that all people receive and experience the Mercy of God.
Jesus Christ also called all people to practice mercy in a spirit of love towards others.

When I was very young, possibly in first grade, I was taught to obey God's Commandments out of Love for God, because God loved me into existance. Below I have listed a summary of the **Spiritual Works of Mercy** and **Corporal Works of Mercy** reworded for clarity.

Spiritual Works of Mercy

1. Instruct the uninformed.
2. Correct those who have separated themselves from God's will.
3. Counsel the doubtful.
4. Comfort the sorrowful.
5. Be patient with those in error.
6. Forgive offenses.
7. Pray for the living and the dead.

Corporal Works of Mercy

1. Feed the hungry.
2. Give drink to the thirsty.
3. Clothe the naked.
4. Shelter the homeless.
5. Comfort the imprisoned.
6. Visit the sick.
7. Bury the dead.

Jesus taught us.

Faith without works is dead.

Whatsoever you did to others you did it to me.

July Joy

Devotions and Celebrations = God and Country

The Military Mailbox

The toll of Flint service men injured in the war on the Pacific was increased by one today with the announcement that Steven Jerome Lukasavitz has been wounded.

His parents, Mr. and Mrs. John Lukasavitz, of 758 Black avenue, received a message from the Navy department informing them of their son's injury. He enlisted here about 18 months ago and was assigned to the Pacific fleet.

The navy's message was as follows: "The Navy department deeply regrets to inform you that your son, Steven Jerome Lukasavitz, has been wounded in action in the performance of his duty and in the service of his country. The department appreciates your great anxiety and will furnish you further information promptly when received. To prevent possible aid to our enemies do not divulge the name of his ship or station."

Lukasavitz

1. 2. 3.

4. 5.

1. Army - Uncle Dominic was my Grandpa John's younger brother, birth 1903, death 1987.
2. Navy - Uncle Steve was my Daddy's younger brother, birth 1918, death 1978.

Survivor of Pearl Harbor Attack Describes His Experience to JF

By JOHN FLINT

DURING the observance of the anniversary of Pearl Harbor Day last Tuesday J.F. recalled a talk he had a few years ago with the Flint area's only survivor of the battleship USS Arizona, which was sunk during the attack.

Steven J. Lukasavitz was a seaman first class when the attack occurred on Dec. 7, 1941.

He recalled that the day began as a sunny, quiet Sunday in Pearl Harbor. Sailors aboard the 94 ships in the harbor were getting ready for church services.

Lukasavitz, who had been in the Navy 18 months, was pressing his suit uniform when the first low-flying Japanese fighter planes began bombing the harbor. This was at 7:50 a.m.

"At first we thought it was a mock air raid," Lukasavitz told J.F. "Then, the guy on the public address system hollered 'This is the real thing.'"

Lukasavitz's air-raid battle station was topside as a fuse-setter for one of the ship's antiaircraft guns. From this position Lukasavitz could see swarms of low-flying dive bombers strafing the harbor.

NINE BATTLESHIPS were the primary objectives of the Japanese attack. Besides the Arizona, the Nevada, Tennessee, Utah, Maryland, Oklahoma, California, Pennsylvania and West Virginia provided choice targets for Japanese torpedo-carrying planes.

Lukasavitz told J.F. he was below decks when the first torpedo slammed in to the Arizona.

"The first explosion knocked the lights out and blew the hatch open," he said.

"A lot of water gushed in. It was up to my ankles and there were flames all over the place. The impact of the blast slammed me against the bulkhead and stunned me."

Lukasavitz said he isn't sure how he managed to make it topside.

"When I got up there I saw the motor launches removing men from the deck," he recalled. "I had to jump to make it into one of the launches."

HE DESCRIBED the harbor as "black with smoke." The damaged ships were lying there twisted and helpless, he said.

"Many of the sailors didn't wait for the launches and jumped overboard to swim ashore," Lukasavitz said. "The water was ablaze because of the oil slick and many of the swimmers burned to death. When I glanced back at the Arizona the water was about even with her lower decks."

Lukasavitz was taken to Ford Island nearby, where a temporary hospital had been set up.

"I was pretty dazed and don't remember too much about the place except that many of the men were burned badly and some wandered into the hospital completely naked," he said.

Lukasavitz was told that he suffered from smoke inhalation and internal burns.

Approximately 1,100 of the Arizona's more than 1,500 men died at Pearl Harbor. Another 43 were wounded in the attack.

"There was no panic aboard the Arizona," Lukasavitz said. "Everything happend so fast at Pearl Harbor that I lost all concept of time. It seemed like a matter of a few seconds."

3. Marines - Uncle George was my Daddy's younger brother, birth 1920, death 1988.
4. Army - Uncle Johnny was my Mother's younger brother, birth 1920, death 2012.
5. Navy - Uncle Bernard is my Mother's younger brother, birth 1925.
5. Navy - Uncle Steve is my Mother's younger brother, birth 1925.

July Joy

Polish–American Recipe = *Wieprzowa Przyjecie*: Pork Barbeque

Melt in Your Mouth Ribs

Preheat Oven to 350º =
The amount of celery and onions depends on the size of your Baking Dish.

1. Place four (4) tablespoons butter in a medium frying pan. Simmer celery and onions separately.
2. Simmer sufficient celery, chopped in bite size pieces, to cover the entire area underneath the "slab of pork ribs" and place in the Baking Dish.

    Step 2.   Onions and celery   Step 2. Place ribs on top.

3. Simmer sufficient onions, sliced in ¼ inch quarters, of onion ring to cover the entire area underneath the "slab of pork ribs" and place in the Baking Dish.
4. Mix the celery and onion pieces together and place the "slab of pork ribs" on top.
5. Onions alone and Celery alone are options; each provides a different flavor to the ribs and is delicious.
6. Cover Baking Dish with foil and bake at 350º for 45 minutes.
7. After 45 Minutes of baking reduce the Oven temperature to 275º. Spoon generous amounts of My Special Ribs Sauce included below on the "slab of pork ribs" cover again with foil.

Step 8. Spoon sauce & bake.   Step 10. Cut ribs into sections.

8. Continue baking the ribs for 1 and 1/2 to 2 hours. After this time, check the internal temperature with a meat thermometer. The thermometer should read at least 140º.
9. Return to oven uncovered for one hour or less. The thermometer should read at least 160º and My Special Ribs Sauce form a glaze and the ribs are falling off the bones. If left in the oven too long the sugar in the "Sauce Glaze" could burn and the ribs dry out.
10. Cut the ribs into three or four sections before placing them on a plate. Using tongs, just tug gently at each bone and the meat will fall off cleanly.
11. Serve with one or two side dishes: corn on the cob, cucumber salad, cole slaw, baked beans, potato Salad, macaroni salad, or even baked or country fired potatoes, yes or potato chips.

Pull out bones. Enjoy!

My Special BAR-B-Q Sauce

INGREDIENTS:

1/2 Cup - Light Brown Sugar
4 Tablespoons – Dill Pickle Juice
4 Tablespoons – Bread & Butter Pickle Juice

1 Full Cup – Ketchup
1 Tablespoon – Yellow Salad Mustard

PROCESS:

In a glass measuring pitcher firmly pack the Brown sugar.
Add all of the pickle juices, stir together, and pour into mixing bowl.
In a glass measuring pitcher place the Ketchup. Add the Mustard and blend together thoroughly.

When the Mustard is added to the Sugar & Pickle Juice mixture, the Mustard curdles.

Slowly pour the Ketchup & Mustard mixture into the Sugar & Pickle Juices mixture, stirring until well blended. This makes about two cups BAR-B-Q SAUCE.

I pour my Special sauce into an empty Ketchup bottle to use as needed.

July   Joy

Polish–American Activity = Patriotic – American Flags

Most Americans still display the American Flag on their homes on Independence Day on July 4th.

    Our celebration of Independence Day on July 4th included a trip to the cemetery. We not only prayed for the dead, but also placed American Flags on the graves of people who served in the military to keep our freedoms. Families would team up to clean the grave sites of those that were not being maintained.

July   Joy

People of Polish Heritage = My Daddy's Parents & Grandparents

1. My Daddy's parents home on Black Avenue in Flint Michigan before Grandpa John had built his Taxidermy Shop. at the back of the driveway.
2. The Fiftieth Wedding Anniversary 1957 – four sons and three daughters. Two of my Daddy's brothers had died - Chester and Joseph. Uncle Steve is taking pictures. My Daddy is first in the second row.
3. Back Row – Left to Right: Victor, Christian my Daddy, Donald, and in front are George and Grandpa John.
4. Back Row – Left to Right are my Daddy's sisters, Clara and Regina, and in front are Busia Pearl and Aunt Agnes.
5. Grandpa John's sister - Sister Mary Cyria and Grandpa John's brother Dominick.

6.

7.

6. John A. Lukasiewicz birth March 10, 1860, Victoria Bohanski birth December 23, 1862. This Picture was taken in Portage, Wisconsin 1942. Great-Grandma died May 21, 1943. Great-Grandpa died November 7, 1951.

7. Grandpa John W. was my Daddy's father. He was a Taxidermist and mounted the animals so realistically that at Christmas time people would stop their cars to take pictures in the life size display with three or more deer pulling a sleigh with room for a fat Santa and a big bag of toys. Most of the animals that he mounted were hunted for food. In later years he would mount animals for the science department in local High Schools.

Grandpa John W. was a great story teller and some of the relatives got tired of him repeating the stories so quite frequently I would be the only one left and then he would ask me if I wanted to go play and I would tell him not until I hear the end of the story. When I was in ninth grade at All Saints High School I was working in the school library when I found a big reference book that could only be used in the library and I found out that two of the relatives in Poland were real and most of the events that my Grandpa told were true. Recently I looked up my two Famous Polish Cousins, Ignacy Lukasiewicz and Jan Lukasiewicz on the Internet if you are interested you can just type the English spelling for the last name Lukasiewicz.

Here are some additional stories from my Grandpa John.

He would say, "They can take Poland off the World Map but they can't take Poland out of the hearts of the Polish people." Starting in 1772 to 1861 the three militaristic countries of Prussia/Germany, Russia, and Austria partitioned Poland among themselves thus taking Poland off the World Map. Poland assisted the United Stares of America in the Revolutionary War of 1776 to 1779.

Ignacy Lukasiewicz was born in 1822 and died in 1882. He was arrested in February 1846 and released December 1847 for lack of evidence are the facts presented in one of his Biographies. Grandpa John told me: When Ignacy and his fellow scientist were arrested they were given vegetable peelings to eat. The scientists made some "Rot-Gut Whiskey" out of the garbage and got their guards drunk and stole the keys and locked the guards up in the prison cells. Ignacy and the others were under surveillance the rest of their lives.

Jan Lukasiewicz was born December 21, 1878 and died February 13, 1956. He married Regina Barwinska in 1928. From 1920 to 1939, Jan was a professor at Warsaw University. Grandpa John related these details and the old book of Famous Scientist corroborated Grandpa John's story. All of the faculty members at Warsaw University were called to a meeting by the NAZI officials but Jan was suspicious and didn't go. Instead they fled to Belgium. When in exile Regina, his wife died of mysterious causes. Many Polish people said that she died of a broken heart because she would never see her beloved Poland without endangering the life of her beloved husband Jan.

From birth through Life to death, My large extended Polish Family brought **JOY** to its members when we spent time Celebrating New Babies, Holy Days, Holidays, Graduations, Weddings and all the time in between. Finally, at funerals and on All Souls Day, November 2, we remembered the times we had spent with the Loved Ones who had passed on to Eternity.

Be glad in the Lord, and rejoice, O righteous, and shout for joy, all you upright in heart!
(Psalm 32:10-11)

August   Goodness

Hostas in My Front Yard

Fruit of the Holy Spirit = Goodness

Liturgical Calendar = The Immaculate Heart of Mary

**Devotions and Celebrations = Sacrament of Matrimony
Mary – Queen of Heaven and Earth**

Polish–American Recipe = *Ciastka z Owsiane:* Oatmeal Cookies

Polish–American Activity = Gardening Fun

People of Polish Heritage = My Polish Wedding Reception

August   Goodness

Fruit of the Holy Spirit = Goodness

Prayer:
　　Holy Spirit, eternal Love of the Father and the Son, kindly bestow on us the fruit of Goodness, that we may be benevolent toward all.

Goodness is holiness put into practice and results from knowing God.

Goodness is consistent with God's nature or will for us.

Goodness inclines us to wish to do good to everyone without distinction.

We exhibit goodness when we honor God by avoiding sin and always trying to do what we know is right.

It is the goodness of God that leads men to repentance. That's why we need to be good to all people. Our witness won't have any power if we are kind to only those who are kind to us.

We are called to be bright lights in a dark world, and we must not pick and choose when to shine that light. (Psalm 52: 5 -7)

The fruit of the Holy Spirit is love, joy, peace, patience, kindness, goodness, faithfulness, gentleness, self-control, against such there is no law. (Galatians 5: 21-24)

Surely goodness and mercy shall follow me all the days of my life; and I shall dwell in the house of the Lord for ever. (Psalm 23: 5 – 6)

I believe that I shall see the goodness of the Lord in the land of the living! (Psalm 27: 12 – 14)

To you who hear I say, "Love your enemies, do good to those who hate you, bless those who curse you, pray for those who mistreat you"- (Luke 6: 27 – 28)

Do good to those of the household faith: "Let us not grow tired of doing good, for in due time we shall reap our harvest, if we do not give up. So then, while we have the opportunity, let us do good to all, but especially to those who belong to the family of the faith." (Galatians 6: 9 – 10)

I preferred to do nothing without your consent in order that your goodness might not be by compulsion but of your own free will. (Philemon 1: 13 – 15)

I myself am satisfied with what I hear about you, my brethren, that you yourselves are full of goodness, filled with all knowledge, and able to instruct one another. (Romans 15: 13 – 15)

August Goodness

Liturgical Calendar = The Immaculate Heart of Mary

With Mary Immaculate, let us adore, thank, implore and console the Most Beloved and Sacred Heart of Jesus in the Blessed Sacrament.

Our Lady of Good Counsel Litany

LEADER PRAYS.	FAITHFUL RESPOND.
Lord, have mercy on us.	Lord, have mercy on us.
Christ, have mercy on us.	Christ, have mercy on us.
Lord, have mercy on us.	Lord, have mercy on us.
Christ, hear us.	Christ, graciously hear us.
God the Father of Heaven,	have mercy on us.
God the Son, Redeemer of the world,	have mercy on us.
God the Holy Spirit,	have mercy on us.
Holy Trinity, One God,	have mercy on us.
Beloved Daughter of the Eternal Father,	pray for us.
August Mother of God the Son,	pray for us.
Blessed Spouse of God the Holy Ghost,	pray for us.
Living temple of the Holy Trinity,	pray for us.
Queen of Heaven and earth,	pray for us.
Seat of Divine wisdom,	pray for us.
Depositary of the secrets of the Most High,	pray for us.
Virgin most prudent,	pray for us.
In our doubts and difficulties,	pray for us.
In our tribulations and anguish,	pray for us.
In our discouragements,	pray for us.
In perils and temptations,	pray for us.
In all our undertakings,	pray for us.
In all our needs,	pray for us.
At the hour of death,	pray for us.
By thine Immaculate Conception,	pray for us.
By thy happy nativity,	pray for us.
By thine admirable presentation,	pray for us.
By thy glorious Annunciation,	pray for us.
By thy charitable Visitation,	pray for us.
By thy Divine Maternity,	pray for us.
By thy holy Purification,	pray for us.
By the sorrows and anguish of thy maternal heart,	pray for us.
By thy precious death,	pray for us.
By thy triumphant Assumption,	pray for us.

Lamb of God, Who takes away the sins of the world,	Spare us, O Lord.
Lamb of God, Who takes away the sins of the world,	Graciously hear us, O Lord.
Lamb of God, Who takes away the sins of the world,	Have mercy on us.
Pray for us, O holy Mother of God,	Obtain for us the gift of good counsel.

Let Us Pray

Lord Jesus, Author and Dispenser of all good, Who in becoming incarnate in the womb of the Blessed Virgin has communicated to her lights above those of all the heavenly intelligences, grant that in honoring her under the title of Our Lady of Good Counsel, we may merit always to receive from her goodness, counsels of wisdom and salvation, which will conduct us to the port of a blessed eternity. Amen.

Novena Prayer to the Immaculate Heart of Mary

O Most Blessed Mother, heart of love, heart of mercy, ever listening, caring, consoling, hear our prayer. As your children, we implore your intercession with Jesus your Son. Receive with understanding and compassion the petitions we place before you today, especially... (Mention your special intention.)

We are comforted in knowing your heart is ever open to those who ask for your prayer. We trust to your gentle care and intercession, those whom we love and who are sick or lonely or hurting. Help all of us, Holy Mother, to bear our burdens in this life until we may share eternal life and peace with God forever. Amen.

The entire month falls within the liturgical season of Ordinary Time, which is represented by the liturgical color green, the symbol of hope. August is often considered the transitional month in our seasonal calendar. It is the time of the year we begin to wind-down from our summer travels and vacations and prepare for Autumn — back to school, fall festivals, harvest time, etc. The Church in her holy wisdom has provided a cycle of events in its liturgical year which allow the faithful to celebrate the major feasts in the life of Christ and Mary. Most notably, during August, we celebrate the feast of the Transfiguration, August 6.

The feast of The Assumption of the Blessed Virgin Mary August 15

On November 1, 1950, Pope Pius XII defined the dogma of the Assumption. He solemnly proclaimed that the belief whereby the Blessed Virgin Mary, at the end of her life on earth, was taken up body and soul, into the glory of heaven, definitively forms part of the deposit of faith, received from the apostles.

18th Sunday of Ordinary Time: Jesus feeds the crowd with five loaves and two fish.
19th Sunday of Ordinary Time: In this Gospel Jesus tells Peter to walk on the water.
20th Sunday of Ordinary Time: Jesus is approached by a Canaanite woman begging for her daughter to be healed.
21st Sunday of Ordinary Time: In this Gospel Peter professes his faith that Christ is the Son of the living God."
22nd Sunday of Ordinary Time: Whoever wishes to come after me must deny himself, take up his cross, and follow me."

August   Goodness

Devotions and Celebrations = Sacrament of Matrimony
Mary – Queen of Heaven and Earth

First Major Compromise – Mass Was Celebrated in My Latin Rite Parish Church - With the Priest from the Byzantine Rite Presiding Over Our Sacrament of Matrimony.

1.

2.

3.

1. The sacrament of Matrimony signifies the union of Christ and the Church. It gives spouses the grace to love each other with the love with which Christ has loved his Church; the grace of the sacrament thus perfects the human love of the spouses, strengthens their indissoluble unity, and sanctifies them on the way to eternal life.

    Marriage is based on the consent of the contracting parties, that is, on their will to give themselves, each to the other, mutually and definitively, in order to live a covenant of faithful and fruitful love. Ronald Philip Miscisin and Jean Marie Lukasavitz administered the Sacrament of Matrimony to each other when they pronounced their wedding vows before a Catholic Priest who officiated as the Primary Witness on August 16, 1958.

2. On August 15, the Feast of the Assumption of Mary, the Mother of Jesus, is celebrated every year. Since my wedding ceremony date was set for Saturday, August 16, 1958, I purchased a special bouquet of flowers from the florist from whom we were purchasing the flowers for our wedding day. The flowers were placed at the feet of the statue of the Blessed Mother of Jesus on August 15.   When I ordered the bouquet I did not know that a special blessing for the Wife after the Byzantine Sacrament of Matrimony would take place with me kneeling before this holy reminder of Mary's Holy Motherhood.

    After exchanging vows in the Sacrament of Matrimony in the Byzantine Rite of the Catholic Church, the Priest prays a special prayer over the Wife. This prayer includes asking for the intercession of Mary for the wife to be faithful to God and her vows, and the blessing of living to see the fifth generation of her children. Both of My Grandmothers lived to see their grandchildren's grandchildren.

    Unity, indissolubility, and openness to fertility are essential to marriage. What God has joined together let no man tear asunder. Fertility in marriage is the "supreme gift," the child. The Christian home is the place where children receive the first proclamation of the faith. For this reason the family home is rightly called "the domestic church," a community of grace and prayer, a school of human virtues and of Christian charity.

3. Why do I have the unusual look on my face?
    The elderly Priest of the Byzantine Rite said, "Here is your passport to the motel."

All Saints Roman Catholic Church –
A Juridical Polish National Catholic Church Founded by a Bishop from Poland in 1910.

Since marriage establishes the couple in a public state of life in the Church, it is fitting that its celebration be public, in the framework of a liturgical celebration, before the priest or a witness authorized by the Church, the witnesses, and the assembly of the faithful. The marriage covenant, by which a man and a woman form with each other an intimate communion of life and love, has been founded and endowed with its own special laws by the Creator. By its very nature it is ordered to the good of the couple, as well as to the generation and education of children. Christ the Lord raised marriage between the baptized to the dignity of a sacrament.

During a High Mass in Latin with Three Concelebrating Priests most of the prayers were sung. Since my parents and I had been long-time choir members, Sister Mary Avila played the organ and both "retired and current" choir members, sang at our wedding Mass.

Old All Saints Catholic Church in Flint, Michigan was on Industrial Avenue and My Mother's Parents Lived Catty-Corner across the street. Our wedding was not the first wedding in the new All Saints Catholic Church on Jennings Road, but it was the first Mass at which the bride and groom celebrated the Holy Sacrament of Matrimony. The Altar is from the Old All Saints Catholic Church in Flint, Michigan. Reverend Father Anthony gave me two small, decorative pieces from the Old Altar after the New Altar was installed.

Bride's Family - Left to right:
Brother Chris, Mother Stefania, Jean Marie, Ronald, Father Christian, Sister Barbara, Brother Raymond.

Groom's Family - Left to right:
Sister Mary, Mother Ella, Jean Marie, Ronald, Father Nicholas.

August Goodness

Polish–American Recipe = *Ciastka z Owsiane:* Oatmeal Cookies

My Special Oatmeal Cookies - Procedure used for Pictures 2014
Baked Cookies from this recipe measure three inches in diameter -
Approximately three dozen cookies

Day 1. To soften the butter, take the butter out of the refrigerator the night before you plan to prepare the Cookie Dough.
Day 2. Mix the Cookie Dough, because it needs to set for three hours or overnight.
Day 3. Bake the cookies and eat some.

1. In 2014, I used the large bowl from my Electric Table Mixer. Place in a large bowl in the following order: 1/2 cup Granulated Sugar (Cane sugar), 1 cup firmly packed Light Brown Sugar. Stir the two sugars together.
2. Add to the sugars: 1 1/4 cups (2 sticks plus 4 Tablespoons) Butter softened to room temperature. Cream together using a spoon or paddle. I cream them together with the "Bread Paddle" attachment on my Electric Table Mixer - on medium speed.

Alternate Method for Day 1: This method speeds up clean-up and mixing on Day 2. I used two plastic containers as in the first picture (I didn't have one "just right" container.), and sprinkled one-third of the sugar mixture in the bottom of each tub. Then I cut one stick and 2 Tablespoons butter the same as in the picture and put half of the pieces on top of the sugar mixture in each container. Next, I sprinkled one-third of the sugar mixture on this layer of butter pieces. Repeat with a layer of butter pieces and top off with the last third of the sugar mixture, cover and let set overnight. On Day 2 I just dumped both tubs of butter/sugar mixture in the large bowl and creamed them together with the "Bread Paddle" attachment on my Electric Table Mixer - on medium speed.

3. In a small one (1) quart bowl, I use an electric "Hand Mixer" to whip together the following until creamy with no bubbles: Crack each egg into a very small dish to check for freshness before placing the egg in the small one (1) quart bowl; 2 Large Eggs or 3 Medium Eggs, 1 teaspoon Vanilla Extract, 1/2 teaspoon Salt.
4. Add Egg mixture to the Creamed Sugar and Butter and mix thoroughly with the "Bread Paddle" unit until fluffy and creamy.
5. In a separate extra large, bowl, I place: 3 cups Rolled Quick Oats or Old Fashioned Oats. I now use a medium plastic bowl with a tight fitting cover.

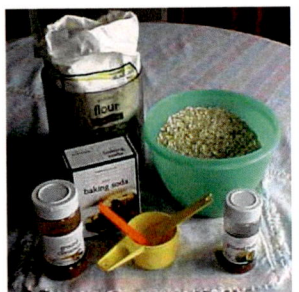  

Step 5 and 6. Step 8. Step 9.

6. Add the following dry ingredients to the Rolled Oats: 1 1/2 cups All-purpose Flour-Unbleached 1 teaspoon Baking Soda, 1 teaspoon Cinnamon, 1/2 teaspoon Nutmeg.
7. Stir Dry Ingredients together with the Rolled Oats. I lift the spoon through the ingredients, and cover the bowl and shake it, instead of sifting like most recipes suggest.
8. Add ALL of the Dry Ingredients to the "creamed Sugar, Butter, and Eggs mixture in the "Electric Mixer Bowl" and mix on the lowest setting.
9. When cookie dough pulls away from the side of the bowl, transfer to a container with a tightly fitting lid, and place in the refrigerator. I spoon the Cookie Dough back into the same plastic bowl with its tight fitting lid.
10. Refrigerate "Cookie Dough" for at least three hours – Over night is better.
11. Before starting to roll the Cookie Balls, Using my blender - Dry Ingredient container, I place one cup rolled oats and "Pulse" two times, shake the oats and "Pulse" again, and place in an empty box from Oat Meal. I write on the box "Coarse Ground" for cookies.
12. Preheat oven to 350º - Take the Cookie Dough bowl out of the refrigerator and using a table knife cut the dough into chunks.

Step 12. Step 14 and Step 15. Step 16

13. Put about one fourth cup of the "Coarse Ground" Oats in a small bowl, and set out a paper plate or other ten inch plate.
14. Take around one rounded tablespoon of dough in your hands and roll into a ball. Flatten the cookie dough ball into a thick disk a little more than one inch in diameter. Place the disk into the "Coarse Ground" oats to coat on both sides and roll the edge so it is also coated.
15. Place each Cookie Disk on the paper plate or other ten inch plate. This size easily fits one dozen Cookie Disks. I prepare all three dozen Cookie Disks before the next step.

16. Using a Tortilla Press, simply place one "coated" Cookie Disk in the center and press lightly enough to make a two inch diameter cookie to place on an ungreased cookie sheet.   My cookie sheets hold only six cookies. I put "easy release" foil on my cookie sheets for easier cleaning. On new pans foil covers are not necessary.
17. Place the two cookie sheets in preheated 350º oven and bake for ten (10) to twelve (12) minutes until golden brown.
18. Then after taking the sheets, with baked cookies on them, out of the oven; place them on the top of the stove (I have an electric oven/stove) and leave the cookies on the cookie sheets for five (5) minutes. Without this "setting time" the cookies will be too soft to take off the cookie sheets. With a longer "setting" time the cookies sometimes stick to the foil.
For a gas stove I think it would be wise to place the cookie sheets on a counter on
    "Trivets or Pot Holders" for the "setting time."

Step 19.   Step 20.

19. Transfer cookies to a "cooling rack" and then, using "Parchment Paper" line a pan with a cover and place a piece of Parchment Paper.
20. I purchased two special pans for My Special Oat Meal Cookies; one for me and one for my husband. In that way I can keep track of the day to "soften the butter" so we have a steady supply of cookies.

    This recipe for My Special oatmeal Cookies has the Polish ingredients.
The American Additions are the steps in the process to accommodate my physical limitations, using different appliances and utensils.

August   Goodness
Polish–American Activity = Gardening Fun

    When I finally retired from California classroom teaching in 2004, we moved to Oscoda, Michigan, and I took my special "Earth Boxes" for container gardening with me. Yes, even in container gardening I used my Busias' advice, "Green beans are planted with tomatoes, because green beans are Nitrogen fixing plants and Tomatoes are Nitrogen using plants."
I prepared and we ate the green beans, so I don't have a picture. These were the tomatoes from just two plants, one plant was "Cherry tomatoes" that explains the differences in size.

    When my granddaughter, Brianna was only three years old she was "playing in the mud" with me when I was preparing the "Earth Boxes". The directions included packing mud in three corners of the tub to draw up the water from the bottom of the tub. When Brianna's Daddy came to pick up her from our home in California, we were in our small backyard. He could see that the two of us had muddy hands, and not just our hands, so he asked, "What are you doing?" Brianna answered, "Playing in the mud." By 2009 my body was not cooperating so I gave my "Earth Boxes" to a family with young children.

    When I was three years young my Busias' called gardening, "Playing in the dirt."
Those were basically the only times I was allowed to get dirty, when I was "helping" my Busias or my Daddy in the gardens. Of course at that age, I had no idea what was meant by "... green beans are Nitrogen fixing plants and Tomatoes are Nitrogen using plants." More scientific facts were taught in simple terms in answer to my question, "Why are the flowers in your vegetable garden, Busia?" She explained that the Marigolds kept little bugs away, and other flowers helped keep other pests away. When I got older my Busias' and my Daddy explained many gardening terms to me, including Companion Gardening.

August　　Goodness

People of Polish Heritage = My Polish Wedding Reception

Polish Tradition – Changing the Bride to Wife

1.

2.

3.

4.

Polish Tradition – Changing the Bride to Wife

1. While friends sing a special Polish song, the mother of the bride removes the bride's veil. My Mother is taking off my Bridal Veil. On my Mother's right is Ciocia Helen. Out of respect we called many of my Mother's women friends Ciocia which means Auntie, even though my Mother did not have any living sisters. Ciocia Helen's brother Frank played Santa Claus and had his own physical "belly and beard" making him more believable than most other men who pretended to be Santa Claus. I enjoyed playing "Let's Pretend" and didn't ruin the fun for other children by saying, "Hi! Uncle Frank."

2. Dust Cap on My Head and Apron around My Waist? I am Transformed into a Wife??? Wait a minute! A dust cap was the symbol for housework and an apron signifies meal preparation. That's not what I thought a wife was. You don't have to use your imagination. Remember, I wanted lots of children.

3. Since my sister was Matron-of-Honor, my veil was put on my Maid-of-Honor, Madeline; we are friends from the time we were toddlers. Ciocia Helen was my Mother's friend and Madeline's Mother. Tradition calls for the woman who wears the bride's veil to be the next bride. Madeline married Tony about two years later.

4. After a Polish Traditional Dance the Couple Left for Their Honeymoon. Before we left the hall, we actually danced one set of wedding songs which included: Blue Skirt Waltz = The first waltz that we danced together before our first date. O How We Danced on the Night We Were Wed, and How Swiftly The Moments Pass Waltz.

When we got to my parent's home all the doors were locked. I had suspected other "games" to frustrate us. I was not surprised, since no one knew in which vehicle we would be leaving - no tin cans were tied to our car. When I explained to Ron that it was easy to climb into the house through my bedroom window in the attic, he teased me. "Why didn't you tell me sooner?" I said, "I don't think my folks knew." I felt secure in knowing that in case of fire I could get out. I had not thought of going in that way or I might have thought of some person who meant harm could have gotten in the same way. So, I showed Ron how to get into my attic bedroom and he went into the house and unlocked the front door for me.

As we were turning off Roberts Street, a car from the opposite direction was turning onto it. I thought that they were expecting to have to let us in the house. I bet they were surprised to find the house unlocked.

My large extended family and our many friends displayed Goodness in all seasons - For better or for worse in sickness and in health from birth to death.

My Niece Susan in My Arms & My Cousins Dancing Around Me

Grand March

Tony Kaczmarek and his Orchestra played for our wedding. We left our wedding reception after the Grand March and the Polish Tradition -- Changing the Bride to Wife. Sunday we drove back to All Saints Church for Mass. Several people remarked, that Tony and his whole Orchestra stayed and played music while the hall was being cleaned and all the cooks and helpers had a chance to dance and they sang:

"... In a year, in a day, in a moment, together we will not be."

So then, while we have the opportunity, let us do good to all,
and especially to those who belong to the family of the faith.
(Galatians 6: 9 – 10)

In my Father's home there are many dwelling places.
If it were not so, would I have told you that I go to prepare a place for you?
(John 14: 2)

My personal belief is that the earth is only our home for a short time compared to eternity. There is a very big place in eternity where the Polish Saints will gather. We are all called to know, love, and serve God, in other words to become Saints. There will be wondrous organ music, and beautiful Polish Hymns praising and thanking God.

In addition, I believe there will be another big place in eternity reserved for Polish Orchestras and festive celebrations as more friends and relatives join them. Tony Kaczmarek, his Orchestra and singers will be there with accordions, violins, base fiddles, tubas, trumpets, trombones, and percussion ensemble, where All the Polish Saints will come dancing in - celebrating their love for our God of Love and Mercy.

We will finally sing "together we all will be for all eternity."

September   Gentleness

Pink Day Lilies in Neighbor's Yard

Fruit of the Holy Spirit = Gentleness

Liturgical Calendar = Our Lady of Sorrows

Devotions and Celebrations = Immaculate Conception

Polish–American Recipe = *Zupa = Krupnik*: Barley Soup

Polish–American Activity = Stage Dramatic Productions

People of Polish Heritage = All Saints Parish Priests

September Gentleness

Fruit of the Holy Spirit = Gentleness

Prayer:

    Holy Spirit, eternal Love of the Father and the Son, kindly bestow on us the fruit of Gentleness, that we may subdue every rising of ill temper.

Gentle people act calmly and avoid actions that might lead others to anger or resentment.

Gentle people have extraordinary patience over a long period of time, even without encouragement.

Gentle people who possess this quality pardon injuries, correct faults, and rule their own spirits well out of love for God.

As for you, man of God, aim at righteousness, godliness, faith, love, steadfastness, and gentleness. (1 Timothy 6: 10 – 12)

In your hearts reverence Christ as Lord. Always be prepared to make a defense to any one who calls you to account for the hope that is in you, yet do it with gentleness and reverence. (1 Peter 3: 14 – 16)

I, then, a prisoner for the Lord, urge you to live in a manner worthy of the call you have received, with all humility and gentleness, with patience, bearing with one another through love of God. (Ephesians 4: 1 – 2)

The fruit of the Holy Spirit is love, joy, peace, patience, kindness, goodness, faithfulness, gentleness, self-control, against such there is no law. (Galatians 5: 21-24)

September Gentleness

Liturgical Calendar = Our Lady of Sorrows

Litany of Our Lady of Seven Sorrows

LEADER PRAYS.	**FAITHFUL RESPOND.**
Lord, have mercy on us.	Lord, have mercy on us.
Christ, have mercy on us.	Christ, have mercy on us.
Lord, have mercy on us.	Lord, have mercy on us.
Christ, hear us.	Christ, graciously hear us.
God, the Father of heaven,	have mercy on us.
God the Son, Redeemer of the world,	have mercy on us.
God the Holy Ghost,	have mercy on us.
Holy Mary, Mother of God,	pray for us.
Holy Virgin of virgins,	pray for us.
Mother of the Crucified,	pray for us.
Sorrowful Mother,	pray for us.
Mournful Mother,	pray for us.
Sighing Mother,	pray for us.
Afflicted Mother,	pray for us.
Foresaken Mother,	pray for us.
Desolate Mother,	pray for us.
Mother most sad,	pray for us.
Mother set around with anguish,	pray for us.
Mother overwhelmed by grief,	pray for us.
Mother transfixed by a sword,	pray for us.
Mother crucified in thy heart,	pray for us.
Mother bereaved of thy Son,	pray for us.
Sighing Dove,	pray for us.
Mother of Dolors,	pray for us.
Fount of tears,	pray for us.
Sea of bitterness,	pray for us.
Field of tribulation,	pray for us.
Mass of suffering,	pray for us.
Mirror of patience,	pray for us.
Rock of constancy,	pray for us.
Remedy in perplexity,	pray for us.
Joy of the afflicted,	pray for us.
Ark of the desolate,	pray for us.
Refuge of the abandoned,	pray for us.
Shield of the oppressed,	pray for us.
Conqueror of the incredulous,	pray for us.
Solace of the wretched,	pray for us.
Medicine of the sick,	pray for us.
Help of the faint,	pray for us.
Strength of the weak,	pray for us.
Protectress of those who fight,	pray for us.
Haven of the shipwrecked,	pray for us.
Calmer of tempests,	pray for us.

Companion of the sorrowful,	pray for us.
Retreat of those who groan,	pray for us.
Terror of the treacherous,	pray for us.
Standard-bearer of the Martyrs,	pray for us.
Treasure of the Faithful,	pray for us.
Light of Confessors,	pray for us.
Pearl of Virgins, pray for us.	pray for us.
Comfort of Widows,	pray for us.
Joy of all Saints,	pray for us.
Queen of thy Servants,	pray for us.
Holy Mary, who alone art unexampled,	pray for us.

Pray for us, most Sorrowful Virgin, that we may be made worthy of the promises of Christ.

Let us pray

O God, in whose Passion, according to the prophecy of Simeon, a sword of grief pierced through the most sweet soul of Thy glorious Blessed Virgin Mother Mary. Grant that we, who celebrate the memory of her Seven Sorrows, may obtain the happy effect of Thy Passion, Who lives and reigns world without end, Amen.

Novena of Our Lady of Seven Sorrows- Intentions

For the nine days between September 7, the vigil of the feast of the Birth of Mary, and September 15, the feast of Our Lady of Sorrows, we pray for the intercession of Mary, the Mother of our Life, our Faith and our Hope.

DAY 1 = Pray for the Suffering Women of the World.

DAY 2 = Pray for Mothers who are pregnant.

DAY 3 = Pray for Fathers at the Birth of their Child.

DAY 4 = Pray for All Children.

DAY 5 = Pray for Families.

DAY 6 = Prayer for Life Begins in the Home.

DAY 7 = Pray to accept Secret Suffering.

DAY 8 = Pray to appreciate the Holy Cross of Jesus.

DAY 9 = Pray to Our Lady of Sorrows to intercede for all of our needs.

September Gentleness

Devotions and Celebrations = Immaculate Conception

September 8, the feast of the Birth of Mary, the Mother of God
Immaculate Conception

When I was only in First Grade at All Saints School, this Doctrine was explained as follows = Jesus is the Savior of ALL People including His Mother Mary. Jesus saved All People making it possible for them to be saved from drowning after falling into the turbulent waters of sin. Mary, His Mother was saved by Jesus who protected her and held her close to Him to keep her safe from falling into the turbulent waters of sin from the time Mother Mary was conceived by her Mother Anne. Yes, of course the Sisters of Saint Joseph vividly explained the word "turbulent" with pictures of rough waters during storms.

DEVOTION TO OUR MOTHER OF SORROWS

Devotion to the Sorrows of Mary has always been a favorite devotion among Catholics. It has been approved by the Catholic Church in order to keep before our minds the inexpressible sufferings endured for us by the Mother of God while she lived here on earth with her Divine Son.

1. **The prophecy of Simeon**: And Simeon blessed them, and said to Mary his mother: Behold this child is set for the fall and for the resurrection of many in Israel, and for a sign which shall be contradicted; And thy own soul a sword shall pierce, that out of many hearts thoughts may be revealed. (Luke 2: 34-35).

2. **The flight into Egypt**: And after they, the wise men, departed, behold an angel of the Lord appeared in sleep to Joseph, saying: Arise and take the child and His mother and flee into Egypt: and stay there until I shall tell thee. For it will come to pass that Herod will seek the child to destroy Him. Joseph arose and took the child and His mother by night, and fled into Egypt: and the Holy Family stayed there until the death of Herod. (Matt. 2: 13-14).

3. **The loss of the Child Jesus in the temple**: Having fulfilled the days, when they returned, the Child Jesus remained in Jerusalem; and His parents knew it not. Thinking that he was in the company, they came a day's journey, and sought him among their kinsfolk and acquaintances. Not finding Him, they returned into Jerusalem, to look for Him. (Luke l2: 43-45).

4. **The meeting of Jesus and Mary on the Way of the Cross**: There followed Him a great multitude of people, and of women, who bewailed and lamented Him. (Luke 23: 27).

5. **The Crucifixion**: They crucified Him. Standing at the foot of the cross of Jesus, was His Mother. When Jesus saw His Mother and the disciple whom he loved, standing there, He said to His Mother: Woman: behold thy son. After that he said to the disciple: Behold thy Mother. (John 19: l8, 25-27).

6. **The taking down of the Body of Jesus from the Cross**: Joseph of Arimathea, a noble counselor, came and went in boldly to Pilate, and begged for the body of Jesus. Joseph had purchased fine linen, and took Jesus down, and wrapped Him up in the fine linen. (Mark 15:43-46)

7. **The burial of Jesus**: Now there was in the place where He was crucified, a garden; and in the garden a new sepulcher, wherein no man yet had been laid. So they laid Jesus there, because of the Jewish preparation day; for the tomb was close by. (John 19: 41-42).

September Gentleness

Polish–American Recipe = *Zupa* = *Krupnik*: Barley Soup

Krupnik = Barley Soup

Krupnik = Barley Soup with Beef

First Day - Braised Beef Short Ribs   -- Preheat Oven to 350º

1. Place two tablespoons butter in a medium frying pan. Simmer two (2) cups celery and two (2) cups onions separately; lightly salt and sprinkle with Poultry seasoning while frying.
2. Line the bottom of an oven-proof, square casserole dish with half of the onions and celery. The dimensions of my dish are four (4) inches deep and ten (10) inches square. Save the rest of the onions and celery in a bowl to use for topping.
3. In the same pan without washing it, place four Tablespoons butter. Take six, large, thawed, Beef Short Ribs
4. Sprinkle each BONE-IN Short Rib with salt and a General seasoning to your taste. The commercial brand that I use has the following ingredients.
5. On a medium high heat, brown two Short Ribs on all six sides for three (3) minutes until browned.
6. Line the RIBS WITH THE THIN SIDE OF THE BONE UP in the dish.
7. In a Tea Ball place six (6) Whole Allspice, and the equivalent of two, dried, Bay Leaves about two inches long each. Place the filled Tea Ball in the middle of the dish.
8. Pour one half cup of purified water into the frying pan to dissolve the spices and pour over the filled Tea Ball.
9. Carefully place some onions and celery that were set aside, on top of each rib.
10. Place casserole dish in the center of the preheated oven, cover and bake for thirty (30) minutes.
11. Turn the oven down to 250º and bake for two (2) hours.
12. Into a dish, place the meat that has been separated from the bones and solid fat particles.
13. Cover the dish and place in the refrigerator.
14. Place all of the onions, celery, and all the juices in a small kettle; add one cup cool purified water.

15. Pat down the onions and celery below the water level. In the morning the fat will lift off easily.
16. Place the bones and solid fat particles into a four quart kettle or slow cooker. Add four cups purified water to the cooker and the Tea Ball.
17. Cook the bones and fat. on low for three more hours. After the three hours strain the clear broth into a large kettle that can be refrigerated and add the Tea Ball. You won't know if it was long enough until the next day. The broth should be semi-solid like Gelatine.
18. Lift off the layers of fat from both kettles and discard the fat.

Second Day – Krupnik = Barley Soup from Braised Beef Short Ribs

1. Prepare barley according to package directions. Do not drain off the water.
2. Place two cups Baby Carrots in a steamer or kettle for twenty minutes.
3. When done drain water into the kettle that has the strained Beef broth.
4. Add barley with the cooking water to the Beef broth.
5. Use a fork and small sharp knife to cut the Baby Carrots into bite sized pieces.
6. With the stove element set on Low, heat up the kettle that has the strained Beef broth mixture to simmer with low bubbles.
7. Add the onions, celery, and cut carrots; simmer for twenty minutes and the Beef Soup is done.
8. Add water and extra seasoning to your preferences.
9. The Beef Soup will freeze well.

September Gentleness

Polish–American Activity = Stage Dramatic Productions

My Mother is seated third from the Left and My Aunt Agatha is seated second from the right.

My Mother's Father was a multi talented individual. In addition to playing the organ at Church he played Classical Music on the piano. I enjoyed hearing melodies composed by Chopin for the piano. My Dzia Dzia Walenty, Valentine in English, could speak and write seven foreign languages fluently and helped immigrants to pass their citizenship tests in English: Polish, Italian, French, Spanish, German, Russian, and Hungarian.

Besides translating famous Scripts from Poland he directed and produced them. This is the only picture I have. Some of them were musicals and had Historical and Religious themes. Dzia Dzia wrote an original script titled, Orphans in a Storm, which he directed and produced.

In a different production about Jesus raising Lazarus from the dead, the actor preempted his cue and started coming out of the tomb too early and Margaret started waving him back. The show must go on so he went back and the rest of the actors managed to stay in character, even while the audience was laughing.

When I went to All Saints School, the students in both the Senior and Junior Grades performed in stage productions, usually one during the Christmas Season and the Passion Play during Lent. The Seniors usually chose also a current Broadway Play for their last dramatic production.

A Variety Show for Father's Feast Day took place every year with students from all twelve grades participating. In the next section of this chapter I share with you my kindergarten performance.

September Gentleness

People of Polish Heritage = All Saints Parish Priests

But many who are first will be last, and the last shall be first.
(Matthew 19: 30)

**Reverend Father Stanislaus Bortnowski may look stern
but he was always gentle with me.**

But many who are first will be last, and the last shall be first. (Matthew 19: 30)
The first time that I heard these words, they came from Reverend Father Stanislaus Bortnowski.
I was in Kindergarten and the smallest child in the classroom, in the whole school for that matter.
We were all taken to our All Saints Church to practice for a Procession. It was early in the school year, and I was very shy, having been a sickly child, I only knew my one Cousin and my next door neighbor who were in my classroom. The top of my head came to their shoulders, so I was sort of lost among the taller children.

Father Bortnowski came to the back of the Church where I was being jostled by the bigger children; he picked me up into his strong arms, carried me to the front of the Church, and sat me down in the front pew. My feet stuck out straight in front of me. I was afraid to move. Much later my Mother came into the Church. I recognized the sound of her high heels, in the side aisle to my right, so I turned to look at her. She had a scowl on her face that usually meant that I was in trouble. I turned away back toward the center aisle and tears welled up in my eyes. I don't know how much longer I was sitting there, but I knew that my Mother had come to take me home so I figured it was getting late.

Suddenly the whole Church was quiet and Father Bortnowski came down the center aisle, and was looking down at me. He took out his big, clean, white handkerchief, and wiped my tears and softly in English with his Polish accent he said, "Oh little one, why are you crying? Don't you know dat Jesus said, "... the last shall be first." He then picked up me and placed me first in the Procession line right behind the Altar Server who was carrying the tall, gold, Crucifix.

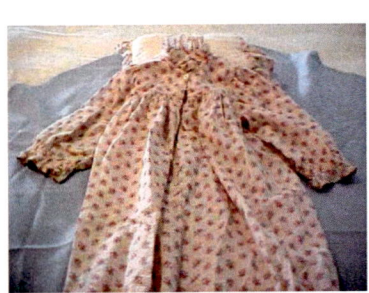  

1. Patron Saint Feast Day   2. My sister's graduation   3. My graduation "Honors Ceremony"

1. For Reverend Father Stanislaus Bortnowski's Patron Saint Stanislaus Feast Day, the whole school put on a "Stage production." In Kindergarten we had partners, and we shared our dreams. I still remember my poem: "I dreamt that I was Reverend Father's cook. I boiled the ice cream and froze the soup. I made hash out of every thing I took." After which we had a "Pillow Fight" – My Partner was a boy, and we "forgot" that we were supposed to pretend to hit each other. He hit me real hard and his pillow popped open and feathers flew all over. The people were laughing even harder when I hit him back real hard. Back then "Good Girls" weren't supposed to fight, you know.

2. My sister Barbara was Valedictorian – All Saints High School, 1952.

3. My graduation "Honors Ceremony" – 1954 I was Valedictorian too.
   At my graduation "Honors Ceremony" – I was Valedictorian and each person's name was called in each of the Categories. Father Bortnowski would mimic my "curtsy steps," the unique way I had to lift my graduation Gown to keep from tripping, as I went up the stairs at the front center of the stage. After my second trip to the stage and back down to my seat, Father Bortnowski shook his finger at me and told me to stand next to him. For the next three medals, Father Bortnowski would mimic my "curtsy steps" and then turn toward me and place the little gold box in my hands. At the very end of the ceremony, Father Bortnowski teased me that I needed bigger hands, and then escorted me down the stairs.

4. Father Bortnowski had a good memory. Christmas Procession 1953 of my Senior year in high school, I was again the shortest one in the group. Again Father Bortnowski came to the back of the Church and escorted me to the front of the line and repeated, 'Remember the last shall be first in the eyes of the Lord." That time I was smiling.

Monsignor Anthony P. Majchrowski

Father Anthony was a friend of my Mother's brothers, so I met him when I was very young and I attended his Ordination to the Priesthood, June 3, 1944. He was one of my high school teachers. Father Anthony contributed generously his time and knowledge toward the accuracy of my research for my Masters Degree in American Culture Studies from the University of Michigan in 1982, titled, Three Polish Parishes.

Father Anthony; the way he preferred that I address him when we talked on the telephone, even after he received the title Monsignor expressed his joy of being a Priest.

"I'm happy being a priest and wouldn't want to be anything else," he said.

"I only have one lifetime to give to the Lord," Monsignor Majchrowski said. "I hope to die in my boots."

At age 93, Monsignor Majchrowski still had no plans to retire. He had made that clear back in 1986 when he wrote to Bishop Kenneth Povish. "I am happy to inform you that that I am perfectly satisfied with my present assignment until death do us part," he wrote.

"I will have all of eternity to retire," he said. At the same time, he did look forward to eternity. "I am eager to see the Lord and his mother, the most beautiful woman in the world. And to see my family, relatives and friends -- What a great reunion that will be."

He joked that the thought of retiring had crossed his mind — at 5 a.m., when his alarm goes off, but passed before he arrived at Church. He was in Church by 5:30 a.m. and celebrated mass at 7 a.m. Monday through Saturday. Then had breakfast and after spending time in the office he visited the sick people. He usually drove his 1988 Chevrolet Blazer, which he joked used to be white but is now two-tone because of the rust spots.

Bishop Earl Boyea Jr. of Lansing, Michigan, called Monsignor Majchrowski "one of the saints at All Saints parish." He said Monsignor Majchrowski — the longest-serving pastor in the Lansing Diocese, known as Father Tony — is humble and hardworking.

Father Anthony said, "If I were to live all over again, I would choose to do the same thing. Being a priest is the greatest vocation in the world. Holding your Creator in your hands while celebrating Mass is mind-boggling. I am thankful to almighty God for the blessings of these many years." -

My Wedding compromise - All Saints Church and Byzantine Priest

Father Anthony was the main celebrant for our Marriage Mass and a Priest from the Byzantine Rite in the Catholic Church presided over the Sacrament of Matrimony. When the Bride and Groom exchange their vows, they administer the Sacrament of Matrimony to each other.

Gentle people have extraordinary patience over a long period of time.

Both Father Bortnowski and Father Anthony displayed gentleness toward me, and I respected both of them. Now I pray to them to intercede for me for perseverance in My Faith.

October   Patience

Rudbeckia in Neighbor's Yard

Fruit of the Holy Spirit = Patience

Liturgical Calendar = Holy Rosary

Devotions and Celebrations = Rosary – Photo Album of the Life of Jesus

Polish–American Recipe = *Jablko Kruchy*: Apple Crisp

Polish–American Activity = Wycinanki – Sceneria = Scenery with Leaves

People of Polish Heritage = Grandparents and the Rosary

October   Patience

Fruit of the Holy Spirit = Patience

Prayer:

    Holy Spirit, eternal Love of the Father and the Son, kindly bestow on us the fruit of patience that we may endure humbly everything that may be opposed to our own desires.

Patience enables us to endure the disagreeable circumstance of life and resigns us to the suffering of deaths. We know that we can overcome the temptations and sufferings of life because God is always with us.

We demonstrate patience by treating others with thoughtfulness and tolerance.

Patience enables us to endure hardship caused by another person in conformity with God's will without sadness or resentment.

And as for that in the good soil, they are those who, hearing the word, hold it fast in an honest and good heart, and bring forth fruit with patience. (Luke 8: 14 – 16)

The signs of a true apostle were performed among you in all patience, with signs and wonders and mighty works. (2 Corinthians 12: 11 – 13)

May you be strengthened with all power, according to his glorious might, for all endurance and patience with joy.   (Colossians 1: 10 – 12)

Put on then, as God's chosen ones, holy and beloved, compassion, kindness, lowliness, meekness, and patience. (Colossians 3: 11 – 13)

Preach the word, be urgent in season and out of season, convince, rebuke, and exhort, be unfailing in patience and in teaching. (2 Timothy 4: 1 – 3)

Love is patient, love is kind. (1 Corinthians 13: 4 – 7)

October   Patience
Liturgical Calendar = Holy Rosary

The month of October is dedicated to the Holy Rosary. The Memorial of Our Lady of the Rosary is celebrated on October 7. October falls during the liturgical season known as Ordinary Time, which is represented by the liturgical color green.

27th Sunday in Ordinary Time = Our Lord tells the parable of the vineyard.
28th Sunday in Ordinary Time = This Gospel recounts the parable of the wedding banquet.
29th Sunday in Ordinary Time = Jesus says to "Render to Caesar what is Caesar's".
30th Sunday in Ordinary Time = In this Gospel Jesus gives us the greatest commandment.

The Miracle of the SUN at Fatima, Portugal on October 13, 1917 was witnessed by hundreds possibly thousands of people of all ages. They were believers, agnostics, atheists, rich, poor, well educated, and those with no formal instruction.

Our Lady of Fatima, pray for our dear country.
Our Lady of Fatima, sanctify our clergy.
Our Lady of Fatima, make our Catholics more fervent.
Our Lady of Fatima, guide and inspire those who govern us.
Our Lady of Fatima, cure the sick who confide in thee.
Our Lady of Fatima, console the sorrowful who trust in thee.
Our Lady of Fatima, help those who invoke your aid.
Our Lady of Fatima, deliver us from all dangers.
Our Lady of Fatima, help us to resist temptation.
Our Lady of Fatima, obtain for us all that we lovingly ask of thee.
Our Lady of Fatima, help those who are dear to us.
Our Lady of Fatima, bring back to the right road our erring brothers.
Our Lady of Fatima, give us back our ancient fervor.
Our Lady of Fatima, obtain for us pardon of our manifold sins and offenses.
Our Lady of Fatima, bring all men to the feet of thy Divine Child.
Our Lady of Fatima, obtain peace for the world.
O Mary conceived without sin, pray for us who have recourse to thee.
Immaculate Heart of Mary, pray for us now and at the hour of our death. Amen.

Let us pray
O God of infinite goodness and mercy, fill our hearts with a great confidence in Thy dear Mother, whom we invoke under the title of Our Lady of the Rosary and our Lady of Fatima, and grant us by her powerful intercession all the graces, spiritual and temporal, which we need. Through Christ our Lord. Amen.

Novena Prayer – Our Lady of the Holy Rosary
Listen, my faithful children; open up your petals, like roses planted near running waters; send up the sweet odor of incense, break forth in blossoms like the lily. Send up the sweet odor of your hymn of praise; bless the Lord for all he has done.? (Sir 39:13-14)

My dearest Mother Mary, behold me, your child, in prayer at your feet. Accept this Holy Rosary, which I offer you in accordance with your requests at Fatima, as a proof of my tender love for you, for the intentions of the Sacred Heart of Jesus, in atonement for the offenses committed against your Immaculate Heart, and for this special favor which I earnestly request in my Rosary Novena: (Mention your request).

I beg you to present my petition to your Divine Son. If you will pray for me, I cannot be refused. I know, dearest Mother, that you want me to seek God's holy Will concerning my request. If what I ask for should not be granted, pray that I may receive that which will be of greater benefit to my soul.

I offer you this spiritual "Bouquet of Roses" because I love you. I put all my confidence in you, since your prayers before God are most powerful. For the greater glory of God and for the sake of Jesus, your loving Son, hear and grant my prayer. Sweet Heart of Mary be my salvation.

October   Patience
Devotions and Celebrations = Rosary – Photo Album of the Life of Jesus

One of the most beautiful ways of praying the Rosary is by meditating on verses from Scripture before each bead on the Rosary. These verses describe an event in the lives of Jesus and His Mother Mary. During Meditation picture the scene in your mind, and think about its meaning and significance. For deeper appreciation of each Mystery, we can spend time in Contemplation by picturing ourselves in the event and thinking how we would have acted if we were in the shoes of the various people in the scene.

The Mysteries of the Rosary

The Joyful Mysteries present the conception, birth, and childhood of Jesus.
The Luminous Mysteries describe the public life of Jesus.
October 2002, Pope John Paul II introduced the Mysteries of Light in order to provide a more complete presentation of the life Jesus when He walked on earth.
The Sorrowful Mysteries follow Jesus during His passion and death.
The Glorious Mysteries celebrate the resurrection and ascension of Jesus, the descent of the Holy Spirit, and the crowning of Mary as Queen of heaven and earth.
When I pray the Rosary – I usually meditate on only 0ne Set of Mysteries each day.
This is one way of learning about the Life of Jesus by looking through the Photos in an Album with the Mother of Jesus as she retells the thoughts she holds close in her heart regarding them.

Sign of the Cross: We start by holding the Crucifix and making the Sign of the Cross: First, by touching the Crucifix to our foreheads while saying, "In the name of the Father." Second, by touching the Crucifix to the bottom center part of our sternums while saying, "- and of the Son." Third, by touching the Crucifix to both shoulders starting with our left and moving to the right in one smooth gesture while saying, "- and of the Holy Spirit." Amen.

Apostles Creed: While still holding the Crucifix, we recite the Apostles Creed:
I believe in God, the Father Almighty, Creator of heaven and earth and in Jesus Christ, His only Son, our Lord; Who was conceived by the Holy Spirit, born of the Virgin Mary, suffered under Pontius Pilate, was crucified, died, and was buried, He descended to the dead. On the third day He arose again. He ascended into Heaven, and is seated at the right hand of God, the Father Almighty, from thence He shall come to judge the living and the dead. I believe in the Holy Spirit, the Holy Catholic Church, the communion of saints, the forgiveness of sins, the resurrection of the body, and life everlasting. Amen.

Our Father: On the large beads we say the Lord's Prayer:
Our Father, who art in heaven, hallowed be Thy Name. Thy kingdom come -Thy will be done on earth, as it is in Heaven. Give us this day our daily bread, and forgive us our trespasses as we forgive those who trespass against us. And lead us not into temptation, but deliver us from evil. Amen.

Hail Mary: On ALL of the small beads, we ask Mary to intercede for us as she did at the wedding in Cana, and Jesus changed water into wine. (John 2:1 - 11) **On the three small beads, pray Hail Mary's for increase in the Virtues of Faith, Hope and Charity.**
Hail Mary, full of grace, the Lord is with thee; blessed are thou amongst women, and blessed is the fruit of thy womb, Jesus. Holy Mary, Mother of God, pray for us sinners now and at the hour of our death. Amen.

Glory be: Between each Mystery we recite this short prayer:
Glory be to the Father, and to the Son, and to the Holy Spirit, as it was in the beginning, is now and ever shall be, world without end. Amen.

First Joyful Mystery - The Annunciation
Lord, Grant Me the Grace of Humility.

Large bead = Our Father...
Presented for meditation before each Hail Mary is a "Scripture Verse."

In the sixth month, the angel Gabriel was sent from God to a town of Galilee called Nazareth, to a virgin betrothed to a man named Joseph, of the house of David, and the virgin's name was Mary.
(Luke 1:26, 27) **Hail Mary...**

And coming to her, he said, "Hail, full of grace! The Lord is with you."
(Luke 1:28) **Hail Mary...**

But she was greatly troubled at what was said and pondered what sort of greeting this might be.
(Luke 1:29) **Hail Mary...**

Then the angel said to her, "Do not be afraid, Mary, for you have found favor with God.
(Luke 1:30) **Hail Mary...**

Behold, you will conceive in your womb and bear a son, and you shall name him Jesus.
(Luke 1:31) **Hail Mary...**

He will be great and will be called Son of the Most High, and the Lord God will give him the throne of David his father, and he will rule over the house of Jacob forever, and of his kingdom there will be no end." (Luke 1:32, 33) **Hail Mary...**

But Mary said to the angel, "How can this be, since I have no relations with a man?"
(Luke 1:34) **Hail Mary...**

And the angel said to her in reply, "The Holy Spirit will come upon you, and the power of the Most High will overshadow you. Therefore the child to be born will be called holy, the Son of God.
(Luke 1:35) **Hail Mary...**

And behold, Elizabeth, your relative, has also conceived a son in her old age, and this is the sixth month for her who was called barren; for nothing will be impossible for God."
(Luke 1:36, 37) **Hail Mary...**

Mary said, "Behold, I am the handmaid of the Lord. May it be done to me according to your word." Then the angel departed from her.(Luke 1:38) **Hail Mary.**   **Glory Be To...**

Second Joyful Mystery – The Visitation
Lord, Grant Me the Grace of Love of Thy Neighbor.

Large bead = Our Father...

During those days Mary set out and traveled to the hill country in haste to a town of Judah, where she entered the house of Zechariah and greeted Elizabeth. (Luke 1:39, 40) **Hail Mary...**

When Elizabeth heard Mary's greeting, the infant leaped in her womb, and Elizabeth, filled with the holy Spirit, cried out in a loud voice and said, "Most blessed are you among women, and blessed is the fruit of your womb." (Luke 1:41, 42) **Hail Mary...**

"And how does this happen to me; that the mother of my Lord should come to me?"
(Luke 1:43) **Hail Mary...**

"For at the moment the sound of your greeting reached my ears, the infant in my womb leaped for joy."
(Luke 1:44) **Hail Mary...**

"Blessed are you who believed that what was spoken to you by the Lord would be fulfilled."
(Luke 1:45) **Hail Mary...**

And Mary said: "My soul proclaims the greatness of the Lord; my spirit rejoices in God my Savior."
(Luke 1:46, 47) **Hail Mary...**

"For he has looked upon his handmaid's lowliness; behold, from now on will all ages call me blessed."
(Luke 1:48) **Hail Mary...**

"The Mighty One has done great things for me, and holy is his name. His mercy is from age to age to those who fear him." (Luke 1:49, 50) **Hail Mary...**

"He has helped Israel his servant, remembering his mercy, according to his promise to our fathers, to Abraham and to his descendants forever." (Luke 1:54, 55) **Hail Mary...**

Mary remained with her cousin Elizabeth about three months and then returned to her home in Nazareth.
(Luke 1:56) **Hail Mary...**   **Glory Be To...**

Third Joyful Mystery – The Nativity
Lord, Grant Me the Grace of Poverty of Spirit.

Large bead = Our Father...

The birth of Jesus Christ came about, when his mother Mary was betrothed to Joseph, but before they lived together, she was found with child through the Holy Spirit. (Matthew 1:18) **Hail Mary...**

Joseph her husband, since he was a righteous man, yet unwilling to expose her to shame, decided to divorce her quietly. (Matthew 1:19) **Hail Mary...**

Such was his intention when, behold, the angel of the Lord appeared to him in a dream and said, "Joseph, son of David, do not be afraid to take Mary your wife into your home. For it is through the Holy Spirit that this child has been conceived in her. (Matthew 1:20) **Hail Mary...**

"She will bear a son and you are to name him Jesus, because he will save his people from their sins." (Matthew 1:21) **Hail Mary...**

All this took place to fulfill what the Lord had said through the prophet: "Behold, the virgin shall be with child and bear a son, and they shall name him Emmanuel," which means "God is with us." (Matthew 1:22, 23) **Hail Mary...**

When Joseph awoke, he did as the angel of the Lord had commanded him and took his wife into his home. (Matthew 1:24) **Hail Mary...**

In those days a decree went out from Caesar Augustus that the whole world should be enrolled. (Luke 2:1) **Hail Mary...**

And Joseph too went up from Galilee from the town of Nazareth to Judea, to the city of David that is called Bethlehem, because he was of the house and family of David, to be enrolled with Mary, his betrothed, who was with child. (Luke 2:4, 5) **Hail Mary...**

While they were there, the time came for her to have her child, and she gave birth to her firstborn son. She wrapped him in swaddling clothes and laid him in a manger, because there was no room for them in the inn. (Luke 2:6, 7) **Hail Mary...**

And suddenly there was a multitude of the heavenly host with the angel, praising God and saying: "Glory to God in the highest and on earth peace to those on whom his favor rests." (Luke 2:13, 14) **Hail Mary...**   **Glory Be To...**

Fourth Joyful Mystery – The Presentation
Lord, Grant Me the Grace of Purity of Mind, Body, Heart and Will.

Large bead = Our Father...

When the days were completed for their purification according to the law of Moses, they took him up to Jerusalem to present him to the Lord... (Luke 2:22) **Hail Mary...**

Now there was a man in Jerusalem whose name was Simeon. This man was righteous and devout, awaiting the consolation of Israel, and the Holy Spirit was upon him. (Luke 2:25) **Hail Mary...**

It had been revealed to him by the Holy Spirit that he should not see death before he had seen the Messiah of the Lord. (Luke 2:26) **Hail Mary...**

He came in the Spirit into the temple; and when the parents brought in the child Jesus to perform the custom of the law in regard to him, he took him into his arms and blessed God, saying: "Now, Master, you may let your servant go in peace, according to your word, for my eyes have seen your salvation, which you prepared in sight of all the peoples, a light for revelation to the Gentiles, and glory for your people Israel." (Luke 2:27-32) **Hail Mary...**

The child's father and mother were amazed at what was said about him. (Luke 2:33) **Hail Mary...**

Simeon blessed them and said to Mary his mother, "Behold, this child is destined for the fall and rise of many in Israel, and to be a sign that will be contradicted and you yourself a sword will pierce, so that the thoughts of many hearts may be revealed." (Luke 2:34, 35) **Hail Mary...**

There was also a prophetess, Anna, of the tribe of Asher. She was advanced in years, having lived seven years with her husband after her marriage - (Luke 2:36) **Hail Mary...**

.Then as a widow until she was eighty-four, She never left the temple, but worshiped night and day with fasting and prayer. (Luke 2:37) **Hail Mary...**

And coming forward at that very time, she gave thanks to God and spoke about the child to all who were awaiting the redemption of Jerusalem. (Luke 2:38) **Hail Mary...**

When they had fulfilled all the prescriptions of the law of the Lord, Joseph took his wife Mary and Jesus and returned to Galilee, to their own town of Nazareth. Luke 2:39) **Hail Mary...**   **Glory Be To...**

Fifth Joyful Mystery – Finding Jesus in the Temple
Lord, Grant Me Wisdom and the Grace of Obedience.

Large bead = Our Father...
Each year his parents went to Jerusalem for the feast of Passover, and when he was twelve years old, they went up according to festival custom. (Luke 2:41, 42) **Hail Mary...**
After they had completed its days, as they were returning, the boy Jesus remained behind in Jerusalem, but his parents did not know it. (Luke 2:43) **Hail Mary...**
Thinking that he was in the caravan, they journeyed for a day and looked for him among their relatives and acquaintances. (Luke 2:44) **Hail Mary...**
Not finding him, they returned to Jerusalem to look for him. (Luke 2:45) **Hail Mary...**
After three days they found him in the temple, sitting in the midst of the teachers, listening to them and asking them questions, and all who heard him were astounded at his understanding and his answers. (Luke 2:46, 47) **Hail Mary...**
When his parents saw him, they were astonished, and his mother said to him, "Son, why have you done this to us? Your father and I have been looking for you with great anxiety." (Luke 2:48) **Hail Mary...**
And he said to them, "Why were you looking for me? Did you not know that I must be about my Father's business?" (Luke 2:49) **Hail Mary...**
But they did not understand what he said to them. (Luke 2:50) **Hail Mary...**
He went down with them and came to Nazareth, and was obedient to them; and Mary his mother kept all these things in her heart. (Luke 2:51) **Hail Mary...**
And Jesus advanced in wisdom and age and favor before God and man. (Luke 2:52) **Hail Mary...**
Glory Be To...

First Luminous Mystery – The Baptism of Jesus
Lord, Grant Me Gratitude for the Gift of Faith.

Large bead = Our Father...
John (the) Baptist appeared in the desert proclaiming a baptism of repentance for the forgiveness of sins. (Mark 1:4) **Hail Mary...**
This is what he proclaimed: "One mightier than I is coming after me. I am not worthy to stoop and loosen the thongs of his sandals." (Mark 1:7) **Hail Mary...**
"I have baptized you with water; he will baptize you with the Holy Spirit." (Mark 1:8) **Hail Mary...**
The next day he saw Jesus coming toward him and said, "Behold, the Lamb of God, who takes away the sin of the world." (John 1:29) **Hail Mary...**
It happened in those days that Jesus came from Nazareth of Galilee and was baptized in the Jordan by John. (Mark 1:9) **Hail Mary...**
"I did not know him, but the reason why I came baptizing with water was that he might be made known to Israel." (John 1:31) **Hail Mary...**
John testified further, saying, "I saw the Spirit come down like a dove from the sky and remain upon him. (John 1:32) **Hail Mary...**
I did not know him, but the one who sent me to baptize with water told me, 'On whomever you see the Spirit come down and remain, he is the one who will baptize with the Holy Spirit.' (John 1:33) **Hail Mary...**
And a voice came from the heavens, "You are my beloved Son; with you I am well pleased." (Mark 1:11) **Hail Mary...**
At once the Spirit drove him out into the desert, and he remained in the desert for forty days, tempted by Satan. He was among wild beasts, and the angels ministered to him. (Mark 1:12, 13) **Hail Mary...**
Glory Be To...

Second Luminous Mystery – The Miracle at the Wedding at Cana
Lord, Grant Me the Grace of Fidelity.

Large bead = Our Father...
On the third day there was a wedding in Cana in Galilee, and the mother of Jesus was there.
  (John 2:1) **Hail Mary...**
Jesus and his disciples were also invited to the wedding. (John 2:2) **Hail Mary...**
When the wine ran short, the mother of Jesus said to him, "They have no wine." (John 2:3) **Hail Mary...**
(And) Jesus said to her, "Woman, how does your concern affect me? My hour has not yet come."
  (John 2:4) **Hail Mary...**
His mother said to the servers, "Do whatever he tells you." (John 2:5) **Hail Mary...**
Now there were six stone water jars there for Jewish ceremonial washings, each holding twenty to thirty
  gallons. Jesus told them, "Fill the jars with water." So they filled them to the brim. (John 2:6, 7)
  Hail Mary...
Then he told them, "Draw some out now and take it to the headwaiter." So they took it. (John 2:8)
  Hail Mary...
When the headwaiter tasted the water that had become wine, without knowing where it came from. The
  servers who had drawn the water knew. The headwaiter called the bridegroom... (John 2:9) **Hail
  Mary...**
He said to the bridegroom, "Everyone serves good wine first, and then when people have drunk freely, an
  inferior one; but you have kept the good wine until now." (John 2:10) **Hail Mary...**
Jesus did this as the beginning of his signs in Cana in Galilee and so revealed his glory, and his disciples
  began to believe in him. (John 2:11) **Hail Mary...**
  Glory Be To...

Third Luminous Mystery – The Proclamation of the Kingdom
Lord, Grant Me the Desire for Holiness.

Large bead = Our Father...
"This is the time of fulfillment. The kingdom of God is at hand. Repent, and believe in the gospel."
  (Mark 1:15) **Hail Mary...**
As he passed by the Sea of Galilee, he saw Simon and his brother Andrew casting their nets into the
  sea; they were fishermen. (Mark 1:16) **Hail Mary...**
Jesus said to them, "Come after me, and I will make you fishers of men." (Mark 1:17) **Hail Mary...**
Then they abandoned their nets and followed him. (Mark 1:18) **Hail Mary...**
They came bringing to him a paralytic carried by four men. Unable to get near Jesus because of the
  crowd, they opened up the roof above him. After they had broken through, they let down the mat
  on which the paralytic was lying. (Mark 2:3, 4) **Hail Mary...**
When Jesus saw their faith, he said to the paralytic, "Child, your sins are forgiven." (Mark 2:5)
  Hail Mary...
Jesus immediately knew in his mind what they were thinking to themselves, so he said, "Why are you
  thinking such things in your hearts? Which is easier, to say to the paralytic, 'Your sins
  are forgiven,' or to say, 'Rise, pick up your mat and walk'? (Mark 2:8, 9) **Hail Mary...**
But that you may know that the Son of Man has authority to forgive sins on earth"-- he said to the
  paralytic, "I say to you, rise, pick up your mat, and go home." (Mark 2:10, 11) **Hail Mary...**
Some scribes who were Pharisees saw that he was eating with sinners and tax collectors and said to his
  disciples, "Why does he eat with tax collectors and sinners?" (Mark 2:16) **Hail Mary...**
Jesus heard this and said to them, "Those who are well do not need a physician, but the sick do. I did not
  come to call the righteous but sinners." (Mark 2:17) **Hail Mary...**
  Glory Be To...

Fourth Luminous Mystery - The Transfiguration
Lord, Grant Me the grace of Spiritual Courage.

Large bead = Our Father...
About eight days after he said this, he took Peter, John, and James and went up the mountain to pray. (Luke 9:28) **Hail Mary...**
While he was praying his face changed in appearance and his clothing became dazzling white. (Luke 9:29) **Hail Mary...**
And behold, two men were conversing with him, Moses and Elijah, who appeared in glory and spoke of his exodus that he was going to accomplish in Jerusalem. (Luke 9:30, 31) **Hail Mary...**
Then Peter said to Jesus in reply, "Rabbi, it is good that we are here! Let us make three tents: one for you, one for Moses, and one for Elijah." (Mark 9:5) **Hail Mary...**
Peter hardly knew what to say, they were so terrified. (Mark 9:6) **Hail Mary...**
Then a cloud came, casting a shadow over them; then from the cloud came a voice, "This is my beloved Son. Listen to him." (Mark 9:6) **Hail Mary...**
When the disciples heard this, they fell prostrate and were even more afraid. (Matthew 17:6) **Hail Mary...**
But Jesus came and touched them, saying, "Rise, and do not be afraid." (Matthew 17:7) **Hail Mary...**
And when the disciples raised their eyes, they saw no one else but Jesus alone. (Matthew 17:8) **Hail Mary...**
As they were coming down from the mountain, Jesus charged them, "Do not tell the vision to anyone until the Son of Man has risen from the dead." (Matthew 17:9) **Hail Mary...**
Glory Be To...

Fifth Luminous Mystery – The First Eucharist
Lord, Grant Me the grace of Love of Our Eucharistic Lord.

Large bead = Our Father...
Before the feast of Passover, Jesus knew that his hour had come to pass from this world to the Father. He loved his own in the world and he loved them to the end. (John 13:1) **Hail Mary...**
"You know that in two days' time it will be Passover, and the Son of Man will be handed over to be crucified." (Matthew 26:2) **Hail Mary...**
On the first day of the Feast of Unleavened Bread, the disciples approached Jesus and said, "Where do you want us to prepare for you to eat the Passover?" (Matthew 26:17) **Hail Mary...**
He said, "Go into the city to a certain man and tell him, 'The teacher says, "My appointed time draws near; in your house I shall celebrate the Passover with my disciples." (Matthew 26:18) **Hail Mary...**
When it was evening, he reclined at table with the Twelve. (Matthew 26:19) **Hail Mary...**
He said to them, "I have eagerly desired to eat this Passover with you before I suffer... (Luke 22:15) **Hail Mary...**
While they were eating, he took bread, said the blessing, broke it, and gave it to them, and said, "Take and eat; this is my body." (Mark 14:22) **Hail Mary...**
Then he took a cup, gave thanks, and gave it to them, saying, "Take and drink for this is my blood of the new covenant, which will be shed on behalf of many for the forgiveness of sins." (Matthew 26:27, 28) **Hail Mary...**
"I tell you, from now on I shall not drink this fruit of the vine until the day when I drink it with you new in the kingdom of my Father." (Matthew 26:29) **Hail Mary...**
Then, after singing a hymn, they went out to the Mount of Olives. (Matthew 26:30) **Hail Mary...**
Glory Be To...

First Sorrowful Mystery – The Agony in the Garden
Lord, Grant Me Contrition for My Sins and the Grace to Forgive Others.

Large bead = Our Father...
Then they came to a place named Gethsemane, and he said to his disciples, "Sit here while I pray." (Mark 14:32) **Hail Mary...**
He took with him Peter, James, and John, and Jesus began to be troubled. (Mark 14:33) **Hail Mary...**
Jesus said to them, "My soul is sorrowful even to death. Remain here and keep watch." (Mark 14:34) **Hail Mary...**
Jesus advanced a little and fell to the ground and prayed that if it were possible the hour might pass; he said, "Abba, Father, all things are possible to you. Take this cup away from me, but not what I will but your will be done." (Mark 14:35, 36) **Hail Mary...**
When he returned he found them asleep. Jesus said to Peter, "Simon, could you not keep watch for one hour with me? Watch and pray that you may not give into temptation." Withdrawing again, he prayed, saying the same thing. (Mark 14:37-39) **Hail Mary...**
Judas got a band of soldiers and guards from the chief priests and the Pharisees and went to the Garden of Olives with lanterns, torches, and weapons. (John 18:3) **Hail Mary...**
Jesus, knowing everything that was going to happen to him, went out and said to them, "For whom are you looking?" (John 18:4) **Hail Mary...**
They answered him, "Jesus the Nazarene." He said to them, "I AM." Judas his betrayer was with them. Jesus said to them, "I AM," they turned away and fell to the ground. (John 18:5, 6) **Hail Mary...**
Then Simon Peter, who had a sword, drew it, struck the high priest's slave, and cut off his right ear. Jesus said to Peter, "Put your sword into its scabbard. Shall I not drink the cup that the Father gave me?" Jesus healed the ear of the servant. (John 18:10, 11) **Hail Mary...**
Then the band of soldiers, the tribune, and the Jewish guards seized Jesus. (John 18:12, 13) **Hail Mary...**
Glory Be To...

Second Sorrowful Mystery – The Scourging at the Pillar
Lord, Grant Me the Grace to Mortify My Senses.

Large bead = Our Father...
They led Jesus away to the high priest, and all the chief priests and the elders and the scribes came together. (Mark 14:53) **Hail Mary...**
The chief priests and the entire Sanhedrin kept trying to obtain testimony against Jesus in order to put him to death, but they found none. (Mark 14:55) **Hail Mary...**
The high priest rose and questioned Jesus, saying, "Have you no answer to what these men are testifying against you?" Jesus was silent and answered nothing. Again the high priest asked him, "Are you the Messiah?" (Mark 14:60, 61) **Hail Mary...**
Then Jesus answered, "I AM; and 'you will see the Son of Man seated at the right hand of the Power and coming with the clouds of heaven.' (Mark 14:62) **Hail Mary...**
At that the high priest tore his garments and said, "What further need have we of witnesses? You have heard the blasphemy. What do you think?" They all condemned him as deserving to die. (Mark 14:63, 64) **Hail Mary...**
As soon as morning came, the chief priests with the elders and the scribes, that is, the whole Sanhedrin, held a council. They bound Jesus, led him away, and handed him over to Pilate. (Mark 15:1) **Hail Mary...**
Now Jesus stood before the governor, and he questioned him, "Are you the king of the Jews?" Jesus said, "You say so." (Matthew 27:11) **Hail Mary...**
Jesus answered, "My kingdom is not of this world. If my kingdom did belong to this world, my attendants would be fighting to keep me from being handed over to my enemies. But as it is, my kingdom is not of this world." (John 18:36) **Hail Mary...**
Pilate said to him, "Then you are a king?" Jesus answered, "You say I am a king. For this I was born and for this I came into the world, to testify to the truth. Everyone who belongs to the truth listens to my voice." (John 18:37) **Hail Mary...**
Then Pilate took Jesus and had him scourged. (John 19:1) **Hail Mary...**   **Glory Be To...**

Third Sorrowful Mystery – The Crowning with Thorns
Lord, Grant Me the Grace to Be in the World, but Not of It.

Large bead = Our Father...
And the soldiers wove a crown out of thorns and placed it on his head, and clothed him in a purple cloak, and they came to him and said, "Hail, King of the Jews!" Then they struck him repeatedly. (John 19:2, 3) **Hail Mary...**
Pilate took some water, washed his hands in front of the crowd and said, "I am innocent of this man's blood. It is your concern." (Matthew 27:24) **Hail Mary...**
Jesus was brought out, wearing the crown of thorns and the purple cloak. Pilate said to them, "Behold, the man!" (John 19:4, 5) **Hail Mary...**
When the chief priests and the guards saw him they cried out, "Crucify him! Crucify him!" Pilate said to them, "Take him yourselves and crucify him. I find no guilt in him." (John 19:6) **Hail Mary...**
So Pilate said to Jesus, "Why do you not speak to me? Do you not know that I have power to release you and I have power to crucify you?" (John 19:10) **Hail Mary...**
Jesus answered him, "You would have no power over me if it had not been given to you from above. For this reason the one who handed me over to you has the greater sin." (John 19:11) **Hail Mary...**
Consequently, Pilate tried to release him; but the Jews cried out, "If you release him, you are not a Friend of Caesar. Everyone who makes himself a king opposes Caesar." (John 19:12) **Hail Mary...**
It was preparation day for Passover, and it was about noon. Pilate said to the crowd, "Behold, your king!" (John 19:14) **Hail Mary...**
They cried out, "Take him away! Crucify him!" Pilate said to them, "Shall I crucify your king?" The chief priests answered, "We have no king but Caesar." (John 19:15) **Hail Mary...**
Then he handed Jesus over to them to be crucified... (John 19:16) **Hail Mary...**
Glory Be To...

Fourth Sorrowful Mystery – Jesus Carries the Cross
Lord, Grant Me the Grace of Patience in Times of Tribulation

Large bead = Our Father...
When they had mocked him, they stripped him of the cloak, dressed him in his own clothes, and led Jesus off to crucify him. (Matthew 27:31) **Hail Mary...**
As they were going out, they met a man, Simon of Cyrene. This man they pressed into service to carry the cross with Jesus. (Matthew 27:32) **Hail Mary...**
A large crowd of people followed Jesus, including many women who mourned and lamented him. (Luke 23:27) **Hail Mary...**
Jesus turned to them and said, "Daughters of Jerusalem, do not weep for me; weep instead for yourselves and for your children. For indeed, the days are coming when people will say, "'Blessed are the barren, the wombs that never bore and the breasts that never nursed." (Luke 23:28, 29) **Hail Mary...**
At that time people will say to the mountains, 'Fall upon us!' and to the hills, 'Cover us!' for if these things are done when the wood is green what will happen when it is dry?" (Luke 23:30, 31) **Hail Mary...**
They brought Jesus to the place of Golgotha, which is translated Place of the Skull. (Mark 15:22) **Hail Mary...**
Now two others, both criminals, were led away with him to be executed. When they came to the place called the Skull, they crucified Jesus and the criminals there, one on his right, the other on his left. (Luke 15:23, 24) **Hail Mary...**
They offered Jesus wine drugged with myrrh, but he did not take it. (Mark 15:23) **Hail Mary...**
Then they crucified Jesus and divided his garments by casting lots for them to see what each should take. It was nine o'clock in the morning when they crucified him. (Mark 15:24, 25) **Hail Mary...**
They placed over his head the written charge against him: This is Jesus, the King of the Jews. (Matthew 27:37) **Hail Mary...**
Glory Be To...

Fifth Sorrowful Mystery – Jesus Breathes His Last and Dies
Lord, Grant Me the Grace of Pardoning Injuries

Large bead = Our Father...
So the chief priests of the Jews said to Pilate, "Do not write 'The King of the Jews,' but that he said, 'I am the King of the Jews.' (John 19:21) **Hail Mary...**
Pilate answered, "What I have written, I have written." (John 19:22) **Hail Mary...**
Now one of the criminals hanging there reviled Jesus, saying, "Are you not the Messiah? Save yourself and us." (Luke 23:39) **Hail Mary...**
The other, however, rebuking him, said in reply, "Have you no fear of God, for you are subject to the same condemnation? And indeed, we have been condemned justly, for the sentence we received corresponds to our crimes, but this man has done nothing criminal." (Luke 23:40, 41)
  Hail Mary...
Then the second criminal said, "Jesus, remember me when you come into your kingdom." (Luke 23:42)
  Hail Mary...
Jesus replied to him, "Amen, I say to you, today you will be with me in Paradise." (Luke 23:43)
  Hail Mary...
When Jesus saw his mother and the young disciple, John there, he said to his mother, "Woman, behold, your son." (John 19:26) **Hail Mary...**
Then he said to the disciple, "Behold, your mother." And from that hour the disciple took her into his home. (John 19:27) **Hail Mary...**
It was now about noon and darkness came over the whole land until three in the afternoon by an eclipse of the sun. Then the veil of the temple was torn down the middle. (Luke 23:44, 45)   **Hail Mary...**
Jesus cried out in a loud voice, "Father, into your hands I commend my spirit"; and when he had said this Jesus breathed his last. (Luke 23:46) **Hail Mary...**
  Glory Be To...

First Glorious Mystery – The Resurrection
Lord, Grant Me the Grace of Faith.

Large bead = Our Father...
Amen, amen, I say to you, you will weep and mourn, while the world rejoices; you will grieve, but your grief will become joy. (John 16:20) **Hail Mary...**
Jesus said, you are now in anguish. But I will see you again, and your hearts will rejoice, and no one will take your joy away from you. (John 16:22) **Hail Mary...**
At daybreak on the first day of the week the women took the spices they had prepared and went to the tomb. (Luke 24:1) **Hail Mary...**
They found the stone rolled away from the tomb; but when they entered, they did not find the body of the Lord Jesus. (Luke 24:2) **Hail Mary...**
While they were puzzling over this, behold, two beings in dazzling white garments appeared to them. (Luke 24:4) **Hail Mary...**
The women were terrified and bowed their faces to the ground. They said to them, "Why do you seek the living one among the dead? (Luke 24:5) **Hail Mary...**
He is not here, but he has been raised. Remember what Jesus said to you while he was still in Galilee - that the Son of Man must be handed over to sinners and be crucified, and rise on the third day." (Luke 24:6, 7) **Hail Mary...**
Behold, Jesus met them on their way and greeted them. They approached, embraced his feet, and did him homage. Then Jesus said to them, "Do not be afraid. Go tell my brothers to go to Galilee, and there they will see me." (Matthew 28:9, 10) **Hail Mary...**
Then the women returned from the tomb and announced all these things to the eleven and to all the others. (Luke 24:9) **Hail Mary...**
Jesus said, "I am the resurrection and the life; whoever believes in me, even if he dies, will live, and everyone who lives and believes in me will never die... John (11:25, 26)   **Hail Mary...**
  Glory Be To...

Second Glorious Mystery – The Ascension
Lord, Grant Me the Grace of Hope

Large bead = Our Father...
He said to them, "These are my words that I spoke to you while I was still with you, that everything written about me in the Law of Moses and in the prophets and psalms must be fulfilled." (Luke 24:44) **Hail Mary...**
Jesus said to them, "Thus it is written that the Messiah would suffer and rise from the dead on the third day and that repentance, for the forgiveness of sins, would be preached in his name to all the nations, beginning from Jerusalem. (Luke 24:47) **Hail Mary...**
You are witnesses of these things. (Luke 24:48) **Hail Mary...**
Then he led them out as far as Bethany, raised his hands, and blessed them. (Luke 24:50) **Hail Mary...**
Jesus approached and said to them, "All power in heaven and on earth has been given to me." (Matthew 28:18) **Hail Mary...**
"Go, therefore, and make disciples of all nations, baptizing them in the name of the Father, and of the Son, and of the Holy Spirit, teaching them to observe all that I have commanded you. And behold, I am with you always, until the end of time." (Matthew 28:19, 20) **Hail Mary...**
Whoever believes and is baptized will be saved; whoever does not believe will be condemned. (Mark 16:16) **Hail Mary...**
While meeting with them, he enjoined them not to depart from Jerusalem, but to wait for "the promise of the Father about which you have heard me speak; for John baptized with water, but in a few days you will be baptized with the Holy Spirit." (Acts 1:4, 5) **Hail Mary...**
When he had said this, as they were looking on, he was lifted up, and a cloud took him from their sight. (Acts 1:9) **Hail Mary...**
While they were looking intently at the sky as he was going, suddenly two men dressed in white garments stood beside them. They said, "Men of Galilee, why are you standing there looking at the sky? This Jesus who has been taken up from you into heaven will return in the same way as you have seen him going into heaven." (Acts 1:10, 11) **Hail Mary...**
Glory Be To...

Third Glorious Mystery – The Descent of the Holy Spirit
Lord, Grant Me the Grace of All of the Gifts from the Holy Spirit

Large bead = Our Father...
When the time for Pentecost was fulfilled, they were all in one place together. (Acts 2:1) **Hail Mary...**
Suddenly there came from the sky a noise like a strong driving wind, and it filled the entire house in which they were. (Acts 2:2) **Hail Mary...**
Then there appeared to them tongues as of fire, which parted and came to rest on each one of them. (Acts 2:3) **Hail Mary...**
And they were all filled with the Holy Spirit and began to speak in different tongues, as the Spirit enabled them to proclaim. (Acts 2:4) **Hail Mary...**
There were devout Jews from every nation under heaven staying in Jerusalem. (Acts 2:5) **Hail Mary...**
At this sound, they gathered in a large crowd, but they were confused because each one heard the Disciples of Jesus speaking in his own language. (Acts 2:6) **Hail Mary...**
Then Peter stood up with the Eleven, raised his voice, and proclaimed to them, "You who are Jews, indeed all of you staying in Jerusalem. Let this be known to you, and listen to my words." (Acts 2:14) **Hail Mary...**
Peter said to them, "Repent and be baptized, every one of you, in the name of Jesus Christ for the forgiveness of your sins; and you will receive the gifts of the Holy Spirit. (Acts 2:38) **Hail Mary...**
Those who accepted his message were baptized, and about three thousand persons were added that day. (Acts 2:41) **Hail Mary...**
...And every day the Lord added to their number those who were being saved. (Acts 2:47) **Hail Mary...**
Glory Be To...

Fourth Glorious Mystery – The Assumption of Mary
Lord, Grant Me the Grace to Love You as Our Lady Desires

Large bead = Our Father...
Then God's temple in heaven was opened... (Revelation 11:19) **Hail Mary...**
As a lily among thorns, so is my beloved among women. (Song of Songs 2:2) **Hail Mary...**
You are all-beautiful, my beloved, and there is no blemish in you. (Song of Songs 4:7) **Hail Mary...**
All glorious is the king's daughter as she enters, her raiment threaded with gold;   (Psalm 45:14)
    Hail Mary...
"Arise, my beloved, my beautiful one, and come! (Song of Songs 2:10) **Hail Mary...**
"For see, the winter is past, the rains are over and gone. (Song of Songs 2:11) **Hail Mary...**
The flowers appear on the earth, the time of pruning the vines has come, and the song of the dove is heard in our land. (Song of Songs 2:12) **Hail Mary...**
The fig tree puts forth its figs, and the vines, in bloom, give forth fragrance. Arise, my beloved, my beautiful one, and come!" (Song of Songs 2:13) **Hail Mary...**
In embroidered apparel she is led to the king.   The maids of her train are presented to the king.
    (Psalm 45:15) **Hail Mary...**
He brings me into the banquet hall and his emblem over me is love.
    (Song of Songs 2:4) **Hail Mary...**
    Glory Be To...

Fifth Glorious Mystery – The Coronation of Mary
Lord, Grant Me the Grace of Final Perseverance in Faith and Good Works.

Large bead = Our Father...
A great sign appeared in the sky. (Revelation 12:1) **Hail Mary...**
A woman clothed with the sun, with the moon under her feet, and on her head a crown of twelve stars.
    (Revelation 12:1) **Hail Mary...**
Who is this that comes forth like the dawn, as beautiful as the moon, as resplendent as the sun, as awe-inspiring as bannered troops? (Song of Songs 6:10) **Hail Mary...**
"I am a flower of Sharon, a lily of the valley." (Song of Songs 2:1) **Hail Mary...**
My heart is stirred by a noble theme, as I sing my ode to the king. (Psalm 45:2) **Hail Mary...**
"Give heed! For noble things I speak; honesty opens my lips." (Proverbs 8:6) **Hail Mary...**
For he who finds me finds life, and wins favor from the Lord. (Proverbs 8:35) **Hail Mary...**
The promises of the Lord I will sing forever... (Proverbs 89:1) **Hail Mary...**
"Blessed are you, daughter, by the Most High God, above all the women on earth.   (Judith 13:18)
    Hail Mary...
The Mighty One has done great things for me, and holy is his name. (Luke 1:49) **Hail Mary...**
    Glory Be To...

October   Patience

Polish–American Recipe = *Jablko Kruchy*: Apple Crisp

Apple Crisp
Margreta - Urbanik Polish Recipe

Busia Helen was my Mother's Mother. When my sister was in school and I was three years old, my Mother would do various errands for the Nuns at All Saints. She would take them shopping for necessities, and to doctor or dentist appointments. She would telephone them in advance and say, "I'll be right over as soon as I dump Jean Marie off at Busia's house." Busia Helen's house was only one block away from the Convent, so it was convenient for everyone involved.

Those words were music to my ears, because to be "... dumped off at Busia's house" meant FUN TO ME. If it was a nice day we would spend some time outside and on inclement days we would enjoy activities indoors.

Busia would get apples from the two trees in her side yard. She would push on the tall branches and catch apples in her apron and put them in one basket, while I stood safely aside.
I would help her collect the apples that fell on the ground and help her sort them. The bruised apples went into a separate box. Busia Helen would talk to me in both Polish and English. I don't remember enough of the Polish so I will share some of her advice.

"Some people take the bruised apples and eat them first because the nice apples will KEEP LONGER. They are so stupid because by the time all the bruised apples are eaten the nice apples are not so nice." Then she would pick out two of the nicest apples and shine them in her apron and take a big bite out of one of them. Satisfied that they were GOOD, she would take the apples into the house and cut them in quarters, cut out the cores and slices them up into two bowls, one for her and one for me. In a third bowl she would mix: Equal amounts of Cinnamon, sugar, and a dash of Nutmeg. We would sit at the kitchen table and dip the tips of our apple slices into the mixture before - we had a "crunching contest" – to see who could make the most noise eating our apple slices.

She would be peeling and chopping some of the apples, the ones with the fewest bruises for APPLE CRISP. Once the APPLE CRISP was in the oven she would take some of the other bruised apples and prepare to make apple sauce. A big bowl full of the nicest apples were polished in her apron and set on the Dining Room Table for my Uncles and any other visitors to enjoy. The rest of the apples were taken down the basement to the "Fruit Cellar." The "Fruit Cellar" wasn't only for fruit, root vegetables like carrots and potatoes were also stored there. Home-canned fruits and vegetables were carefully labeled and dated then placed in neat rows on the shelves.

Early in December 1985, I telephoned my Mother asking for two of my favorite recipes that I knew were only in her head. They had been handed down for at least three generations from my Mother's side of the family. I received a short typed letter from her that was dated, Friday, December 6, 1985.

Dear Jeanie-
It was nice hearing from you, but I'll tell you like I tell the others – it's cheaper to write.
Here are the recipes you wanted:

Apple Crisp

Place 5 to 6 pared or unpared tart apples on a greased 6 x 10 baking dish.
Mix the following together with a fork until crumbly, and sprinkle over the apples.
1 cup sifted flour
½ to 1 cup sugar – depending on the tartness of the apples.
¾ teaspoon salt
1 teaspoon baking powder
1 unbeaten egg
Melt and cool 1/3 cup shortening and pour over apples
Sprinkle with ½ teaspoon Cinnamon
Bake 30 to 40 minutes at 350
Love, Mother

That's it? That is the whole recipe? No Directions????
My Mother typed proficiently with only two fingers.
The other recipe for Quick Cake in the May chapter of this book was the other recipe.
Yes, a person had to watch this delicious recipe being prepared to know what steps were missing.
This letter is fading so I typed this exactly as it came to me.

Apple Crisp with American Additions by Jean Marie Miscisin

1. Use real butter to grease a glass baking dish 8" X 8" =
2. Wash with purified water - four large Granny Smith Tart apples.
    Peel and cut into ¾ inch cubes.
    Place apple pieces in the prepared glass baking dish.
3. Sprinkle the apple pieces with a mixture of granulated sugar and Cinnamon.

2.

9.

10.

4. Preheat oven to 350º
5. In a sifter place:
    1 cup flour, add ¾ teaspoon salt, ½ teaspoon Cinnamon,
    1/8 teaspoon Nutmeg and 1 teaspoon Baking Powder.
    Sift this mixture into a two quart bowl.
6. Add 1 cup sugar on top of flour mixture and whisk with a fork until well blended.
    Make four indentations into the Flour-Sugar mixture.
7. Crack the egg into a small bowl – yes, and throw away the shell.
    Smell the egg or the shell to make sure the egg is fresh.
    The egg should have no order at all.
    Stir the egg with a fork until the whites and yolks are blended with no bubbles.

8. Pour the "stirred" egg into the indentations in the Flour-Sugar mixture.
    Mix together until crumbly by using two plain table knives, not sharp,
    to cut the egg into the Flour-Sugar mixture.
For this step - you cut by passing each knife past the other and turn the bowl after each set of four or five cuts.

9. Pour the crumbly mixture on top of the apple chunks, and use the knives to spread the ingredients over the apples.

10. The melted and cooled 1/3 cup of real butter is now poured – drizzled over the "Crumbly Mixture."

11. Sprinkle lightly with Cinnamon.

11.

12.

12. Bake for exactly 40 minutes then shut off the oven, open the oven door, and leave the Apple Crisp in the oven to cool slowly for at least 15 minutes.

Scoop out portions into bowls, enjoy with "Half N' Half" poured around the warm dessert or top with Vanilla Ice Cream.

October   Patience

Polish–American Activity = Wycinanki – Sceneria = Scenery with Leaves

1. Autumn Trees on a Hill   2. Autumn Trees on a River Bank

In Michigan the Autumn colors are spectacular. Various hues and shades of Green stay through the winter in some of the grass and Evergreen trees like Balsam Spruce, and Pine Trees. Early in October the shorter days bring on the colors. The blustery winds blow them off the trees. Adults rake them in piles to grind into mulch but not before the children jump in the piles and throw them up into the wind. My Daddy frequently joined in the fun and sometimes waited for the wind to blow the leaves away.

My Mother encouraged creative play on the rainy days. When I was seven or eight she taught me how to dry the leaves and press them between waxed-paper with a warm iron and a cloth to protect the iron from getting coated with wax. To create the back ground sky, water, and grass only green paper was torn to shape the hill and the river bank and then attached to a full sheet of blue paper. The Maple leaves were picked off the ground so I am not sure if they came from the same tree.

When I was taking an entry level Botany Course at Flint Junior College 1955, these experiences came in handy. I already knew where to find most of the trees in our Michigan Trees Textbook. The Professor marked strictly on a percentage based rubric, I was the only student that earned an "A" for my Michigan Leaves Project. I still have it in my cedar chest. Yes, Professor, she had a Ph. D. in Botany/Plant Science and taught at the college level for over twenty years, much of the time at the University of Michigan.

October   Patience

People of Polish Heritage = Grandparents and the Rosary

    Starting at the top left corner of the frame is a picture of Matka Boska = Mother of God – Czestochowa = the final place for the picture. Tradition told to me was that it was painted on a wooden table top by Saint Luke, the author of one of the Gospels. It has a long beautiful history which can be found on the Internet. The picture, Matka Boska Czestochowa, was given to me by My Mother's Father, Dzia Dzia, who was also my Baptismal Sponsor. He died Good Friday morning 1943. Portrait of My Mother's parents' wedding and Busia Helena's "week day" Rosary which she kept in the pocket of her apron complete the top row. The corpus of Jesus on Busia's Rosary is worn almost smooth. I remember praying the Rosary in Polish with her using this Rosary to count the prayers. When Busia died in 1986, nobody wanted this worn out Rosary. To me it is a very special treasure.

    Busia Pearl's "week day" Rosary which she kept in the pocket of her apron is displayed in the bottom left corner. Yes, it too is worn from years of prayers. She died in February 1988. My Daddy's Parents' wedding picture is in the center. Grandpa John would sit in his rocker in the dining room of their home and pray the Rosary on Sunday afternoons and some of the family members joined him. His Rosary is only slightly worn and the beads are very large. When he retired from Buick Factory he would walk to Mass daily and open the front doors of Sacred Heart Church in Flint, Michigan so the Priests wouldn't have to go outside before Mass. There was easy access to the Church from the rectory through the basement. The day before he went to the hospital for exploratory surgery he gave his key to his friend. Grandpa John died the next day. I share more about all of my Grandparents in other chapters of this book.

    All of these dear Grandparents modeled the virtue of patience when dealing with my lively spirit and questioning mind. All of my visits were enjoyable for me and they always appeared happy to see me.

Love is patient, love is kind. (1 Corinthians 13: 4 – 7)

November Generosity

Pink Petunias in Neighbor's Yard

Fruit of the Holy Spirit = Generosity

Liturgical Calendar = Souls in Purgatory

Devotions and Celebrations = All Saints Day

Polish–American Recipe = *Pasztecik*: Pasty and Pasty Roll

Polish–American Activity = House Plants Care with Prayer

People of Polish Heritage = Uncles, Aunts, and Cousins

November   Generosity

Fruit of the Holy Spirit = Generosity

Prayer:

    Holy Spirit, be pleased to infuse in us the fruit of Generosity, that we may willingly relieve our neighbor's necessities.

We demonstrate the fruit of generosity when we are share our gifts and possessions with others.

What good is it my brothers, if someone says he has faith but does not have works? Can that faith save him? If a brother or sister has nothing to wear and has no food for the day, and one of you says to them, "Go in peace, keep warm, and eat well," but you do not give them the necessities of the body, what good is it? So also faith of itself, if it does not have works is dead. (James 2: 14 – 17)

You will be enriched in every way for great generosity, which through us will produce thanksgiving to God. (2 Corinthians 9: 10 – 12)

Under the test of this service, you will glorify God by your obedience in acknowledging the gospel of Christ, and by the generosity of your contribution for them and for all others. (2 Corinthians 9: 12 – 14)

November   Generosity

Liturgical Calendar = Souls in Purgatory

Communion of Saints = Our Family in Faith

The Saints in Heaven, The Faithful on Earth, and The Souls in Purgatory.

    The Catholic Church teaches us about the Communion of Saints. This doctrine means that we are united through Prayers for each other. The Faithful on earth pray for each other and the Souls in Purgatory, the Departed who have not been recognized as being Saints in Heaven. The Souls in Purgatory are the souls of the people who have not been canonized as Saints in Heaven. The Souls in Purgatory can pray for us but not for each other. The Canonized Saints in Heaven are the souls of people who lived holy lives on earth, and after a long process outlined in four stages by the Catholic Church Magisterium the people are canonized as Saints in Heaven.

    The Souls in Purgatory may need an explanation. I am only sharing my understanding of the Souls in Purgatory. They are the souls who by God's mercy are being purified before entering Heaven. This place could be compared to the Vestibule of a Catholic Church or a back door mud-room on a house. Using the definition for purified as: being cleaned-up and getting ready to meet some one special. In the Polish Catholic Churches, worshipers took off their boots, set down umbrellas, and hung-up their coats before entering the Church to meet the Lord. A Bride on her wedding day would make last minute adjustments getting ready to meet her groom. So the Souls in Purgatory are getting cleaned–up to be ready to meet their Creator.

Each country may celebrate the Memorial Feast Day of different Saints who have been canonized in the Catholic Church. After a "saintly" person dies there is a grieving period. There are four required steps for a person to be declared a Canonized Saint and it is frequently a lengthy process taking many years; the steps are Servant of God, Venerable, Blessed, and Canonization. All Baptized Christians are called to accept the love, mercy, and grace from God to follow Jesus Christ. The Saints are people who have demonstrated heroic virtue in one or more of the virtues, at least the last ten years of their lives or have been martyred for their beliefs in the teachings of Jesus Christ. As Catholics we are encouraged to imitate their virtues while they were living on earth.

1. Servant of God = People who knew the person and believe that the person displayed heroic virtue ask the local Bishop to open the "cause for Canonization. In this step usually the last ten years of the person's life are given the most attention. Testimonies are recorded, and any material written by the "potential saint" is read carefully.

2. Venerable = When the person has been declared venerable the cause for Canonization is opened, local people can began intercessory prayers for a miracle.

3. Blessed = One, fully investigated miracle is needed before the person can be declared Blessed.

4. Canonization = A second, fully investigated miracle is needed before the person can be declared a Saint.

At All Saints School, we learned to read using Little Biographical Books of Lives of the Saints. There was a picture of each Saint on the even numbered pages and four or more simple sentences about the virtue that we were to learn to emulate not merely imitate. The length and complexity of the biographies increased until we were reading large hard bound volumes of our favorite Saints. In 2003, I purchased the book, Voices of the Saints, which has three-hundred-sixty-five (365) biographies. Under the Title: Resources" - Biographical information about each Saint can range from several Books to just a few small articles = many lifetimes of reading.

New holy people are being recognized as worthy of investigation by the Church every year. All of the Saints are unique individuals. Many of them led fascinating lives and others were able to lead Holy lives doing every day tasks with love for God and others.

My Patron Saint John Vianney was baptized Jean Marie. He is also the Patron Saint of Parish Priests. One of His prayers is so beautiful I want to share it with you. "I love you, O my God, and my only desire is to love You until the last breath of my life. I love You, O my infinitely lovable God, and I would rather die loving You, than live without loving You. I love You Lord, and the only grace I ask is to love You eternally... My God if my tongue cannot say in every moment that I love You, I want my heart to repeat it to You as often as I draw breath."

The year 2013 was particularly tumultuous so I wrote two short prayers inspired by the prayer of my Patron Saint. "Dear God, grant me the grace to Love You every moment of my life on earth and for all eternity." "Dear God, I trust in Your Love for me, my children, grandchildren, and my loved ones."

November   Generosity

Devotions and Celebrations = All Saints Day

Litany of All Saints

Lord, have mercy on us.	Lord, have mercy on us.
Christ, have mercy on us.	*Christ, have mercy on us.*
Lord, have mercy on us.	Lord, have mercy on us
God, the Father of heaven,	*have mercy on us*
God the Son, Redeemer of the world,	*have mercy on us*
God the Holy Spirit,	*have mercy on us*
Holy Trinity, one God,	*have mercy on us*
Holy Mary,	*pray for us.*
Holy Mother of God,	*pray for us.*
Holy Virgin of virgins,	*pray for us.*
St. Michael,	*pray for us.*
St. Gabriel,	*pray for us.*
St. Raphael,	*pray for us.*
All you Holy Angels and Archangels,	*pray for us.*
St. John the Baptist,	*pray for us.*
St. Joseph,	*pray for us.*
All you Holy Patriarchs and Prophets,	*pray for us.*
St. Peter,	*pray for us.*
St. Paul,	*pray for us.*
St. Andrew,	*pray for us.*
St. James,	*pray for us.*
St. John,	*pray for us.*
St. Thomas,	*pray for us.*
St. James,	*pray for us.*
St. Philip,	*pray for us.*
St. Bartholomew,	*pray for us.*
St. Matthew,	*pray for us.*
St. Simon,	*pray for us.*
St. Jude,	*pray for us.*
St. Matthias,	*pray for us.*
St. Barnabas,	*pray for us.*
St. Luke,	*pray for us.*
St. Mark,	*pray for us.*
All you holy Apostles and Evangelists,	*pray for us.*
All you holy Disciples of the Lord,	*pray for us.*
All you holy Innocents,	*pray for us.*
St. Stephen,	*pray for us.*
St. Lawrence,	*pray for us.*
St. Vincent,	*pray for us.*

Sts. Fabian and Sebastian,	*pray for us.*
Sts. John and Paul,	*pray for us.*
Sts. Cosmas and Damian,	*pray for us.*
All you holy Martyrs,	*pray for us.*
St. Sylvester,	*pray for us.*
St. Gregory,	*pray for us.*
St. Ambrose,	*pray for us.*
St. Augustine,	*pray for us.*
St. Jerome,	*pray for us.*
St. Martin,	*pray for us.*
St. Nicholas,	*pray for us.*
All you holy Bishops and Confessors,	*pray for us.*
All you holy Doctors,	*pray for us.*
St. Anthony,	*pray for us.*
St. Benedict,	*pray for us.*
St. Bernard,	*pray for us.*
St. Dominic,	*pray for us.*
St. Francis,	*pray for us.*
All you holy Priests and Levites,	*pray for us.*
All you holy Monks and Hermits,	*pray for us.*
St. Mary Magdalene,	*pray for us.*
St. Agatha,	*pray for us.*
St. Lucy,	*pray for us.*
St. Agnes,	*pray for us.*
St. Cecilia,	*pray for us.*
St. Anastasia,	*pray for us.*
St. Catherine,	*pray for us.*
St. Clare,	*pray for us.*
All you holy Virgins and Widows,	*pray for us.*
All you holy Saints of God,	*pray for us.*
Lord, be merciful,	*Lord, save your people.*
From all evil,	*Lord, save your people.*
From all sin,	*Lord, save your people.*
From your wrath,	*Lord, save your people.*
From a sudden and unprovided death,	*Lord, save your people.*
From the snares of the devil,	*Lord, save your people.*
From anger, hatred, and all ill-will,	*Lord, save your people.*
From the spirit of uncleanness,	*Lord, save your people.*
From lightning and tempest,	*Lord, save your people.*
From the scourge of earthquake,	*Lord, save your people.*
From plague, famine, and war,	*Lord, save your people.*
From everlasting death,	*Lord, save your people.*
By the mystery of your holy Incarnation,	*Lord, save your people.*
By your Coming,	*Lord, save your people.*
By your Birth, *Lord, save your people.*	*Lord, save your people.*
By your Baptism and holy fasting,	*Lord, save your people.*
By your Cross and Passion,	*Lord, save your people.*
By your Death and Burial,	*Lord, save your people.*
By your holy Resurrection,	*Lord, save your people.*
By your wonderful Ascension,	*Lord, save your people.*
By the coming of the Holy Spirit,	*Lord, save your people.*

On the day of judgment,	*Lord, save your people.*

Be merciful to us sinners,	*Lord, hear our prayer.*
That you will spare us,	*Lord, hear our prayer.*
That you will pardon us,	*Lord, hear our prayer.*
That it may please you to bring us to true penance,	*Lord, hear our prayer.*
Guide and protect your holy Church,	*Lord, hear our prayer.*
Preserve in holy religion the Pope, and all those in holy Orders,	*Lord, hear our prayer.*
Humble the enemies of holy Church,	*Lord, hear our prayer.*
Give peace and unity to the whole Christian people,	*Lord, hear our prayer.*

Bring back to the unity of the Church all those who are straying, and bring all unbelievers to the light of the Gospel,   *Lord, hear our prayer.*

Strengthen and preserve us in your holy service,	*Lord, hear our prayer.*
Raise our minds to desire the things of heaven,	*Lord, hear our prayer.*
Reward all our benefactors with eternal blessings,	*Lord, hear our prayer.*

Deliver our souls from eternal damnation, and the souls of our brethren, relatives, and benefactors,   *Lord, hear our prayer.*

Give and preserve the fruits of the earth,	*Lord, hear our prayer.*
Grant eternal rest to all the faithful departed,	*Lord, hear our prayer.*

That it may please You to hear and heed us, Jesus, Son of the Living God,   *Lord, hear our prayer.*

Lamb of God, who takes away the sins of the world,	*Spare us, O Lord!*
Lamb of God, who takes away the sins of the world,	*Graciously hear us, O Lord!*
Lamb of God, who takes away the sins of the world,	Have mercy on us.

Christ, hear us,	*Christ, graciously hear us*
Lord Jesus, hear our prayer.	*Lord Jesus, hear our prayer.*

Lord, have mercy on us.	*Lord, have mercy on us.*
Christ, have mercy on us.	*Christ, have mercy on us.*
Lord, have mercy on us.	*Lord, have mercy on us.*

November   Generosity

Polish–American Recipe = *Pasztecik*: Pasty and Pasty Roll

Turnover Pasties (Modified from Grandma Pearl Lukasavitz's Recipe)
This recipe makes four large Pasties or Two Large Pasty-Rolls

Preparation by one person does not need timing of the vegetables with the original process.
If two people are working together, put the chopped ingredients in separate bowls to be added as the previous vegetable becomes "just tender" to poke a fork in and pull out without the vegetable piece mashing. Then you add the next vegetable.

July 2013 Method =. I used a steamer for the vegetables, 1 cup chopped rutabaga (Bite sized pieces = ½ inch cubes), and 1 cup chopped carrots (Bite sized pieces = ½ inch cubes) were steamed together (Carrots in the basket) for one hour. The juices from the tray were poured into a glass kettle to be saved for gravy. 2 cups chopped potatoes (Bite sized pieces slightly larger than ½ inch cubes) were steamed separately and the juices from the tray were added to the glass kettle covered and placed in the refrigerator.

Prepare in advance and put to cool in refrigerator =
One large glass bowl put in sequence the following:

1 ½ lb Ground Beef 85% Lean = coat a large fry pan with Bacon Grease and make one big patty and cut into four even patties (Shape doesn't matter). Sprinkle lightly with Poultry Seasoning, and brown 5 to 7 minutes on both sides, break into one-inch chunks and put in the large glass bowl. Cover bowl with foil or plastic wrap and put in the refrigerator. Leave the browning coating that is on the pan. (Discard most of the drippings - leave a light coating Bacon Grease. Leave the browning coating that is on the pan.)

1 cup chopped sweet onions (Small pieces = ½ inch) Place onions in the same large fry pan, sprinkle with salt, and cook until caramelized and translucent. Stir onions into the meat, cover, and return to refrigerator.

1 cup chopped celery (Small pieces = ½ inch) Place celery in the same large fry pan, sprinkle with salt, and cook until translucent. Stir celery into the meat, cover, and return to refrigerator.

If a steamer is not used then follow these directions
1 cup chopped rutabaga (Bite sized pieces = ½ inch cubes). Put into a medium size kettle/sauce pan.
Pour cold water over them to cover them. Put on "Low heat" on stove.
Bring to a simmer on "Low heat" on stove (Slightly bubbling water).

In a metal "Tea Ball" I place six, whole ALLSPICE, and add one large Bay Leaf or two small ones crumbled to fit without floating out the holes of the "Tea Ball."
Place the "Tea Ball" in the center of the pot of water.

<u>1 cup chopped carrots</u> (Bite sized pieces = ½ inch cubes). Put into the medium size kettle/sauce pan with the rutabaga. Pour more cold water over them to cover them.
Continue to simmer on "Low heat" on stove (Slightly bubbling water).

<u>2 cups chopped potatoes</u> (Bite sized pieces) = Put into the medium size kettle/sauce pan with the rutabaga and carrots. Pour more cold water over them to cover them.
Continue to simmer on "Low heat" on stove (Slightly bubbling water).

When the vegetables are tender pour off the water and save for making gravy.
Take-out the "Tea Ball" and throw away the spices, and rinse the "Tea Ball" thoroughly right away. I don't use detergent on the "Tea Ball."

Gently stir the vegetables in with the meat, onions, and celery.
Take one-half = ½ cup of Original Biscuit Mix and sprinkle it over the mixture, mix gently, and return to the refrigerator while you prepare the Original Biscuit Mix dough. After using three other brands of Biscuit Mixes and I prefer the Original Biscuit Mix.

I now use a "Tortilla Press" instead of a rolling pin to make each pasty.

5 1/3 cups = Original Biscuit Mix = measure into a large mixing bowl

8 ounces cream cheese (One 8 oz package) House brands work equally well.
Place softened to room temperature cream cheese into a medium size mixing bowl.
Add 1 1/3 cups of milk (whole milk) to the softened cream cheese.
Using a "Hand electric mixer" beat on low until well blended.

Make four indentations in the Biscuit in the mixing bowl.
Pour the cream cheese and milk mixture in all at once into the four indentations.
Using two table knives cut the mixture until it makes a soft dough.

Flour a board when using a rolling pin, flour both sides of a "Tortilla Press" with biscuit mix to roll-out or press-out the balls of dough into a circle.
Use ½ cup of dough and roll or press thinly without holes
I put the ball of dough in the middle and press down until I see the dough coming out of the sides just a little, then I place the dough on an eight (8) inch glass plate and press the dough out to the edges.

Put approximately on (1) cup of meat mixture on one half of the circle.
Fold the circle in half.
With a biscuit-floured fork seal the edges of each turnover.
Cut three slits in the top to allow steam to escape.

Use parchment paper to line cookie sheets or "clay tray" as seen in these pictures.
Leave space around each pasty for it to rise.

Bake at 400 degrees for 15 to 20 minutes until golden brown on top.
Oven temperatures will vary and opening the oven door to check will affect the time needed.

To make gravy I prefer to fry on a low heat in two tablespoons butter some fresh onion and celery chopped very fine pieces. When the onions and celery pieces are caramelized and translucent sprinkle in three tablespoons of Biscuit Mix and stir until all the pieces are coated and tinged with golden brown color.

Take out about ½ cup vegetable water/broth into a cup. Pour the broth in slowly until smooth and slightly thin, the gravy will thicken as it simmers for at least ten (10) minutes. Stir steadily. Stay close by and add more water/broth if necessary. The best gravy usually takes ten minutes to simmer to correct pouring smoothness and creamy taste.

When Pasties are done, they are very hot inside, so cut them in half and wait to taste them.

I put the gravy on the side, because I like the texture of the Pasty crust, and it might get soggy with lots of gravy on it.

Yes, this recipe takes long. Pasties freeze well. Cool them in the refrigerator overnight lightly covered with foil. The next day, cover each pasty tightly in foil and put them flat in the freezer. When you want to eat one, take it out of the freezer while you heat a toaster oven to 350 degrees. Leave Pasty in the foil packaging and bake about ten minutes.

The foil covered Pasty can be placed on an oven-proof plate or metal pan before placing them in the oven for ease of handling. To reheat several pasties just place on a cookie sheet and heat in a regular oven.

Pasty Vege – Roll

VEGE ROLL RECIPE

This makes more than enough for the VEGE ROLL and the leftover VEGE-MIX, I served over "Bow Tie Pasta" for another meal.

In a large bowl combine the following ingredients:

1 ½ cups chopped broccoli florets
　　(I steamed frozen broccoli before adding and the recipe was just as good.)

1 ½ cups fresh corn kernels (about 3 ears) (One can, well drained corn works well.)

1 cup Shredded part-skim mozzarella cheese

¾ cup reduced-fat ricotta cheese (I used regular ricotta cheese and it was great.)

4 scallions, thinly sliced (I chop one small onion into tiny pieces and sauté before adding.)

¼ cup chopped fresh basil (I didn't have any one time, and it still tasted delicious.)

½ teaspoon garlic powder

¼ teaspoon salt

¼ teaspoon freshly ground pepper

½ jar of Marinara Sauce, 32 ounce jar

Use a large sheet of aluminum foil the size of the baking/cookie sheet pan and place on the bottom of the pan with enough foil to cover the whole top.(My pan is 10 inches by 14 inches.)
Mound the VEGE-MIX mixture to approximately four inches wide and twelve inches long.
The VEGE-MIX will be set in the center of the PASTRY DOUGH for baking.
Wrap the foil around the mixture and return to the refrigerator while you prepare the dough.

VARIATION = "POLISH PASTY" INGREDIENTS

PASTY DOUGH

Prepare in advance:
Cut parchment paper to cover the "cookie sheet" - My pan is 10 inches by 14 inches.
 Place parchment on a hard surface; I use my counter top for this step.
Sprinkle the parchment generously with biscuit mix, and "flour" a "rolling pin" with biscuit mix.

2 cups biscuit mix AND 3 – 4 ounces cream cheese – softened to room temperature
½ cup of milk (whole milk) room temperature is best
In a very large bowl and using a hand mixer/electric mixer, beat the cream cheese with the milk.
Add the 2 cups biscuit mix to the large bowl with the milk and cream cheese mixture.
Using a ½ cup measuring cup add the biscuit mix all at once placed on top around the bowl in four evenly spaced mounds.

Using two table knives, cut the biscuit mix into the milk and cream cheese mixture until the dough pulls away from the sides of the bowl. Gently roll the dough out of the bowl onto the "prepared parchment paper."

Roll out a rectangle that reaches to the outer sides of the "prepared parchment paper."

Take the foil off the VEGE ROLL MIXTURE or POLISH PASTY INGREDIENTS ROLL and place the ROLL in the center of the ROLLED OUT RECTANGLE of PASTRY DOUGH.

I just roll out the dough to extend to the edge of the "Parchment Paper" that is cut a little larger than the "cookie sheet" and carefully fold the long sides to the middle and "pinch the dough" together in the middle, then I fold the two shorter ends, and "Pinch into place."
Finally, I use a "pizza cutter" to cut approximately two inches each to look like "braided top."

OPTIONAL: After the PASTRY DOUGH is braided like in the pictures below, separate one egg and use only the egg-white. In a one quart size bowl, beat one egg-white with 1 tablespoon purified water to a light fluffy foam consistency. Spoon the egg-white foam over the WHOLE TOP OF THE ROLL.

Pre-heat oven to 400 degrees, place the "cookie sheet" pan on the rack in the middle of the oven, and bake at the 400 degrees for 22 – 30 minutes until the top is GOLDEN BROWN.
Some ovens may take even longer. The top will brown before the bottom of the crust.

Cut Pasty-Roll into thick slices before freezing. Treat the slices the same as the regular Pasties.

November   Generosity

Polish–American Activity = House Plants Care with Prayer

1. Starter plants from other plants – I do not recall which plant is in the smallest pot.
2. Less than one year's growth on this spider plant.
3. This Christmas Cactus is the actual plant pictured in 1. Starter plant after three years growth.

4. Overview of Fern – Aloe plant and Peace Lily in background.
5. Detail of Fern in picture 4.
6. Detail of Aloe plant and Peace Lily.

    Busia Pearl had glass shelving along the only window in her "Pullman Kitchen" where she grew herbs and starter plants. She had Ferns and "Mother-in-law's tongue," and decorative flowering plants including some cacti.

    Busia Helen only had room for a few plant in her dining room. In the April chapter in this book there is a side view of her home. The middle window is the dining room. She had two metal plant stands that held three large flower pots. I don't remember where she had her "starter plants" yet she had abundant vegetables from her garden.

    The Aloe plant that you see in my pictures came from my back yard in California. When we moved back to Michigan in 2004, I brought four baby Aloe plants in a pot on the floor of my car. Luckily there was no ban on taking Aloe plants out of California at the time. The Aloe plant in picture 6 is the fifth generation from the Original Great-great-grandmother Plant.

    The secret for the abundant growth is prayer and benign neglect. More plants die from too much water and plant food than from not enough. All plant life needs carbon-dioxide for healthy growth, so both of my Busias would pray or sing when they were working near their house plants.

November   Generosity

People of Polish Heritage = Uncles, Aunts, and Cousins

1.

    We frequently had Lukasavitz family reunions out on my Uncle Chester's Farm. This is the only good picture when I was about five years old. Back Row – Left to Right: Uncle Donald has his first son ,Carl in his arms. Carl was killed by a driver who dragged his body four blocks before stopping when Carl was only six years old. Aunt Angeline, Christian my Daddy, Aunt Agatha, Grandpa John. Middle Row – Left to Right: Busia Pearl. a Nun that accompanied Sister Mary Cyria, Aunt Agnes Laskowski, Stefania my Mother, Sister Mary Cyria, Cousin Bernadette. Front Row – Left to Right: Aunt Regina holding her son Richard, Colette her daughter is facing backwards, Barbara my sister, and ME Jean Marie.

    The farm did not have indoor plumbing. It had a pump house for water that had to be carried into the house kitchen in a pail. The water was always cold and delicious. Aunt Agatha had to cook on a wood burning stove. There was only an outhouse on the property with two holes, one size for adults and a smaller one for children. We still had a wonderful time preparing the meat, potatoes, and corn on the cob on a camp-fire and the vegetables and salads in the house.

    Bernie and I played together. She is two years older than I am, and we still contact each other two or more times per month. She lives on the same farm and has modernized the house with electricity, modern kitchen appliances, and indoor plumbing.

Yes, Bernadette drove the tractor and was basically her father's hired-hand but did not get paid with money. She had chores to do every day including before Mass on Sunday and before school on week days, in addition to more chores later in the day. When my family visited my sister and I helped Bernie with some of her chores such as picking strawberries and green beans, so she had time to play.

One sunny day we were running out to the woods behind the house when Bernie spotted a thicket and suspected that a doe and her fawn could be nearby. She stayed down wind so her body scent wouldn't spook the doe. She stopped quickly and motioned for me lay down. We stayed very still which was hard for two lively girls who loved to run everywhere. Sure enough, a doe and two yearlings came over to the thicket. The white of the doe's tail was pointed up straight. She pushed her yearlings into the thicket and moved branches to cover the opening. We were very sunburned when we reached the house and we were scolded by our Mothers, but to my knowledge we did not share our special experience with the doe and her yearlings. It was our special secret.

2.

3.

2. Uncle Chester, my Daddy's elder brother and Aunt Agatha's wedding.
3. The Bride is Aunt Angeline and the groom is Uncle Donald, one of my Daddy's younger brothers. When I think of Aunt Angeline parties come to mind . She would play with the children and taught us games like Skip-to-my-loo My Darling, and Blue Bird Through My Window. She sang off key some of the time and it didn't matter to us because we were having so much fun.

4.

5.

4. Aunt Regina, my Daddy's sister, married Bruno Zelinski and they had four children. Back Row – Left to Right Collette, Richard, Aunt Regina, Uncle Bruno, Front – Left to Right Joseph, and Loraine. Frequently when our family visited their home, Uncle Bruno would invite us to recite the Rosary with their family.
5. On my sixteenth birthday, I invited my closest friends. My cousins Bernadette is near the door jam in the back row. My cousin Hania/Ann is standing in the back row, second from the right. Barbara my cousin is the second from the right in the middle row. The rest of the young ladies are friends from All Saints High School.

My Daddy's Sister, Ciocia Clara

One of the first gifts I received from my Ciocia Clara was a Poem to Dear Little Baby Girl. When I was around age three, the same time that I got my first Library Card; my Ciocia Clara gave me hard bound high quality books for my birthdays and Christmas. Since I took good care of my books they lasted until I had grandchildren, who also enjoy reading.

Throughout my life before my marriage, I remember not just the gifts but Ciocia Clara's sunny disposition. She always welcomed me to their home even after I was married and we happened to have our ten children with us.

The last time that I was in Flint to visit my Ciocia Clara and Uncle Joe was Christmas Time 2005 and Ciocia Clara was wrapping presents in their bedroom and she was giggling that she had purchased them early because everything took her longer after age eighty-four, so she had written male and female on each gift then put on the wrapping paper. Now she was putting bows on them and couldn't remember what was in some of them. She had a neat stack of boxes on the vanity that she knew had Ribbon Candy in them. So Ciocia Clara pretended that we were in a Game Show. "So which gift do you choose? The sure thing = Red and Green sweet delicious Ribbon Candy???   Or?? One of the surprise boxes???"   When I chose one of the surprise boxes - Ciocia Clara giggled and said, "Open it now - so I can see what I gave you." The sweet kissing angels were in the box, so I gave it a prominent place in my Curio Cabinet, took a picture of it and made a thank you note, which I sent to her. That was my last visit to Flint before my physical limitations began interfering with my travel plans.

My Daddy's Youngest Sister, Aunt Agnes

    I was Flower Girl for my Aunt Agnes and Uncle Bob's wedding. Aunt Agnes loved being Mother to their four sons. She treated me like her daughter until she had a granddaughter. When other people brought baby presents when I had a baby, she brought special presents for me and said, "After all you did all the work." My Aunt Agnes was and is also an excellent example of the virtue of Goodness.

Gifts from My Aunt Agnes – My Daddy's Youngest Sister

1. Bloomers: Bridle Shower Gift from My Aunt Agnes
Words on the Attached Note =
    Now don't get excited
    Now don't get misled
    These aren't for you,
    But your dishes instead
    So when you have read this
    With all my GOOD WISHES
    Just untie the Ribbons
    And go wash your dishes.

2. More of her gifts are pictured here.
   A. The three pictures at the left are hand-crafted decoupage.
   B. Three dimensional decoupage, Andy survived and Ann was loved to pieces.
   C. A Baby's First Year, book is top center.
   D. In the top right-hand corner are two Cartoon Party Napkins with Pre-Born Babies talking to each other.
   E. Bottom center is a picture of a couple with lots of children on an Island.
The caption says, "We need a bigger Island."

You will be enriched in every way for great generosity, which through us will produce thanksgiving to God.
(2 Corinthians 9: 10 – 12)

December   Peace

Christmas Cactus is Four Years Old

Fruit of the Holy Spirit = Peace

Liturgical Calendar = Immaculate Conception of Mary

Devotions and Celebrations = Advent and Christmas Traditions

**Polish–American Recipes = *Chrust – Faworki* = Favors
& Kolacky = Thumbprint Cookies**

**Polish–American Activity = Wycinanki –
Sniegu-platek = Snowflake**

People of Polish Heritage = My Daddy

December Peace

Fruit of the Holy Spirit = Peace

Prayer:

    Holy Spirit, eternal Love of the Father and the Son, kindly bestow on us the Fruit of Peace that we may enjoy tranquility of soul.

We are freed from worrying about trivial things because of the inner peace we experience with God in our hearts. We work and pray for peace throughout the world.

But the fruit of the Holy Spirit is love, joy, peace, patience, kindness, goodness, faithfulness, gentleness, self-control, against such there is no law. (Galatians 5: 21-24)

The peace of God, which passes all understanding, will keep your hearts and your minds in Christ Jesus. (Philippians 4:7)

The wisdom that is from above is first of all chaste, then peaceable, moderate, docile, in harmony with good things, full of mercy and good fruits, without judging. (James 3: 17)

Jesus said to his disciples: "Peace I leave with you; my peace I give to you. Not as the world gives do I give it to you. Do not let your hearts be troubled or afraid." (John 14: 27-31)

I have said this to you, that in me you may have peace. In the world you have tribulation; but be of good cheer, I have overcome the world." (John 16: 32 – 33)

May the Lord give strength to his people! May the Lord bless his people with peace! (Psalm 29: 10 – 11)

"Blessed are the peacemakers, for they shall be called sons of God. (Matthew 5: 8 – 10)

May the God of hope fill you with all joy and peace in believing, so that by the power of the Holy Spirit you may abound in hope. (Romans 15: 12 – 14)

Thou dost keep him in perfect peace, whose mind is stayed on thee, because he trusts in thee. (Isaiah 26: 2 – 4)

"Glory to God in the highest, and on earth peace to men of good will." (Luke 2: 13 – 15)

Now may the Lord of peace give you peace at all times in all ways. The Lord be with you all. (2 Thessalonians 3: 15 – 17)

December Peace

Liturgical Calendar = Immaculate Conception of Mary

When I was only in First Grade at All Saints School, this Doctrine was explained as follows = Jesus is the Savior of ALL People including His Mother Mary. Jesus saved All People making it possible for them to be saved from drowning after falling into the turbulent waters of sin. Mary, His Mother was saved by Jesus who protected her and held her close to Him to keep her safe from falling into the turbulent waters of sin from the time Mother Mary was conceived by her Mother Anne. Yes, of course the Sisters of Saint Joseph vividly explained the word "turbulent" with pictures of rough waters during storms.

Prayer to the Immaculate Conception

O God, who by the Immaculate Conception of the Blessed Virgin Mary, did prepare a worthy dwelling place for Your Son, we beseech You that, as by the foreseen death of this, Your Son, You did preserve Her from all stain, so too You would permit us, purified through Her intercession, to come unto You. Through the same Lord Jesus Christ, Your Son, who lives and reigns with You in the unity of the Holy Spirit, God, world without end. Amen.

Litany of the Blessed Virgin

LEADER PRAYS.	**FAITHFUL RESPOND.**
Lord, have mercy on us.	Lord, have mercy on us.
Christ, have mercy on us.	Christ, have mercy on us.
Lord, have mercy on us.	Lord, have mercy on us.
Christ, hear us.	Christ, graciously hear us
God the Father of heaven,	have mercy on us.
God the Son, Redeemer of the World,	have mercy on us.
God the Holy Spirit,	have mercy on us.
Holy Trinity, one God,	have mercy on us.
Holy Mary,	pray for us.
Holy Mother of God,	pray for us
Holy Virgin of virgins,	pray for us.
Mother of Christ,	pray for us.
Mother of Divine Grace,	pray for us.
Mother most pure,	pray for us.
Mother most chaste,	pray for us.
Mother inviolate,	pray for us.
Mother undefiled,	pray for us.
Mother most amiable,	pray for us.
Mother most admirable,	pray for us.
Mother of good counsel,	pray for us.
Mother of our Creator,	pray for us.
Mother of our Saviour,	pray for us.
Virgin most prudent,	pray for us.
Virgin most venerable,	pray for us.
Virgin most renowned,	pray for us.
Virgin most powerful,	pray for us.
Virgin most merciful,	pray for us.

Virgin most faithful,	pray for us.
Mirror of justice,	pray for us.
Seat of wisdom,	pray for us.
Cause of our joy,	pray for us.
Spiritual vessel,	pray for us.
Vessel of honour,	pray for us.
Singular vessel of devotion,	pray for us.
Mystical rose,	pray for us.
Tower of David,	pray for us.
Tower of ivory,	pray for us.
House of gold,	pray for us.
Ark of the Covenant,	pray for us.
Gate of heaven,	pray for us.
Morning star,	pray for us.
Health of the sick,	pray for us.
Refuge of sinners,	pray for us.
Comforter of the afflicted,	pray for us.
Help of Christians,	pray for us.
Queen of Angels,	pray for us.
Queen of Patriarchs,	pray for us.
Queen of Prophets,	pray for us.
Queen of Apostles,	pray for us.
Queen of Martyrs,	pray for us.
Queen of Confessors,	pray for us.
Queen of Virgins,	pray for us.
Queen of all Saints,	pray for us.
Queen conceived without original sin,	pray for us.
Queen assumed into heaven,	pray for us.
Queen of the most holy Rosary,	pray for us.
Queen of Peace,	pray for us.
Lamb of God, who takes away the sins of the world,	spare us, O Lord.
Lamb of God, who takes away the sins of the world,	graciously hear us, O Lord.
Lamb of God, who takes away the sins of the world,	have mercy on us.

Grant we beseech Thee, O Lord God, that we, Thy servants, may enjoy perpetual health of mind and body, and, by the glorious intercession of the blessed Mary, ever Virgin, be delivered from present sorrow and enjoy eternal gladness, through Christ, our Lord. Amen.

Immaculate Conception Novena

Day One

O most Holy Virgin, who was pleasing to the Lord and became His mother, immaculate in body and spirit, in faith and in love, look kindly on me as I implore your powerful intercession. O most Holy Mother, who by your blessed Immaculate Conception, from the first moment of your conception did crush the head of the enemy, receive our prayers as we implore you to present at the throne of God the favor we now request... *(State your intention here...)*

O Mary of the Immaculate Conception, Mother of Christ, you had influence with your Divine Son while upon this earth; you have the same influence now in heaven. Pray for us and obtain for us from him the granting of my petition if it be the Divine Will. Amen.

Day Two

O Mary, ever blessed Virgin, Mother of God, Queen of angels and of saints, we salute you with the most profound veneration and filial devotion as we contemplate your holy Immaculate Conception, We thank you for your maternal protection and for the many blessings that we have received through your wondrous mercy and most powerful intercession. In all our necessities we have recourse to you with unbounded confidence. O Mother of Mercy, we beseech you now to hear our prayer and to obtain for us of your Divine Son the favor that we so earnestly request in this novena...*(State your intention here...)*

O Mary of the Immaculate Conception, Mother of Christ, you had influence with your Divine Son while upon this earth; you have the same influence now in heaven. Pray for us and obtain for us from him the granting of my petition if it be the Divine Will. Amen.

Day Three

O Blessed Virgin Mary, glory of the Christian people, joy of the universal Church and Mother of Our Lord, speak for us to the Heart of Jesus, who is your Son and our brother. O Mary, who by your holy Immaculate Conception did enter the world free from stain, in your mercy obtain for us from Jesus the special favor which we now so earnestly seek... *(State your intention here...)*

O Mary of the Immaculate Conception, Mother of Christ, you had influence with your Divine Son while upon this earth; you have the same influence now in heaven. Pray for us and obtain for us from him the granting of my petition if it be the Divine Will. Amen.

Day Four

O Mary, Mother of God, endowed in your glorious Immaculate Conception with the fullness of grace; unique among women in that you are both mother and virgin; Mother of Christ and Virgin of Christ, we ask you to look down with a tender heart from your throne and listen to our prayers as we earnestly ask that you obtain for us the favor for which we now plead... *(State your intention here...)*

O Mary of the Immaculate Conception, Mother of Christ, you had influence with your Divine Son while upon this earth; you have the same influence now in heaven. Pray for us and obtain for us from him the granting of my petition if it be the Divine Will. Amen.

Day Five

O Lord, who, by the Immaculate Conception of the Virgin Mary, did prepare a fitting dwelling for your Son, we beseech you that as by the foreseen death of your Son, you did preserve her from all stain of sin, grant that through her intercession, we may be favored with the granting of the grace that we seek for at this time... *(State your intention here...)*

O Mary of the Immaculate Conception, Mother of Christ, you had influence with your Divine Son while upon this earth; you have the same influence now in heaven. Pray for us and obtain for us from him the granting of my petition if it be the Divine Will. Amen.

Day Six

Glorious and immortal Queen of Heaven, we profess our firm belief in your Immaculate Conception preordained for you in the merits of your Divine Son. We rejoice with you in your Immaculate Conception. To the one ever-reigning God, Father, Son, and Holy Spirit, three in Person, one in nature, we offer thanks for your blessed Immaculate Conception. O Mother of the Word made Flesh, listen to our petition as we ask this special grace during this novena... *(State your intention here...)*

O Mary of the Immaculate Conception, Mother of Christ, you had influence with your Divine Son while upon this earth; you have the same influence now in heaven. Pray for us and obtain for us from him the granting of my petition if it be the Divine Will. Amen.

Day Seven

O Immaculate Virgin, Mother of God, and my mother, from the sublime heights of your dignity turn your merciful eyes upon me while I, full of confidence in your bounty and keeping in mind your Immaculate conception and fully conscious of your power, beg of you to come to our aid and ask your Divine Son to grant the favor we earnestly seek in this novena... if it be beneficial for our immortal souls and the souls for whom we pray. *(State your intention here...)*

O Mary of the Immaculate Conception, Mother of Christ, you had influence with your Divine Son while upon this earth; you have the same influence now in heaven. Pray for us and obtain for us from him the granting of my petition if it be the Divine Will. Amen.

Day Eight

O Most gracious Virgin Mary, beloved Mother of Jesus Christ, our Redeemer, intercede with him for us that we be granted the favor which we petition for so earnestly in this novena...O Mother of the Word Incarnate, we feel animated with confidence that your prayers in our behalf will be graciously heard before the throne of God. O Glorious Mother of God, in memory of your joyous Immaculate Conception, hear our prayers and obtain for us our petitions. *(State your intention here...)*

O Mary of the Immaculate Conception, Mother of Christ, you had influence with your Divine Son while upon this earth; you have the same influence now in heaven. Pray for us and obtain for us from him the granting of my petition if it be the Divine Will. Amen.

Day Nine

O Mother of the King of the Universe, most perfect member of the human race, "our tainted nature's solitary boast," we turn to you as mother, advocate, and mediatrix. O Holy Mary, assist us in our present necessity. By your Immaculate Conception, O Mary conceived without sin, we humbly beseech you from the bottom of our heart to intercede for us with your Divine Son and ask that we be granted the favor for which we now plead... *(State your intention here..)*

O Mary of the Immaculate Conception, Mother of Christ, you had influence with your Divine Son while upon this earth; you have the same influence now in heaven. Pray for us and obtain for us from him the granting of my petition if it be the Divine Will. Amen.

December

The month of December is dedicated to the Immaculate Conception, which is celebrated on December 8. The first 24 days of December fall during the liturgical season known as Advent are represented by the liturgical color purple. The remaining days of December mark the beginning of the Christmas season during which the liturgical color changes to white or gold — Symbols of joy, purity and innocence.

The best person we can turn to for help during Advent is Mary, Christ's and our Mother. Mary awaited the day of His birth with more eagerness than any other human being. Her preparation was complete in every respect. In our preparation we attempt to emulate Mary's prayerfulness, her purity and whole-hearted submission to God's will.

MIDNIGHT MASS

Only the Polish traditions surrounding Midnight Mass celebrated on December 24 by the Polish people in the community in which I grew up are presented here. For deeper understanding of the Liturgy of the Mass please refer to books approved by the Catholic Church.

Are you just curious? For a quick start go to Catholicscomehome.org on the Internet; you don't have to be Catholic to ask questions on this site.

During the daylight hours on Christmas Eve we would visit some family members and friends for lunch and dinner. We would sing carols and exchange presents and most times we would not open them. Usually My immediate Family visited with Family Members and Friends on Christmas Eve and again on Christmas Day and broke Oplatek = Angel Bread.

We would come home around 9:00 pm and the whole family took a nap. I do suspect that most parents took shorter naps than the children. When we awoke our clothes were ready and we got dressed quickly. My parents sang on the choir so we usually arrived at Church before 11:00 PM and sang our hearts out with Christmas Hymns while the other people were entering the Church. A beautiful procession of young women in formals, little children in simple gowns and First Communion attire, Acolytes of all ages, Priests, Sisters of Saint Joseph, people of all ages, and finally a young woman dressed in a white gown and light blue veil carried a life-sized statue of the Infant Jesus and placed Him in the manger. We all knew that Jesus was wrapped in swaddling clothes, and we still enjoyed seeing Jesus dressed in beautiful satin clothing. The carol, O come All Ye Faithful, was sung in three languages: English, Polish, and Latin.

December   Peace

Devotions and Celebrations = Advent and Christmas Traditions

Manger Scene

Opłatek = One – Opłateki = Plural
Unleavened Bread – Bread Without Yeast

My American – Polish Heritage - Advent and Christmas Traditions
© 2008 Jean Marie Miscisin

Each person received a piece of Opłatek - about one/sixth of the large wafer and did not eat any of their own pieces. They would then exchange good wishes for each other and break off a piece of the other person's Opłatek and eat the small piece. Usually wishes were for good health, employment, and for those in the military that they would return home safely. The last wish was for Peace on Earth.

Advent "Prayer Cards" and "Opłatek" are available through most web sites that market "Catholic Materials" or through a Catholic Parish gift shop.

First Sunday of Advent
Prayers/Songs Card *
Empty "Manger/Crib" placed in the center of the star.
Light First Purple Candle.
Place stable and animals in Manger Scene.
Sing songs to the suggested melodies.

Second Sunday of Advent
Prayers/Songs Card
Empty "Manger/Crib" is still in center of star.
Light First and Second, Purple Candles.
Add shepherd and sheep to Manger Scene.
Sing songs to the suggested melodies.

Pray the prayers: Priest = P   Congregation = C
In our homes the Father or Mother = P   Children = C

Third Sunday of Advent
Prayers/Songs Card
Empty "Manger/Crib" is still in center of the star.
Light First and Second, Purple Candles.
Light Rose Colored Candle.
Add Three Kings/Three Wise Men
     and camel to Manger Scene.
Sing songs to the suggested melodies.

Fourth Sunday of Advent
Prayers/Songs Card
Empty "Manger/Crib" is still in center of star.
Light First, Second, Third, Purple Candles.
Light Rose Colored Candle.
Add Mary and Joseph to Manger Scene.
Sing songs to the suggested melodies.

Christmas Eve
Baby Jesus is carried by the youngest child
     in procession and then placed in the
"Manger Crib." which is still in center of star.
Light all of the Candles.
Turn on all the Christmas Lights.
Sing Christmas Carols.
Break Oplatek * = Angel Bread
Baby Jesus is placed in the "Manger/Crib"
Christmas Eve before breaking Oplatek.

Christmas Day
Baby Jesus in "Manger/Crib" is in the stable.

Light all of the Candles.
Turn on all the Christmas Lights.

Sing Christmas Carols and
Break Oplatek = Angel Bread,

     Usually My immediate Family visited with Family Members and Friends on Christmas Eve
         and again on Christmas Day and broke Oplatek = Angel Bread.

My Dzia Dzia Walenty my Mother's Tata would use large irons with long handles similar to bake the wafers for Mass and save the broken ones to give to the Polish people for Christmas Celebrations.

December Peace

Polish–American Recipe = *Chrust – Faworki*: Favors

Polish ingredients and procedures worked best. I tried electric appliances and my Tortilla Press. Taste was the same but texture was not light and delicate; it was more like hard, stale cookies, so I threw them out. Now I know why we only made them in a group at Christmas time. Two hands are not enough.

Ingredients and Directions:

A two or three quart size bowl, large sturdy spoon, hand beater, rolling pin, large cutting board, electric frying pan or deep fryer, two quarts cooking oil or lard.

2 Eggs – I used large   2 Egg Yolks   1/4 teaspoon Salt
Beat the Eggs, Egg Yolks, and Salt until creamy.

1/2 cup Confectioner's Sugar
Add the Confectioner's Sugar and beat some more.

2 cups Flour – I used unbleached   1/4 cup Brandy   1/4 cup soft Butter
Add the Flour, Brandy, and Butter.
Knead the dough for ten (10) minutes on the floured cutting board.
Place dough back into the bowl. Take out 1/3 of the dough and place on the floured board. Each third makes twelve Favors. Cover the bowl with the remaining dough.
Roll out first portion to "potato chip" thinness.

KNEADING

1. Flour lightly & pat flat.

2. Push down with heal of palm.

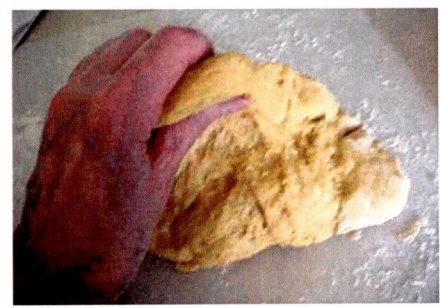
3. Lift with thumb.

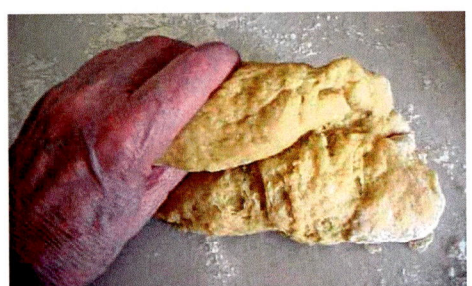
4. Roll over & form a pocket

5. Repeat these 4 steps 10 times.

6. Rotate 90º and repeat 4 steps 10 times.   7. Rotate 90º and repeat 4 steps 10 times.

8. Completing 360º rotations takes about ten minutes.

ROLLING

1. Board and rolling pin.

2. Put extra flour on the board and rolling pin.

I was having trouble rolling out the dough and my husband had to help me.
My board was too small so I could only roll out six even Favors at a time.
I took pictures of the best batch - - the dough was irregular shaped when rolled out, so there were nine different sized Favors.

3. Only 1/12 of dough.

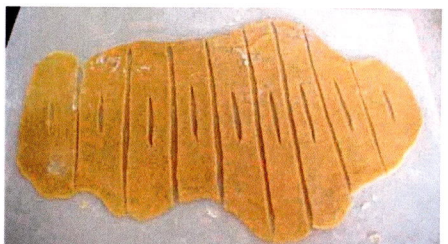
4. Cut slits 2 inches long in center.

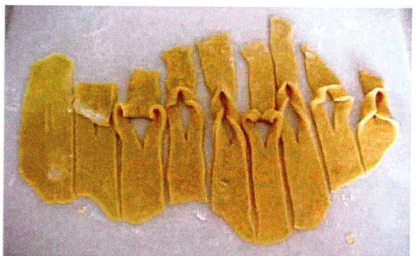
5. Fold dough over and insert through slit and pull dough up to top again.

Frying was difficult even with a small batch. I couldn't turn them fast enough in the frying pan, so some Favors were browned more than the others; Maintain 350º F, temperature.

FRYING and TOPPING WITH SUGAR

1. Quickly place each strip in cooking oil.
2. When each strip floats to the top it is ready to turn over.

3. Second side takes even fewer seconds.

If I make them again, I will make sure that there are at least three more women who Like to Cook in the kitchen with me.

4. After only a few seconds each strip will have to be lifted out onto paper toweling.
The two Favors in the middle were the closest to texture and color of Polish Faworki.

After a big Polish feast most tummies were full; these little Polish Faworki were the "just right" end to the visit before going to the next home about three hours later to another feast.

Polish–American Recipe = Kolacky = Thumbprint Cookies

Since I couldn't find the Original Recipe with the Ingredients that were used by my Busias, I combined the ingredients from a Polish Cookbook with those from a recent Magazine. I used my Table-top electric mixer with the "paddle attachment.

Mix the Ingredients for each Recipe separately, next combine them. Finally, refrigerate the dough over night. Measure out a rounded tablespoon of dough into an oblong shape for each cookie, press down lightly to 1/2 inch thick, and press your thumb to make a 1/4 inch depression. An iced-teaspoon took the place of my thumb. Top off with a little bit of jam; being careful, too much makes a big mess. Bake for 12 to 15 minutes in a 350º oven until light golden brown around the edges.

Kolacky
1 cup butter (room temperature)
1 cup softened cream cheese = 8 oz package
1/4 teaspoon vanilla extract
2 1/4 cups flour
1/2 teaspoon salt
Thick jam or fruit
1. Cream butter and cream cheese until fluffy; beat in vanilla extract.
2. Combine flour and salt and add to butter mixture.

Thumbprint
1 cup butter (room temperature)
2/3 cup granulated sugar
1 /2 teaspoon almond extract
1 /2 teaspoon vanilla extract
2 cups plus 3 tablespoons flour
Raspberry Jam
1. Combine first four ingredients in bowl until creamy.
2. Add flour and beat on low speed until well mixed.

In most Polish Catholic homes, The Holy Family, Jesus, Mary, and Joseph are the unseen guests at every meal and party.

December Peace

Polish–American Activity = Wycinanki – Sniegu-platek = Snowflake

These three snowflakes began by folding a square piece of paper as directed below. Folding lines and cutting designs can be drawn on the back, and are not necessary.

1. Whole sheet   2. Half fold   3. Quarter fold   4. Eighth fold

All cutting takes place on the Eighth Fold.

Carefully unfold to discover the intricate designs.

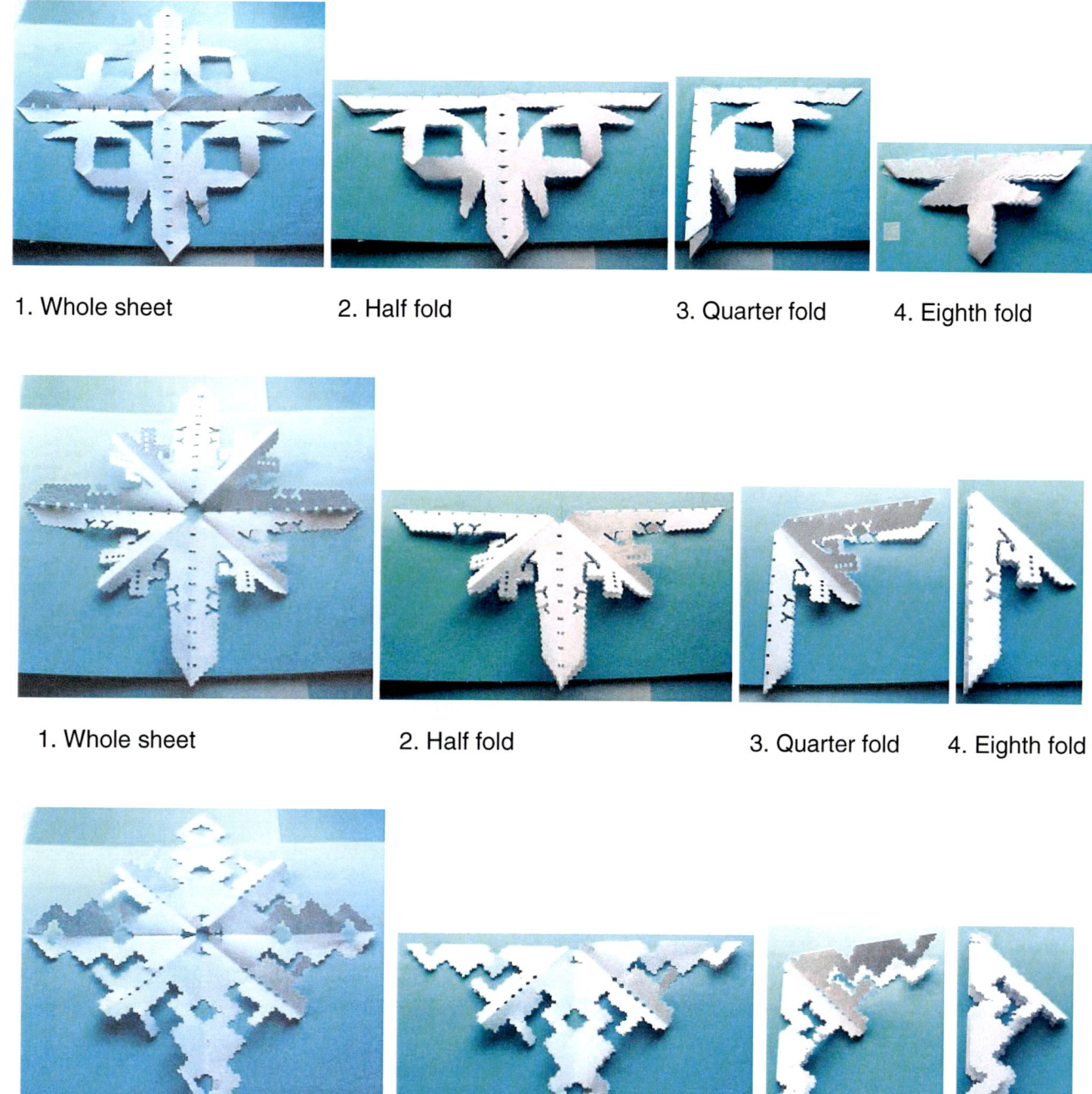

1. Whole sheet
2. Half fold
3. Quarter fold
4. Eighth fold

1. Whole sheet
2. Half fold
3. Quarter fold
4. Eighth fold

1. Whole sheet
2. Half fold
3. Quarter fold
4. Eighth fold

Play around with different colors and textures of paper.
Enjoy time well spent with your families and friends.

December Peace

People of Polish Heritage = My Daddy

1. September 5, 1933   2. May 1994   3. August 16, 1958

1. My Parents' Wedding: - Couple on the left = Aunt Agatha and Uncle Chester, my Daddy's brother - Couple on the right = Philomena Pinder and Uncle Albin, my Mother's brother.

2. My Daddy went to his eternal rest on October 20, 1994.

3. My wedding day -- Before every "first date with a young man," I introduced him to My Daddy. Usually I said, this boy, this guy, or this male friend. When I went into the kitchen to call My Daddy to meet Ronald Miscisin, I said, "Daddy, I want you to meet the finest gentleman I have ever met," My Daddy replied, "Oh Dear!" On our wedding day, he said, "Take care of my little girl."

Around the age of four, I could recite this poem in both Polish and English:

Each time I pass a Church, I stop and make a visit, so when I'm carried in feet first; The Lord won't say, "Who is it?"

When I was in grade school my parents would take us to Mass on special occasions to other Catholic Churches in Flint, Michigan. All the time that I lived with my parents, the main parts of the Mass were in Latin. We could attend Mass anywhere in the world and know what was being said.

Our prayer books/ Missals had the Latin Words for the Mass on the even numbered pages with the English translation on the facing odd numbered pages.

At All Saints Church most of the parishioners spoke Polish and some of our prayer books had Polish translations on the facing odd numbered pages.   As soon as children learned to read English or Polish they easily and quickly learned to recognize that the word, "Sanctus" = "Holy," the word, "Pacem" = "Peace," and "Amen" = "So be it." is the same in every language. By third grade most children were singing in three languages Polish, English, and Latin; fully participating in the celebration of the Mass.

At Our Lady of Guadalupe Church most of the parishioners spoke Spanish.

At Christ the King Church all of the parishioners spoke English. They sang lively songs called out "Amen" whenever they wished and they had brown to black, dark skin. Most of them were born in Flint, Michigan.

These Roman Catholic Churches were open 24 /7 and my parents would stop to pray a short prayer when they were driving past them. We also attended Mass at other Catholic Churches the United States most of them in Michigan, Wisconsin, Illinois, Ohio, Indiana, and New York, also Catholic Churches in Canada, when we were visiting relatives.

We also learned about the Byzantine Rite where Mass was celebrated in Greek, During Mass we could recognize the Liturgy of the Word and the Liturgy of the Eucharist but not the language except for Kýrie Eléison. = Lord have mercy. .Christe Eléison. = Christ have mercy. These Greek words are included in all of the Masses throughout the world to this day and in 2015 it doesn't matter in which language the rest of the Mass is celebrated.

Protestant Churches were just called Other Churches and we knew that they were only open during services and other events, not for private visiting hours.

**We all got along peacefully because at All Saints Church and in our homes –
We were taught that - We are ALL God's children.**

Our family attended most of our Sunday Masses at All Saints Catholic Church.
My Parents sang in the Adult Choir for at least one Sunday Mass until the All Saints Property on Industrial Avenue was sold to Buick Factory.

Lord make me an instrument of your Peace!

CULTURAL BAGGAGE -- © 1995 Jean Marie Miscisin

My cultural baggage was getting heavier every day. "Just dump out the things that no longer have meaning," is all that the experts say.
I opened one big piece, as I dug deeper I found another, and another tucked deep inside, full and treasured as the one before.
So, I opened one and examined the contents carefully too. For how do you know what to do with it until you do?
But now I have a problem greater than the first, I tried to repack my baggage, but it is so full, about to burst.
Now, I wonder if I should listen to those "experts," or the voice inside of me?
Because without my "Cultural Baggage," would I still be ME?

More Autobiographical Books by Jean Marie Miscisin

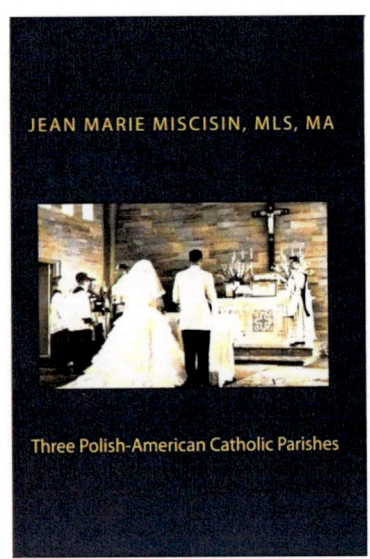

1.

2.

1. Three Polish - American Catholic Parishes = Research completed for my Masters Degree in American Culture Studies earned at the University of Michigan, 1982

2. Life! A Work of Heart = Practical goal getting steps are outlined for achieving Time - Frame Goals and for making progress on Life - Time Goals.

3.

4.

3. God Carries Me! Like My Daddy = Anecdotal vignettes provide a glimpse into some character traits of My Daddy who by his actions and his words introduced me to God, My Father in Heaven.

4. Christmas In Our Living Room = This Historical – Fiction Screen Play reveals the love, faith and hope of a Polish - American family in the tumultuous times during World War II, from one Christmas to another Christmas.

Made in the USA
San Bernardino, CA
21 December 2017